DELIBERATING IN THE REAL WORLD

Deliberating in the Real World

Problems of Legitimacy in
Deliberative Democracy

JOHN PARKINSON

OXFORD
UNIVERSITY PRESS

*This book has been printed digitally and produced in a standard specification
in order to ensure its continuing availability*

OXFORD
UNIVERSITY PRESS

Great Clarendon Street, Oxford OX2 6DP

Oxford University Press is a department of the University of Oxford.
It furthers the University's objective of excellence in research, scholarship,
and education by publishing worldwide in

Oxford New York

Auckland Cape Town Dar es Salaam Hong Kong Karachi
Kuala Lumpur Madrid Melbourne Mexico City Nairobi
New Delhi Shanghai Taipei Toronto
With offices in
Argentina Austria Brazil Chile Czech Republic France Greece
Guatemala Hungary Italy Japan South Korea Poland Portugal
Singapore Switzerland Thailand Turkey Ukraine Vietnam

Oxford is a registered trade mark of Oxford University Press
in the UK and in certain other countries

Published in the United States
by Oxford University Press Inc., New York

ISBN 978-0-19-929111-3

For Carolyn

Contents

Preface

This book grew out of a long-standing interest in the capacity of ordinary people to order their own lives, and the lack of opportunities for them to exercise that capacity in the political arena in modern democracies.

I had not always been an optimist about popular capacities. A campaign to decriminalize homosexuality in New Zealand in 1985 had left me more than a little wary, not because the campaign failed, but because it took elite action to push through change in the face of sometimes hysterical opposition. However, my interest was rekindled a few years later when working as a consultant with businesses on internal communication projects. I was often hired by managers convinced that their staff were stuck in the mud, resistant to any form of change. Instead, I frequently found the opposite: that it was managers who were more often resistant to change and staff who embraced it, coming up with creative solutions to problems that had creased more senior brows. What made the difference, it seemed to me, was whether or not people were given the power to design and implement the changes themselves, as well as some well-designed procedures to help them make those decisions. This caused me to review some of my elitist assumptions, and eventually, as a political scientist, led me to look at the role that power and institutions played in providing opportunity structures for different human capacities.

Given that starting point, deliberative democracy held an instant appeal. Here was an approach to democracy that, at least in some variants, was built on a fundamental respect for people and their capacity for self-government. As with anything instantly appealing in social and political theory, one quickly finds problems, both in theory and in practice, and deliberative democracy is no different. This book explores some of those problems, and presents what I think are significant challenges to proponents of small-scale, participatory variants of deliberative democracy. Much of the current enthusiasm for 'the new localism' in Britain, for example, strikes me as either somewhat naive or downright manipulative. But while I am sceptical about some aspects of deliberative democracy and its practical implementation, that original impression of the remarkable capacities of ordinary people has been reinforced. I approach the subject as a sceptic, not as a cynic. I am sympathetic to what Robert Dahl calls 'the idea of intrinsic equality', that basic sense of respect for people which underlies all but the most elitist democratic theory. While my focus in this book is almost entirely on institutions, and some of the macro conditions that frame political experience, I would hope that my critical comments on those institutions are not used as an excuse to denigrate the capacities of those people who work within them: that conclusion would, I think, be wholly unwarranted.

This is not just a critically oriented book: I offer solutions to the problems I raise, proposing an approach to institutional design that tries to manage the tensions inherent in deliberative democracy. The scheme I suggest is not a million miles away from familiar institutions, and on this point some readers might feel disappointed that I have not been more imaginative. In response, I would say that lack of imagination is not deliberative democracy's problem right now; the literature abounds with ideas for institutions that instantiate deliberative ideals one way or another, and is growing at a fair old pace. Rather, the problem as I see it is making those imaginings a practical reality given the complex social, political, and institutional settings in which they must operate, dealing with the competing pressures created by that setting. Dreaming up schemes of how things might be seems to me to be a very important activity; but we need also to consider how to get to those end points from where we stand now. Otherwise, the dream of a genuinely deliberative democracy remains just that, a dream. I think that would be a great pity.

J.R.P.

York, August 2005

Acknowledgements

The vast majority of the work on this book was conducted while in Social and Political Theory, Research School of Social Sciences at the Australian National University. My particular thanks go to John Dryzek: the opportunity to work with someone whose own work I admire so much was a great privilege. Special thanks also to Bob Goodin, who commented incisively at every step.

Other valuable contributions came from John Uhr; Steve Harrison, who gave specialist advice on UK health policy; Mick Moran and Albert Weale, who commented on the original text; and the anonymous reviewers for Oxford University Press. During my fieldwork, Su Jones, Dave Marsh, and Jeremy Jennings were wonderful hosts at the University of Birmingham, as were Jacqui Burgess at UCL and Eithne McLaughlin at Queen's University, Belfast. The fieldwork was conducted under ANU Human Research Ethics Committee protocol number 2001/16. Thanks to Issues Deliberation Australia for allowing me to observe the second Australian deliberative poll; the numerous participants at conferences in Australia, New Zealand, and the UK for their comments on ideas as they were taking shape; and to all my interviewees for giving so much of their time and experience. Jeff Wood and Kay Lipson assisted on the sampling issues and calculations in Chapter 4, while Elizabeth Minchin coined the term 'thorubocracy' for me, used in Chapter 7.

Others who chipped in with ideas, criticisms, and great company along the way include Graham Smith; Michelle Buxton, Wendy Goodlet, Sandra Grey, Carolyn Hendriks, Simon Niemeyer, and Wynne Russell at the ANU; and Andrew Knops and Therese O'Toole at Birmingham. Helena Catt set my feet firmly on the path.

I am grateful to publishers for permission to reprint material from the following:

John Parkinson (2003). 'Legitimacy Problems in Deliberative Democracy', *Political Studies*, 51: 180–96;

John Parkinson (2004). 'Why Deliberate? The Encounter Between Deliberation and New Public Managers', *Public Administration*, 82: 377–95;

John Parkinson (2004). 'Hearing Voices: Negotiating Representation Claims in Public Deliberation', *British Journal of Politics and International Relations*, 6: 349–63, all by permission of Blackwell Publishers Ltd;

John Parkinson (2006). 'Rickety Bridges: Using the Media in Deliberative Democracy', *British Journal of Political Science*, 36: 175–83 by permission of Cambridge University Press.

Finally, my thanks to the ANU, and the Gordon Watson Scholarship administered by the New Zealand Vice-Chancellors' Committee, for the generous financial support to the University of York for the Anniversary Lectureship, which gave me the time to complete the manuscript; to my colleagues at York who bore the burdens caused by my extended leave with patience and extraordinary good humour; and to Dominic Byatt and Claire Croft at Oxford University Press for their support and enthusiasm throughout.

List of Figures

List of Tables

1

Deliberative democracy and legitimacy

In March 2000, a group of sixteen randomly selected citizens sat down in a conference room at the Leicester City Football Club to hear arguments from witnesses about whether or not hospital services in their English Midlands city should be reorganized; and if so, how? Over the next four days, this 'citizens' jury' would hear from doctors, health authority managers, patients' support group advocates, city council managers, and many others. Their job would be to sort through the often conflicting claims and come up with recommendations for the health authority to implement. At the same time, however, patients' groups had organized one of Leicester's largest ever petitions against any reorganization, and some of their members were picketing outside the stadium. After months of lobbying, protests, petitions, and media campaigning against any change, it seemed they were not going to take 'yes' for an answer.

What reasons did the protesters have for agreeing with the jury's decisions? On what grounds could they be persuaded to accept the outcome without participating in the debate directly? Why should they think, after months of hard work, that this group of sixteen people chosen by a market research firm should have the decisive voice?

The Leicester citizens' jury illustrates a central issue in an approach to democratic theory and practice that has become very significant over the last decade or so. Citizens' juries and a number of similar processes have been linked with, or directly inspired by, deliberative democracy. The term was coined by Bessette (1980) to refer to the deliberations of elected members of the US Congress, but has come to mean much more. Deliberative democracy is a way of thinking about politics which emphasizes the give and take of public reasoning between citizens rather than the counting of votes or the authority of representatives. For some, it is a response to the apparent irrationality of mass politics, which is illegitimate because it is too dominated by powerful interests, unresponsive representatives, and an uninformed public. For others it is a response to the dominance of experts and technocrats in public decision-making, which is illegitimate because it so often fails to take people's experience and preferences seriously enough. Both the term and its principles have been taken up with so much fervour by so many theorists that it sometimes seems as though we are not just all democrats (Fukuyama 1989), but deliberative democrats now.

However, it has only recently been noticed that deliberative democracy faces significant legitimacy challenges of its own, both in theory and in practice. Two problems arise in the classic formulations of deliberative theory: they offer no account of why outsiders should confer legitimacy on the agreements reached inside a deliberative forum, and they seem to be so procedurally demanding that not many people would choose to be inside anyway. These are not just problems of theoretical interest: they cause difficulty whenever any small group of people is asked to resolve a conflict of strongly held views on behalf of their fellows (e.g. Davies et al. 1998: 3).

This book explores those legitimacy challenges and asks whether they can be overcome. I tackle the questions neither purely in theory nor practice but through a combination of the two. The starting point is to reconsider the theory of legitimacy and deliberative democracy, but I also mine deliberative practice for further insights and solutions, drawing on some health policy debates in the UK. Thus, while my starting point is to consider two quite specific theoretical problems, the search for a solution is fairly wide-ranging, and one that leads to a fundamental reconsideration of deliberative democracy and its institutional possibilities. This approach can be very fruitful: the theoretical analysis gives one a normative frame against which to challenge implicit or explicit claims made for particular political practices, while the practices can bring to light new answers to theoretical questions at the same time as providing a reality check on theorists' wilder claims. Such an approach is not without its problems, and I will discuss some of those shortly. What I want to do first is to describe the 'deliberative turn' in democratic theory (Dryzek 2000: v), setting out the nature of the starting questions in a little more detail. I then discuss the empirical work, outlining the cases, and give an overview of the argument before setting out the theoretical issues in more detail in Chapter 2.

1.1   DELIBERATIVE DEMOCRACY AND ITS ACCOUNT OF LEGITIMACY

Like most political concepts, deliberative democracy means many things to many people, a plurality which may be useful if it is to have any vitality (Dryzek 1996*a*: 4–5). Theorists and practitioners from starkly contrasting traditions have applied the deliberative democratic label to everything from radical activism and protest, to consultative forums engaged with the state, to representative assemblies, to the deliberations of small groups of judges, even to the internal processes of making others 'present' in an individual's own internal deliberations.[1]

And yet, despite the bewildering variety of perspectives and prescriptions, deliberative democracy does have a core set of propositions which distinguish it from its rivals. In its normative version, deliberative democracy is based on two principles: it insists on *reasoning* between people as the guiding political procedure, rather than bargaining between competing interests or the aggregation of private preferences; and the essential political act—the giving, weighing, acceptance, or rejection of reasons—is a *public* act, as opposed to the purely private act of voting. Thus democracy is conceived of less as a market for the exchange of private preferences, more as a forum for the creation of public agreements (Elster 1997), a forum in which, ideally, 'no force except that of the better argument is exercised' (Habermas 1975: 108). To ensure that public reason and not private power dominates public discussion, deliberative democracy requires equality between participants, as do other versions of democracy. This means that the franchise should be inclusive, that agreements be decisive, that participants agree to reciprocity in their discussions, giving each other equal speaking time, and equality of enforcement power (Gutmann and Thompson 1996; 2004).

It is also worth stressing that it is democratic deliberation, not deliberation without modifier, despite some undemocratic usages of the term. Democratic deliberation is therefore about making binding collective decisions, covering all the stages of the decision-making process from problem definition and agenda-setting, discussion of solutions, decision-making, and implementation; it should not be disconnected from questions of agendas, decisions, and actions. It should also embody the essential democratic principles of responsiveness to reflective public wishes and the political equality of every member of that public (Beetham 1994: 26–31; May 1978). Otherwise we are talking about deliberation, not deliberative democracy.

Under such conditions, people's arguments for and against certain views must be made in public if they are to persuade others, and so can be examined and challenged by those others; preferences which may be more or less vague, unreflective, ill-informed, and private, are transformed into more firm,

---

[1] For a more radical participatory account of deliberative democracy see Benhabib (1996), Dryzek (1990), and Schlosberg (1999). Cohen and Rogers (1992), Renn, Webler and Wiedemann (1995), and Fung (2003) discuss examples of mediating institutions between state and civil society (see also Habermas 1996: 229). The parliamentary example comes from Bessette (1994) and Uhr (1998), while the last two are discussed by (Rawls 1996: 231–40) and Goodin (2000).

reflective, informed, and other-regarding ones through the deliberative encounter (Cohen 1989). Two prerequisites for such transformation are: that
the participants are communicatively competent, which means that they can
understand and critically assess the arguments of others and make sound
arguments of their own (Outhwaite 1994: 38; Renn, Webler, and Wiedemann
1995: 44); and that participants are willing to be persuaded, to have their
preferences transformed in the face of a better argument, and thus to set aside
strategic concerns and behaviour in the pursuit of those preferences (Dryzek
2000: 2; Miller 1992). Thus, deliberative democracy is a highly rationalist
ideal of democracy, a reaction to the apparent irrationality of processes based
on bargaining and strategy.

These procedural features make deliberation much more than mere talk: it is
a very particular kind of public talk. This point is often missed by writers who
label as deliberative practices which exhibit none of the procedural conditions
of deliberative democratic theory (e.g. Button and Mattson 1999). Often this is
a function of scale: beyond a very small number of participants deliberation
breaks down, 'with speech-making replacing conversation and rhetorical
appeals replacing reasoned arguments' (Goodin 2000: 83n). Thus one should
be cautious about describing large-scale referendum processes, public meetings, or a great deal of media debate as deliberative, at least when considering
such processes in isolation (Parkinson 2001*a*).

Above all, however, deliberative democracy in its classic formulations is an
account of political legitimacy: 'that outcomes are legitimate to the extent
they receive reflective assent through participation in authentic deliberation
by all those subject to the decision in question'.[2] While some authors emphasize the legitimacy of specific decisions, and others the legitimacy of the broad
terms of association within which those decisions are made, the deliberative
ideal is that all those subject to collective rules should have helped make those
rules. But if we accept that classic formulation, then there is a contradiction at
the heart of deliberative democracy. Because the deliberation of *all* those
subject to a decision or regime is impossible, deliberative democratic practices
cannot deliver legitimate outcomes as the theory defines them.

The problem is not just one of getting everyone together in one place at one
time to deliberate: while we might be able to get many more people virtually
present through information technology or the media, they could not *deliberate* together, at least not in the technical sense given above. Most of the
people will simply listen to others' arguments without having the opportunity
to challenge them directly, while only a very few will ever get to speak for

---

[2] Dryzek (2001: 651), summarizing Benhabib (1996: 68), Cohen (1989: 145–6), and Manin
(1987: 360). See also Bessette (1994) and Bohman and Rehg (1997: ix).

themselves. Beyond that, however, is the fact that in a complex society characterized by rapid change and fluid boundaries identifying 'those affected' is an imprecise art at best, entirely arbitrary at worst.

This is deliberative democracy's scale problem: deliberative decisions appear to be illegitimate for those left outside the forum, while bringing more than a few people in would seem to turn the event into speech-making, not deliberation. It also has legitimacy problems to do with motivations. The major issue concerns the requirement that participants be willing to have their preferences transformed, to go into the forum with an open mind. And yet, people's pre-formed preferences, interests, and goals are an essential part of what motivates them to enter political arenas in the first place (Rawls 1996: 82). If deliberative democracy rules those things out of court, it may seem to people that deliberative democracy is procedurally unfair, and thus illegitimate (Shapiro 1999). Even if we can solve the scale problem and uncover reasons why people *should* operate according to deliberative principles, there may be few reasons why they *would*. Other issues to do with motivations will emerge from the more detailed theoretical discussion in Chapter 2.

1.2 THE INSTITUTIONS OF DELIBERATIVE DEMOCRACY

Because different institutions activate different behaviour, the legitimacy problems can be more or less severe depending on the various ways in which deliberative democratic principles have been given institutional form.

From many of the more abstract discussions of deliberative principles, one could be forgiven for thinking that deliberative democracy is only applicable in small sites. Many theorists imply that deliberation occurs in one room at one moment, with a relatively small number of participants applying the somewhat stringent procedures of public reason, sometimes held together by a moderator. This impression is certainly conveyed by the metaphor of 'the forum' (Elster 1997), and strengthened by Cohen (1989) and Gutmann and Thompson (1996) in their discussions. Many other authors have taken the hint and applied deliberative principles to relatively small-scale decision-making sites like citizens' juries (Stewart, Kendall, and Coote 1994; Smith and Wales 2000), deliberative polls (Fishkin 1997), consensus conferences (Joss and Durant 1995), and parliaments (Bessette 1994). Sometimes this has a constructive agenda, attempting to design institutions which embody deliberative principles; sometimes it has a critical agenda, using the principles as a yardstick against which to measure the claims made on behalf of real institutions.

It is at this level that the problem of scale is most sharp, and yet it is sometimes hard to see how it might be otherwise. It is difficult to see how hundreds, let alone millions, of people can 'plausibly "reason together"' (Walzer 1999: 68) given the need for all participants to have equal time to raise proposals and to have those subjected to critical exploration in any depth (Dahl 1989: 225–31, makes a similar point). Indeed, the literature on small groups suggests that the actual deliberative limit is very much smaller than Walzer's most pessimistic number. While the limit may depend on the purpose of the group, the optimum for active decision-making is generally agreed to be between five and seven.[3] This is because the group must 'be small enough that each member knows, and is able to react to, every other member' (Fisher and Ellis 1990). This is not just so from an external point of view: it is also reported to be the most satisfactory size by group members themselves.

However, deliberative democracy is thought of another way. As well as the 'micro' deliberative processes mentioned above, deliberative democracy also comes in 'macro' forms.[4] One version of this conceives of deliberation as conversations carried on across time and space, the threads of which are picked up by people at different times, in different places, and with different interlocutors.[5] At any one moment, people will be engaged in many such threads which change and interact over time. Thus the conversation threads are said to have, to some extent, a life of their own; they are subjectless, decentred. Rationality, on this view, is not necessarily a feature of each individual conversation, because each has only a part of the picture. Rationality is a feature of all the discourses on a topic to the extent that such conversations are openly accessible to communicatively competent publics. It is democratic to the extent that government action is determined by the provisional outcome of the contestation of discourses, discourses which are controlled by communicatively competent people in decentred, flat-structured networks.

This discursive view can seem a little abstract. Another version is tied to more familiar institutions. Mansbridge (1999) talks about a 'deliberative system' which includes formal representative structures but extends well beyond them to include the informal public sphere and private talk that is recognizably political (1999: 215). It is a spectrum along which outcomes become progressively less binding on participants, and demand less accountability to non-participants, the closer the forum is to the informal end. In his

---

[3] See Goodall (1990), Ridgeway (1983), and Rudestam (1982).

[4] I have borrowed the micro/macro distinction from Hendriks 2002*b*, but use the terms more loosely to describe different approaches to deliberative processes as well as deliberative theory.

[5] Benhabib (1996: 75), Dryzek (2000: 74–5), Habermas (1984), Rehg (1996: 87–8), Schlosberg (1999), and Young (2000: 167).

more recent work, Habermas (1996) makes a similar move. Instead of insisting that civil society alone is the arena for democratization, he now offers a 'two-track model' of deliberation which distinguishes the roles of the informal public sphere of civil society and the formal public sphere of representative institutions.[6] Opinions are transmitted to the formal public sphere for action by virtue of a number of mechanisms, all of which can be more or less inclusive, deliberative, and democratic in practice. These include the tools which reach out from the informal public sphere, such as direct protest, representations to government, and commissioned reports; those which reach out from the formal public sphere, like commissions of inquiry, select committee hearings, consultative processes, even government-commissioned opinion research; and many other techniques which inhabit that area that Gutmann and Thompson (1996: 12) call 'middle democracy', including the micro-deliberative processes like deliberative polls and citizens' juries. At the same time, decision-makers are themselves participants in discourses, and the results of discursive contests are said to be 'transmitted to the state' quite automatically, simply by virtue of the fact that governments are made up of people in society. They participate by means of the news media, through dramatizations on stage and screen, in books, in conversations, and so on.

While a particular deliberative moment might have as its focal point a relatively small group of people in one room—whether it be parliament or a group of jurors—thousands, even millions, of people can engage with it in other ways, such as if various news media pick it up; if it is the subject of conversations at work, over a drink, or at home; if interest groups engage with it; if people are mobilized by protests or petitions; if various elected representatives pick up the issue and run with it; if other micro-deliberative forums are set up to grapple with the issue. Each element in such a system may not be perfectly deliberative or democratic in its own right, but may still perform a useful function in the system as a whole, although it would be a strange deliberative system indeed if *none* of its elements met deliberative democratic criteria.

Deliberative institutions, macro and micro, are affected by the legitimacy problems in different ways. For example, the scale problem is particularly

---

[6] For Habermas the informal public sphere is the site of opinion formation only, while the formal public sphere is the site of decision-making; Fennema and Maussen (2000) make a similar distinction. This view has drawn sharp criticism from other critical theorists. Dryzek (2000), appealing to egalitarian democratic values, argues that Habermas has given away too much ground to liberals, especially elite-minded liberals, by theorizing the informal public sphere as subservient to the state rather than as a critical and powerful master. Dryzek insists on a more 'insurgent' model of discursive democracy in which networks in the informal public sphere make strategic calculations about when to engage constructively, and when to do battle, with the state.

acute for the micro version of deliberative democracy simply because it is the one in which the insider/outsider distinction is most sharp; at first glance, macro deliberation avoids the scale problem because everyone is inside the deliberative system to some extent. However, in that 'to some extent' is a great deal of room for slippage: not everyone can be attentive to every issue which affects them, let alone actively participate in their resolution, even to a modest extent. I will discuss the details of how the different models are affected by the legitimacy problems in Chapter 2, and as the book progresses.

1.3   APPROACH AND METHODS

My aim is to find out if there is such a thing as a democracy that embodies deliberative principles, yet solves the legitimacy problems. I start by reconsidering the nature of legitimacy and deliberative democracy in Chapter 2, then use some empirical research to cover two main issues: whether the theoretical problems have been solved in practice, or at least whether they have been managed successfully; and whether new problems arise and are dealt with in practice. The empirical element is what gives the later institutional recommendations some practical foundation. The aim, however, is not to conduct a thorough evaluation of particular processes; it is to use practical experience with deliberative principles to develop further our theoretical account of legitimacy, deliberative democracy, and its institutional possibilities.

Anyone attempting to connect deliberative democratic theory and practice must, however, face up to a serious difficulty: it is hard to ask empirical questions about fully deliberative institutions when such institutions do not exist in the real world. While some authors like Bessette (1994) treat deliberative democracy as a description of some actual practice, I tend more to a position which treats the theory as a counterfactual ideal, an ideal which real institutions can approximate more or less closely. This is because real practices are embedded in our present liberal democratic system, and are fundamentally affected by the assumptions, motivations, discourses, and power structures of that system. Nor have so-called deliberative processes like citizens' juries, deliberative polls, and consensus conferences arisen pure from deliberative theory like Venus from the waves: they are the result of a complex mix of the results of previous democratic experiments and their originators' varied theories, experiences, and biases which, in all but the case of the deliberative poll, owe nothing directly to deliberative democratic theory. Given that, the conclusions I draw about legitimacy in practice need to be treated with some caution: I cannot say what results would have been found from an investigation of the same processes embedded in a different, more fully deliberative institutional setting. What I can say instead, and with some confidence, is that certain issues will be faced in moving from our current institutional starting point towards a more deliberative system. For that reason the aim needs to become a little more modest. Rather than using the results to put forward a model of an ideal, fully legitimate deliberative democracy, the proposals I make in Chapter 7 concern the next steps which move current institutions in a more deliberative democratic direction.

The empirical sections draw on five cases, described in Section 1.4. In order to limit other institutional variables as much as possible, I chose to look for cases in one broad policy area in one country: health and disability services in the UK. The location and topic are logical for a number of reasons. Health politics is instructive because it is one of the fields in which the tension between technocratic and democratic control is most acute. As I discuss in Chapter 3, health politics is characterized by multilateral tensions between a highly professionalized guild, a demanding public, and managers and governments trying to meet demand while controlling costs (Moran 1999). This makes democratic deliberation on health policy fraught with conflict, and, thus a tough test of the ability of any process to deliver legitimate agreements. The UK is an interesting location for such a study because, since the Blair government took office in 1997, it has seen a significant, state-driven programme of experimentation with 'public and patient involvement' initiatives, some of which were designed with deliberative democratic principles in mind. Still, while this meant that my choice of cases was better than it might have been elsewhere, it remained small: although deliberative democracy has taken the little world of democratic theory by storm, its influence on daily political life can easily be overstated. This is reflected in the literature on the use of deliberative techniques in Britain which is still quite limited, concentrating on how a given practice embodies deliberative democratic principles, or on instrumental criticism of a few techniques.[7] So, choosing the cases was more a matter of using what was to hand than deploying an elaborate selection process.

Nonetheless, the cases do vary on a number of key dimensions which means that I can at least offer some limited generalizations based on analytic

---

[7] This is a feature of much of the deliberative democracy literature, not just that focused on health. There is a growing literature on public involvement initiatives in health generally—see, for example, Bowie, Richardson, and Sykes (1995), Klein (2000), Milewa, Valentine, and Calnan (1999), Mullen (2000), Rowe and Shepherd (2002), and Shackley and Ryan (1994). For discussions of specifically deliberative processes in UK health policy, see Barnes (1999), Davies et al. (1998), Dolan, Cookson and Ferguson (1999), Lenaghan, New, and Mitchell (1996), Lenaghan (1999) and McIver (1997).

representativeness (Hamel, Dufour, and Fortin 1993: 44; Yin 1984: 21). The cases vary on the micro/macro dimension; they occupy different points on Mansbridge's deliberative continuum (see Section 1.2); they are based on different conceptions of representation; and they differ according to scale, from the very small-scale to the fairly inclusive. As will be seen, variation on any of these dimensions should have an influence on a process's legitimacy. These differences allowed me to find out under what conditions legitimacy problems are most acute, and what kinds of processes deal with those problems more successfully than others.

As for the empirical research itself, it was based on thirty interviews with facilitators, National Health Service (NHS) managers, health academics, interest group leaders, politicians, and journalists conducted between May and July 2001 in England and Northern Ireland, as well as a range of documentary material on each case. The pressures of time and money meant I was not able to locate and interview lay participants, but I did gain access to transcripts, reports, and broadcast tapes of some of their discussions. The interviews were as non-directive as possible, allowing participants to steer the discussion (Berg 2001; Jorgenson 1991: 211) and using their own words to construct the codes I used in subsequent analysis (Coffey and Atkinson 1996).

Given all this, what follows cannot be taken as applying to all recent deliberative experiments, and this is not meant to be a comprehensive evaluation of the cases, least of all the British government's programme. Nonetheless, I can be confident that certain patterns of discourse, certain dominant ideas, certain perceptions of events were present, and this is quite enough for my purposes.

1.4   THE CASES

The book is organized thematically rather than on a case-by-case basis, because it is the theoretical questions which drive it, not the details of the cases. This helps to draw out the key contrasts between different institutional forms, but can do so at the expense of narrative flow, and so it is worth outlining the cases now to provide a reference point for later discussion.

1.4.1   The Belfast citizens' jury

The first case I use is a citizens' jury held in Belfast in July 1998, commissioned jointly by the Eastern Health & Social Services Board (EHSSB), responsible for the planning and delivery of health services in Belfast, most of County

Down and southern Antrim, and the Eastern Health & Social Services Council (EHSSC), the Board's patient watchdog.

The citizens' jury process is said to fit the deliberative democratic ideal well (Hendriks 2002*a*; Lenaghan, New, and Mitchell 1996; Smith and Wales 2000), although, being developed in the 1970s, it predates the deliberative turn in democratic theory, and has had the deliberative label applied to it *post hoc*. Developed independently in the United States and Germany (where, taking a slightly different form, it is known as the 'planning cell'),[8] the citizens' jury is designed to address policy problems. Evidence from 'witnesses' from various sides of the issue is presented to a jury of lay people who deliberate and make recommendations based on the evidence.[9] The jury selection is not strictly random: it is usually a quota sample of anywhere between twelve and twenty-four people (sixteen seems to be common), with the quotas determined by age, gender, ethnicity, and whatever other demographic variables might be important on a given issue. The events themselves are generally managed by professional facilitators and overseen by steering groups made up of the commissioning body and key stakeholders including, sometimes, a media representative. Citizens' juries were introduced into the UK health policy community in mid-1996 when the Institute of Public Policy Research (IPPR) and the King's Fund, a London-based health foundation, ran six pilots with five health authorities in England (McIver 1997). This followed a trial earlier in 1996 with five local authorities, sponsored by the Local Government Management Board and managed by the IPPR and the Institute of Local Government Research at the University of Birmingham (Hall and Stewart 1996). Interviewees estimated that around 200 citizens' juries had been run in the UK by mid-2001, most commissioned by health and local authorities, although usage is on the wane after an initial flurry of experimentation, due at least in part to perceptions of high costs in time and resources.

The Belfast jury's aim was to help develop a response to a white paper entitled *The New NHS: Modern, Dependable* (Secretary of State for Health 1997) which set out the government's 'modernization' agenda for the NHS. Rather than go through the whole document, the organizers selected just one

---

[8] In the USA, the originator was Ned Crosby, who registered the name 'citizens' jury' to protect both the intellectual property and to ensure consistency of process. The planning cell was developed by Peter Dienel, and features five or more cells running concurrently in different locations, each of which sends representatives to a final cell which puts together the final recommendations. See Crosby (1998) and Dienel and Renn (1995).

[9] Robin Clarke, formerly of the IPPR, suggests that the analogy with the legal jury should not be taken too far: for example, there are no lawyers or judge, but a facilitator who directs proceedings; and juries can make a range of recommendations, not just binary choices.

area of it, the establishment of Primary Care Groups,[10] and asked, 'What are the advantages and disadvantages of a move to primary care groups, how can our concerns be met?' In addition, they asked two general questions to elicit people's values surrounding health and social services generally, as well as public involvement in health decision-making. Thus a key feature of the Belfast jury was that, while it did have an external focus in the shape of the government's white paper, the decision to run it was made, and the agenda set, by the commissioning bodies, not by any central organization in Belfast or Westminster, nor driven by demand from local people (see Barnes 1999, for a comprehensive evaluation). It was a case of micro deliberation largely in isolation from more macro processes, but one that formed a link between the agencies of formal deliberation and the wider public sphere.

1.4.2   The NHS deliberative poll

The deliberative poll on the NHS was even more the creature of its commissioners, being timed to coincide with the 50th anniversary of the NHS rather than being triggered by any particular policy event.

By contrast with the citizens' jury, the deliberative poll was consciously created with deliberative principles in mind. Its developer, James Fishkin, is a political theorist and his inspiration was flaws in ordinary opinion polls preceding elections, particularly the flaw that people are required to offer opinions on topics whether they know anything about them or not. To correct this, the deliberative poll first puts standard survey questions about a topic to a random sample of the relevant population, brings them together to a conference venue where they are systematically informed about the topic and get the chance to debate it with panels of experts, then polls them again to see how their opinions have changed. Thus, the deliberative poll is really a pre-test/post-test quantitative research design with some limited deliberation in between. It is claimed to bridge 'the gap between *actual* public opinion and *well informed* public opinion' (Park, Jowell, and McPherson 1998: 2, original emphasis); it 'models what the electorate *would* think if, hypothetically, it could be immersed in intensive deliberative processes' (Fishkin 1991: 81). The gap between the informed participants and the uninformed audience is bridged by televizing proceedings, although in Chapter 5 I question how effective that bridge really is.

---

[10] Primary Care Groups were the precursors of free-standing Primary Care Trusts, groups of GP surgeries, district nurses, dentists, and other health services which took over some of the health service commissioning role of health authorities. Their role, and the staged process of their creation, is described in the white paper (Secretary of State for Health 1997) and by Wright (1998: 5).

The NHS deliberative poll was the last of five run in Britain, the first being held in 1994. Like the others, it was organized by Fishkin and Robert Luskin of the Center for Deliberative Polling at the University of Texas, with their UK partners Social & Community Planning Research (SCPR),[11] a London-based not-for-profit social research organization, and their broadcast partner, Channel 4. Following a household survey and questionnaire, a random stratified sample of people were invited to attend a three-day event from Friday, 3 July to Sunday, 5 July 1998, held partly at Manchester Metropolitan University, partly at the studios of Granada Television, one of Channel 4's funders.[12] A total of 228 people accepted the invitation.

The deliberations included three short sessions in discussion groups on the Saturday totalling just over four hours, run by SCPR facilitators. Each small-group session was followed by a plenary session chaired by Sheena Macdonald, a high-profile political journalist working for Channel 4. In the plenary sessions, the groups submitted questions to be asked of two different panels of health policy experts (largely academics), plus another three question-and-answer sessions with the health spokespeople from the three main political parties. The whole event, including some of the small-group discussions, was broadcast in three one-hour programmes called *The Prescription* on 4–5 July (Channel 4 1998).

The deliberative poll is supposed to have 'recommending force', allowing 'a microcosm of the country to make recommendations to us all after it has had the chance to think through the issues' (Fishkin 1997: 162). However, in this case there was no broader macro deliberation going on about the topic, nor did it connect with any particular debate in government. So, while the process's designers might think of it in macro terms, this particular case was another example of micro deliberation, and one that sits roughly in the middle of Mansbridge's deliberative continuum.

1.4.3 The Leicester hospitals debate

The case with which I introduced the study contrasts starkly with the first two, featuring another citizens' jury which this time was the focal point of a high-profile, intense public debate: a case of a micro-deliberative event being used to give a sharp point to a more diffuse macro-deliberative process.

---

[11] SCPR is now called the National Centre for Social Research (www.natcen.org.uk), having changed its name in 1999. To avoid awkwardness in the text and references, I will refer to it by the older name throughout.

[12] Relevant detail about the nature and structure of Channel 4 appears in Chapter 5.

The issue was a Leicestershire Health Authority proposal to reconfigure services at Leicester's three main hospitals, the Leicester Royal Infirmary (LRI), Leicester General, and Glenfield.[13] The health authority felt that 'planned care' services were suffering because acute care was taking up too many resources. Following four years of consultation and planning with hospital-based specialists and other medical interests, they proposed concentrating accident and emergency (A&E) services at the LRI and the General, moving most acute services from Glenfield, and devoting Glenfield to planned care services. When the announcement was made in November 1999, however, a storm of protest erupted: the authority's planning approach had not taken into account the large investment people had in Glenfield hospital. This was for several reasons, among them the fact that it was a relatively new facility, unlike the Victorian-era General, and because of widespread public fear about the closure of A&E units around the country. The key, however, was the fact that a heart unit and breast care services had recently been set up at Glenfield largely thanks to major public appeals for donations rather than direct government spending. These units would have to move, at great expense, and the fundraisers felt they had been kept in the dark over something for which they had paid in time, money, and emotional investment.

In response, a petition was organized by the fundraisers which gathered at least 150,000 signatures;[14] the media were mobilized; members of parliament and local councillors weighed in. In the face of the storm, the health authority tried to find some means of resolving the situation. The means chosen, thanks to a suggestion from Patricia Hewitt—government minister, MP for Leicester West, and former deputy director of the IPPR—was a citizens' jury, which met in March 2000, managed and facilitated by consultants from the non-profit Office for Public Management (OPM). After four days of hearing witnesses and deliberating, the jury accepted the case for a planned care site, but recommended that it be the General, not Glenfield, to the delight of the protestors.

The key features of this case to keep in mind are that the jury was not the only element, but just the end point of a much bigger, Leicester-wide debate;

---

[13] Neither the Leicestershire Health Authority nor its watchdog, the Leicestershire Community Health Council (CHC), exist any longer, following restructuring in 2002 and 2003, respectively.

[14] The 150,000 figure is the lowest estimate I was given; the highest was 190,000. To put those figures in context, the population of the County of Leicestershire at the 2001 census was 610,300, of which 279,923 were in Leicester City, and 458,856 were of voting age (statistics available from www.leics.gov.uk). Thus, even the low figure represents just under a quarter of the total, and a third of the voting age population.

and that it was chosen not simply by decision-makers in the health authority, as in the Belfast case, but under great pressure from numerous others.

1.4.4   The NHS Plan

The next case is the development of *The NHS Plan* (Secretary of State for Health 2000*b*), a white paper setting out institutional and regulatory reforms for the NHS for the following decade. It is interesting for two reasons: its emphasis on putting public and patient involvement at the heart of the NHS, drawing explicitly on deliberative principles in the design of the institutions it recommended; and the use of deliberative principles to create the Plan in the first place. As I stressed earlier, this is not an evaluation of the government's programme, and I will be focusing on the Plan's creation process rather than the institutions it recommended.

The NHS Plan process was created by the Department of Health's (DoH) Strategy Unit, led by health policy academic Chris Ham of the University of Birmingham (see Ham 2004), which advised the then-Secretary of State, Alan Milburn.[15] Particularly important was unit member Jo Lenaghan, a former analyst at the IPPR who ran some of the UK's first citizens' juries in 1996. It was Lenaghan who largely designed and ran the consultation process that informed *The NHS Plan*.

The process had four main elements. The first was a series of focus groups with patients to identify health needs for the next ten years. The second was two day-long public meetings with about 200 participants each who were given presentations on the key policy problems facing the health service and asked to prioritize those problems. The third element was not obviously deliberative in itself but had the broadest reach. In a highly publicized release, a postcard was sent to hospitals, GP surgeries, supermarkets, and other retail outlets that asked, 'What are the top three things which you think would make the NHS better for you and your family?', with space inviting further comment 'on any aspect of NHS care' (Secretary of State for Health 2000*a*). The department received 151,999 replies from the public and 48,961 from staff. This was a low response rate given the salience of the issue in Britain at the time, despite assertions to the contrary by the Department (DoH 2000). The responses were sorted into broad categories by department staff, with the public overwhelmingly wanting shorter waiting times and staff wanting

---

[15] The Strategy Unit and Milburn were directly credited by current or past NHS Executive members and those health policy academics closely involved with the Plan's development and implementation. He became Health Secretary in October 1999; the Secretary at the time of the Belfast citizens' jury and the NHS poll was Frank Dobson.

improved facilities. All three of these public elements were then used as inputs into the fourth, a series of working groups made up of stakeholders from the various medical and nursing colleges, branches of the NHS, and patient advocacy groups. These groups worked on the detail of the plan and, as Modernization Action Teams (MATs), continued to work on implementation issues well after the plan's launch.

Thus the process as a whole was an attempt to generate deliberation in the macro sense, made up of a number of different micro processes, but driven from the formal end of Mansbridge's deliberative spectrum. Of the four elements, three had clearly deliberative features in their own right. While the postcard was not deliberative in the micro sense, it nonetheless fulfilled a useful macro-deliberative function, informing a much wider audience that the detailed deliberation was going on and giving them at least some input into that process.

1.4.5   Disability activist networks

Finally, I occasionally draw on material about macro-deliberative engagement driven from the opposite end of Mansbridge's spectrum, the informal public sphere. My example is the disability movement which is characterized by strong participatory norms, modelled as it is on other civil rights and new social movements (Driedger 1989; Shakespeare 1993); these norms are an essential part of deliberative models which draw on radical, participatory democracy for inspiration (Schlosberg 1995). Organizations like the British Council Of Disabled People, the Long-Term Medical Conditions Alliance, Choices and Rights, and the Disabled People's Direct Action Network are all multinoded networks with loose structures. They de-emphasize hierarchy and emphasize collective decision-making and collective action, although their internal decision-making processes do have majoritarian features thanks to the UK's legal requirements for registration as a charity which impose certain rules of governance.

When engaging in external deliberations, things are quite different. For one, disability activists are deeply suspicious of formal deliberative processes like citizens' juries, rejecting them as a 'top-down' model of citizen engagement which constructs disability as a medical problem, incompatible both with their 'bottom up' stress on self-determination and their model of disability as being socially constructed (Oliver 1990). Further, they see many consultation processes, deliberative or otherwise, as loaded in favour of the interests of those with financial interest in the outcomes, such as bus companies who do not want to have to make their vehicles accessible, or large charities which are disability 'industries' in their own right (DAN 1998). Instead the movement engages with the rest of public sphere in ways which try to ensure that it does not get co-opted by such powerful interests (Barnes and Oliver 1995). Like the environmental movement in Germany, described by Dryzek (2000), the movement has both 'insurgent' and 'collaborative' wings, using both direct action to generate publicity for its messages and, within strict limits, collaborative work with government agencies and charities. Operating in such ways, the movement has had some considerable successes, including the creation of the Disability Discrimination Act in 1995, the Disability Rights Commission in 1999, and new employment controls in 2004, although the detail of each of these remains the subject of controversy within the movement.

I do not spend as much time on the disability movement as I do on the other cases, partly because the movement prefers to support the work of disabled academics. Nonetheless, their activities often provide a useful contrast to the more formal, top-down processes that dominated the other cases, and so now and then I draw on secondary sources, including internet sites of disabled people's networks.

1.5 OUTLINE OF THE ARGUMENT

So far the key questions have been asked, the approach explained, and the cases introduced. All that remains is to give a brief outline of the argument to come before launching into the detailed discussion.

I have noted that the classic deliberative conception of legitimacy leads to the scale and motivations problems. But what if that conception is faulty in some way? Can we avoid the problems simply by reconsidering the nature of legitimacy? Chapter 2 tackles this question, building a more complete theoretical picture and expanding the deliberative account to include two different means of establishing links between participants and non-participants: representation and the publicity principle. The former helps take the sting out of the scale problem by allowing a legitimate basis for including relatively few participants; the latter helps both issues by greatly expanding the institutional possibilities of deliberative democracy. It helps us move away from a reliance on small, micro-deliberative forums towards a more discursive, macro conception of democracy in which a variety of institutions at various points of the public sphere are connected together in a deliberative system. Along the way I consider how other authors have dealt with the problems, drawing on them where that is fruitful. Neither solution is perfect, however: they both contain elements which buttress some aspects of legitimacy while undermining others.

Having established a new set of ideals, I then examine how three key features of my theoretical solution play out in real deliberations, using the cases. These chapters address the questions posed above: have the theoretical problems been solved, or at least managed, in practice; and what new problems arise in practice and how are they dealt with?

Before getting into the detail, however, I ask 'why deliberation?' in Chapter 3. The history and discourse surrounding deliberative experiments in the NHS is instructive because it reveals points of contact and conflict between deliberative and bureaucratic norms, which helps explain both why deliberative techniques were taken up with such enthusiasm by some policymakers and why legitimacy problems plagued some of those attempts. This provides some valuable insights into the challenges and opportunities to be faced when recommending a new way of thinking about deliberative institutions, as I do in Chapter 7. One of the challenges is to make sure that deliberation happens not just on small, local problems but on the big issues which frame them; otherwise we may end up with sophisticated deliberation on things which do not matter very much, a state of affairs which would not have much motivational power, let alone much democratic appeal. This may mean, however, that we need to move away from some of the micro-deliberative approaches which have attracted a lot of theoretical and experimental attention recently. I consider the possibility that these processes are best suited to small, local, self-contained issues rather than the big, complex, and ill-defined ones. Our democratic need in health policy, as perhaps in other fields, is for more democratic deliberation on the latter kind of issues, less on the former.

Chapters 2, 3, and 4 then dive into the case material in more detail. Chapter 4 looks at how competing representation claims are managed in practice, arguing that different claims have strengths and weaknesses depending on context. This has implications for the kind of process used at different points of a policy debate, with particular implications for participant selection. For example, random selection has been the preferred means for the designers of micro-deliberative processes, but its benefits come with significant costs when it comes to making legitimately binding collective decisions, since such representatives lack accountability to non-participants. Similarly, I look at the advantages and disadvantages of elected representation and what a few interviewees called 'championing' to see what they add to, and subtract from, legitimate outcomes. An important conclusion from this chapter is that no one micro process can be fully legitimate because no one representative can claim fully legitimate authority to speak on behalf of others. Once again the analysis drives us away from a reliance on micro deliberation and towards thinking about the contribution that many different micro moments can make to a deliberative system.

The second major form of establishing links between insiders and outsiders, publicity, seems to lessen our reliance on problematic representative solutions. However, it presents difficulties of its own to do with salience and the dramatization of communication, issues which I consider in Chapter 5. I pay particular attention here to the structure of the media as the primary means by which information and arguments are exchanged between deliberative sites, or between insiders and outsiders, drawing on some interesting contrasts between the deliberative poll as experienced by its participants and the poll as presented to its television audience. The major issue that emerges here is that the media is a necessary but unreliable transmitter of arguments around a deliberative system, but for fundamental reasons to do with the nature of news, not so much because of the individual failings of journalists. These features make it easier to transmit narratives which are simplified, personalized, and polarized, and not so good at transmitting complexities, abstractions, or information about impersonal forces. This in turn creates serious risks that the deliberative system is weighted in favour of those whose arguments can be dramatized and against those whose arguments cannot.

Chapter 6 develops some earlier concerns further by looking at how battles over what counts as rational are crucial for establishing legitimacy. The agenda-setting issue turns up again, the discussion reinforcing the earlier point that tightly focused agendas are best for micro deliberation but undermine the legitimacy of the outcome if the issue is inherently ill-defined and features battles over problem definitions, although some processes handle this better than others. Picking up on the rhetoric concerns in Chapter 5, it turns out that narration is one of the ways people reason together, having a positive role in forming communicative bridges, helping people understand what it is like to be in another's shoes. Nonetheless, the worry remains that such narrative privileges certain viewpoints over others, giving too much deliberative power to those skilled in public rhetoric and with a sympathetic story to tell.

As the discussion progresses, a somewhat pessimistic conclusion emerges, which is that one can only have good deliberation on things which do not matter all that much. Once something is important to a lot of people—that is, if one solves the motivational problem—the participation and publicity needed for legitimacy go up significantly; but so do the incentives to use rhetoric manipulatively and act strategically, undermining the deliberative quality that is also necessary for legitimacy. This implies that, at least given the present uneven distribution of power, state regulation will be necessary to enforce compliance with deliberative procedures, enforcement which some argue is counterproductive. Nonetheless, the cases show that these conflicts are manageable. At the start of Chapter 7 I restate the principles of a legitimate deliberative democracy, and argue that while we may have to give up on the idea of a perfectly legitimate deliberative institution, it may be possible to connect several different types of institution, operating at different points in time and space in the deliberative system, to create legitimate agreements. After going through the pros and cons for legitimacy of each of the deliberative models under study here, drawing out the major contrasts between micro and macro deliberation, I then sketch a scheme in which different kinds of process make different contributions at different stages of the decision-making process. While it clearly has some antecedents, this is a new kind of deliberative democracy. My model does not solve the legitimacy problems completely, but it makes positive progress on all the legitimacy criteria while managing the negative consequences. Chapter 8 summarizes the main conclusions, makes some suggestions for further research, and answers the question with which I began: what reasons did the protestors in Leicester have for conferring legitimacy on a process which seemed to hand decisive power to a group of sixteen strangers?

There are two final caveats before I start to answer that in detail. First, I reiterate that this is not a comprehensive analysis of the pros and cons of particular processes or decisions, least of all the British government's policy prescriptions for the NHS, although I do offer a limited comparative assessment of the processes in Chapter 7. Second, this is not a comprehensive critique of deliberative democracy, but an attempt to throw light on one set of little remarked but significant problems. I stay away from questions of whether deliberative democracy is a 'good thing' or not because the range of evaluative criteria I bring to bear is far from complete (for some discussion of this, see Macedo 1999). What I do hope to achieve is to give deliberative democrats, both theorists and practitioners, a richer understanding of legitimacy than the classic model provides, give a richer understanding of how the inevitable legitimacy tensions can be managed, and provide some ideas on how we can take the next step from current political institutions towards a more legitimate deliberative democracy.

2

Legitimacy reconsidered: theoretical solutions

The exploration of legitimacy issues in deliberative democracy starts by looking for theoretical solutions to the scale and motivations problems. The first task is to re-examine the concept of legitimacy itself, and in so doing we come across some interesting tensions between the demands of deliberation on the one hand, and democracy on the other. This reconsideration leads away from the possibility of achieving legitimacy in any one micro-deliberative process, and towards thinking about legitimacy created within macro-deliberative systems, with different micro moments making different kinds of contribution. However, while I conclude by summarizing the key legitimacy criteria which emerge from the theoretical discussion, the criteria stand in tension with one another. The later chapters will show how real policy actors manage those tensions, given their own views of what legitimacy and deliberation mean.

The argument will remain at a fairly abstract level for the moment, avoiding much discussion of specific institutions. The reason for this is that I want to resist the common tendency to equate deliberative democracy with specific micro institutions such as citizens' juries, consensus conferences, and deliberative polls. Instead, I want to establish some normative principles which allow us to be insistently critical of institutions. If we take the opposite approach and discuss deliberative democracy only in terms of practice, we have no means of criticizing those practices chosen, somewhat arbitrarily, as paradigms; Saward (1998: 8) makes the same point about liberal democratic principles and institutions. Nonetheless, some institutional implications will become obvious as the argument progresses.

2.1 THE CONCEPT OF LEGITIMACY

At its most abstract level, legitimacy is 'the moralization of authority' (Crook 1987: 553), the moral grounds for obedience to power, as opposed to grounds of self-interest or coercion (Poggi 1978: 101–2). It is only when decisions or regimes are legitimate that those who refuse to accept them should be coerced into following them, on the grounds that their refusal is illegitimate. As well as value which springs from our moral convictions, legitimacy also has instrumental value: legitimacy makes political processes more efficient by reducing the costs of enforcing compliance. Regimes, institutions, or decisions with low legitimacy face higher costs associated with uncooperative, strategic behaviour.

This, it must be noted, is quite a different kind of account of legitimacy from that implicit in a lot of political science. Particularly in the 1960s in the USA, but evident elsewhere and to this day (e.g. Thompson 2002: 2–4), scholars have drawn not on a moral account of legitimacy but a sociological account, starting with Max Weber and his famous categorization of claims to authority: traditional, charismatic, and legal-rational (Weber, Roth, and Wittich 1978: 215). Following Weber's view that authority systems are the result of psychological phenomena, scholars looked for evidence that such claims were accepted; in other words, they thought that the belief in legitimacy was all there was to legitimacy, and that acts like voting were indicative of widespread belief in the legitimacy of regimes. The classic expression of this view comes from Lipset (1984: 88) who writes: 'Legitimacy involves the capacity of its political system to engender and maintain the belief that the existing political institutions are the most appropriate for the society.'

This is clearly problematic: it equates legitimacy with 'stable and effective political power, reducing it to a routine submission to authority' (Grafstein 1981: 456). Such submissive belief cannot be all there is to legitimacy. Belief is important: it is people's belief in the legitimacy of regimes that helps render them stable; and political actors expend a great deal of effort making various Weberian legitimation claims by means of symbolic and verbal communication. But these claims can be tested against normative standards (Habermas 1975: 97–102). The point is further clarified by Barker (2001: 22–3), who offers a useful working distinction 'between legitimacy as an ascribed attribute' of objects and their properties, used in normative enquiry, and legitimation as 'the action of ascribing' such properties to an object, used 'for the discussion of observable human activity'. Legitimacy is the grounds, legitimation the social, symbolic, and political processes by which those grounds are claimed.

Beetham (1991), in one of the few thorough explorations of the concept, also makes this distinction between legitimacy and legitimation, but introduces a further distinction between these two ideas and legality. Legality concerns the rules of the political game, and is fairly uncontroversially subordinate to the other two, because the rules themselves may be just or unjust according to some external standard, and could have been established by just or unjust means. As such, legality tends not to get much ink in discussions of legitimacy, but this could be a mistake. This is because political procedures and other rules of the game need to have a certain amount of stability because people need to be able to learn the rules and use them if they are to be equally effective members of the polity; if the rules change all the time, only those who can bear the cost of relearning the rules will be enfranchised. Thus legitimacy includes what Flathman (1972) calls a stability requirement. Legitimacy involves a balance between the deliberative ideal that the rules should be the result of, or defensible in, public debate, and the need to ensure that the rules of debate are not up for grabs every single time.

Beetham's scheme has a great deal more to it, and it is worth pointing out a few more of its features. First, Beetham divides legitimacy into what he calls source norms and content norms. The source norms of legitimacy concern the rightful source of authoritative decisions. Given the democratic concern with the moral equality of persons, the legitimate source of authoritative decisions in a democracy is considered to be all those people affected, rather than tradition or external sources like scientific doctrine, revelation, or tradition, though of course 'those affected' may themselves be adherents of a particular tradition which defines them and their goals in particular ways (Bell 1993).[1] Beetham, however, takes the facts of scale into account, and argues that, because there will always be more people affected than active deciders, the deciders should be both authorized to decide by everyone else, and held accountable to everyone else for the procedures and quality of their decisions.

This means that legitimacy has a substantive element. The substantive grounds are of two kinds: the degree to which policy outcomes match the goals of the people affected; and the degree to which they achieve normatively justifiable or desirable ends. The important point here is that legitimacy includes a concern about the ends of political life, not just its procedures (see Estlund 1997). Now, we should only go so far as to give labels to these ends: freedom, equality, justice, as well as the meeting of basic physical, emotional, and educational needs of an autonomous life. In a fully legitimate

---

[1] Beetham's scheme does not include future generations or non-human subjects for whom present humans are the only spokespersons, but this is not essential to my argument. For a discussion of the representation of non-human subjects, see Goodin (1996a), as well as Eckersley (2000), and O'Neill (2001) who deal with specifically deliberative solutions.

polity the meanings of those terms will themselves be determined by the people in whose names they are invoked, although experts such as technical specialists, political scientists, public servants, and philosophers have a role in informing the decision-making process, and criticizing and challenging the results. In liberal democracies we tend to demand that those most able to serve the common good get leadership positions, and judge that ability partly in terms of expertise and experience; that is, we apply a meritocratic principle (Beetham 1991: 80–1). However, in liberal democracies we also tend to differentiate between the legitimate decision-making power of representatives and the more limited advisory power of experts on the basis that representatives derive their authority from, and are accountable to, the people; while experts derive their authority from 'external' sources which we regard as less legitimate. In terms of deliberative ethics, this means that experts' opinions have weight, but only inasmuch as they are offered in a process of public deliberation, and are found persuasive by those to whom they are offered, in a context in which the substantive goals of society are plural and essentially contested (a similar point is made by Dryzek 1990: 126–32). The legitimacy of expertise is derived from the discursively determined ends of the people at large, and is not internal to expertise itself.

One important implication of this discussion of the source and content of legitimacy claims is that appeals to rationality should have less force. As an appeal to an external source, the rationality claim is an important factor in the decision-making process, but it should not predetermine the outcome—it is one input among several, along with values such as efficiency, the environment, and freedom. As Walzer (1981: 386) puts it, 'rightness' may be a reason for promoting an answer, for hoping it will be; it is not necessarily so that because something is right, it is legitimate that it be imposed.

This leads to the final element, the procedures of legitimation. There are two possible angles of approach here, one which focuses on the bottom-up processes of granting consent, the other which focuses on the top-down exercise of authority and persuasion. Beetham emphasizes the former in his normative scheme, arguing that deciders should be both authorized to exercise decision-making power by those who are led through specific acts of consent, and made accountable to them by a variety of mechanisms (see also O'Neill 2001; Weale 1999: 112). Procedurally, political scientists have traditionally concentrated on acts of consent like voting (which is also the primary accountability mechanism), party membership, interactions with elected representatives and interest group participation. Now one would include a much wider range of participation in civil society, either directly oppositional like grass-roots campaigning and protests, or more collaborative, like public participation initiatives and interest group activity. It is the collaborative procedures for the creation of public agreements that have particularly occupied the minds of those interested in practical experiments with deliberative democracy (Stewart, Kendall, and Coote 1994: iii).

But there is also a communicative dimension to legitimation that often comes from the opposite direction: legitimation depends not just on consent processes, but on having claims made in public speech acts or on the unspoken, symbolic acts which leaders use to establish their legitimacy (Barker 2001). It is in this context that the Weberian, social-scientific approach to legitimation is still useful. As I turn to empirical material in later chapters I will examine the implicit and explicit legitimacy claims that are made by all sorts of actors, asking which ones are accepted or rejected, and for what reasons, and using the answers to add further depth to our understanding of legitimacy in deliberative democracy.

Because of the threefold nature of legitimacy, it is important to emphasize that there is no magic line to draw between decisions or regimes that are clearly legitimate or illegitimate, even without taking the communicative nature of legitimation claims into account. Citizens may, for instance, agree that certain decision-making procedures are fair, but still retain the right to challenge specific decisions reached using those procedures. That is, the granting of consent, either to decision-making procedures or to decisions themselves, is not enough: legitimacy is built over time through the critical examination of political action such that 'people actually consider institutional arrangements to be in their interest' *and* such that 'institutional arrangements actually are in everyone's interest' (Chambers 1996: 194). Real institutions and decisions will rarely feature such perfect congruence between perceptions and reality, not least because what is 'really' in people's interests can be a matter for intense debate, but this simply reinforces the point: legitimacy is a regulative ideal, not a fixed point on a scale.

Summing all this up in the context of deliberative democracy, the conception of legitimacy set out in Chapter 1—that outcomes are legitimate to the extent they receive reflective assent through participation in authentic deliberation by all those subject to the decision in question—is only a partial account. It deals with procedural conditions for granting consent (in broad terms) and one source norm, albeit the most important one. It does not take into account substantive standards and the advisory role of experts regarding those standards, the bonds of authorization and accountability, or the contribution of legality broadly conceived. Nor does it take into account the Weberian insight into the communicative nature of legitimation claims. I suggest that sensitivity to these other aspects of legitimacy will partly lift deliberative theory out of its legitimacy contradictions—but only partly, of which more later.

2.2   CURRENT SOLUTIONS TO THE SCALE PROBLEM

Let us now turn to the problems raised in Chapter 1 to see if this expanded idea of legitimacy helps overcome them. In this section I survey the available solutions to the scale problem, constructing my own solution in Section 2.3, before moving on to the motivations issue.

The first solution is to ask: What if bringing more than a few people into the forum could still constitute deliberation in some way? We would have to relax deliberative theory's strictures on the exchange of reasons between *all* participants, allowing many more people to take part in deliberation as listeners, rather than insisting, impossibly, that each of them take an active part as speakers (Urbinati 2000: 762).

Some theorists are very wary of this kind of move, because they argue that it gives too prominent a role to rhetoric. For them, democratic communication and rhetoric are polar opposites (Habermas 1996: 318; Webler 1995: 43–5). For them, 'communication' is used to designate the exchange of, and critical reflection on, validity claims which have their basis in a range of experiences, values, beliefs, and norms, while 'rhetoric' is used to denote speech which conceals or misrepresents its basis or coerces people by tugging at the emotions for strategic ends (Chambers 1996: 206). Even Remer (2000: 88), who examines the role that rhetoric played in classical Greek conceptions of deliberation and admires its persuasive power, is nonetheless resigned to the idea that its moral basis is 'murky'. Others disagree with the contrast. John O'Neill (1998), for one, argues that there is no incompatibility between rhetoric and reason because rhetorical claims can be subjected to rational analysis, and that rhetoric is necessary for persuading and coming to decisions. From another angle, Young (1999) and Gutmann and Thompson (1996: 135–6) point out that the pursuit of reasoned consensus and the civilizing norms of deliberative democracy submerge the genuine injustices suffered by 'other voices', and that rhetorical acts are often required to make those voices heard: protests, resistance, and emotional speech-making designed to shock dominant groups into perceiving what they have been blind to. Indeed, such appeals may sometimes be the only things that can reach across difference, 'to reach a particular audience by framing points in a language that will move the audience in question' (Dryzek 2000: 52).

This is not to say that rhetoric should replace reasoned debate, but only that it has a legitimate role in prising open the doors of deliberative moments, and building communicative bridges between participants. However, Goodin (2000: 83n) argues that, beyond a certain scale, replacement of reason with manipulation does in fact occur, regardless of good intentions: that reasoned communication in the deliberative sense is only possible at the small scale. If Goodin is right, rhetoric is redeemed only in so far as it is an accessory to a still small-scale deliberative process, leaving us with the scale problem. That accessory value may still be valuable, however, and I will have more to say about this in Chapter 6 when I consider how participants in deliberative moments actually do reason together.

Dryzek (2001) summarizes three other solutions: (*a*) to restrict the number of deliberative occasions to major constitutional moments (Ackerman 1991) or where the basic structure of society is at stake (Rawls 1996); (*b*) to restrict the number of people who deliberate and ensure they are representative of those who do not (the option pursued by most real deliberative institutions); and (*c*) partially to substitute internal-individual deliberation for social-interactive deliberation, making others 'present' in one's own thoughts and words (Eckersley 2000; Goodin 2000; O'Neill 2001). As Dryzek points out, the first solution is no solution at all, since restricting the number of times that genuine deliberation can occur society-wide simply restricts the number of times the scale problem emerges rather than dealing with it. The second, representative solution, strikes problems if we select our representatives by mass, competitive-elitist elections, since such elections themselves do not match the criteria for creating genuine public deliberation; thus, the representative solution simply recreates the problem in a new location. The third may be inevitable in any given deliberative forum because not every relevant difference can be made physically present without the scale problem rapidly becoming unmanageable. Nonetheless, it is problematic if some groups of people are regularly more spoken for than speakers: in their absence, minority people's views or interests are either not transmitted accurately or not taken as seriously as those of the dominant groups (Kymlicka 1995: 138–9; Williams 1998: 75–82).

Dryzek's own suggestion is much more creative and intriguing, drawing on a discursive idea of democracy. What he proposes is 'detaching the idea of legitimacy from a head count of... reflectively consenting individuals' and instead conferring legitimacy on provisional agreements which are consistent with the constellation of discourses in the public sphere, 'in the degree to which this constellation is subject to the reflective control of competent actors' participating in particular kinds of networks in civil society (Dryzek 2001: 660–5). In such a situation, Dryzek argues, reflective citizens will perceive the provisional outcome of the contest of discourses in the public sphere, a contest which results in transmitting the outcome to the state for policy action. They will either approve of it, thus conferring legitimacy, or will contest it where distortions have emerged, rebuilding legitimacy through such 'insurgent' activity. Thus, for Dryzek, legitimacy occurs in the interface between the public sphere and the state, not in individual, micro deliberations.

I am not convinced that legitimacy can be so easily disconnected from head-counts. First of all, discourses are not themselves disconnected from people; they are partially constitutive of identities on the one hand, and are tools which reflective people use to achieve their goals. For any given public conversation, real people have a stake in seeing a given discourse victorious in the contest in the public sphere and, although they may not think of it in these terms, may undertake strategic action (which is by definition not deliberative action) to achieve those goals. Thus, victory in the contestation of discourses may not depend on the reasonableness of the discourse; rather, it may depend on the existing power structure within which the discourses are embedded, and the way that structure changes either through direct human challenge or by more indirect or impersonal activities such as tech-nological and cultural changes. This idea receives some support from Fraser (1992), who argues that certain discourses are systematically dominated in 'the' public sphere, and that to be heard, their adherents create 'counter publics', parallel public spheres, in which they can engage in contestation. Even in their ideal form, however, provisional outcomes in the public sphere will be challenged precisely in terms of the numbers of people who subscribe to, owe allegiance to, or co-author the contending discourses: a discourse that commands the reflective assent of only some of the people, or only of those people in powerful positions, should not be decisive. In trying to detach legitimacy from headcounts, therefore, we still encounter standard problems in political theory about majority rule and minority rights, inclusion and exclusion, power and interests.[2]

Having raised those concerns, however, I think there is something worth-while in the idea that legitimacy is created in the interface between the public sphere and the state; and value in thinking about deliberative democracy as much more than a series of small-scale, self-enclosed deliberative moments, valuable though they may be at that interface. Before taking up those ideas, however, I want to return to a closer examination of one of the solutions that Dryzek rejected, the representative solution, because this raises some key questions that will be important when I examine the cases.

---

[2] Shapiro (2003) makes a similar point about deliberative democracy generally; a more concise version of the argument appears in his (1999) critique of Gutmann and Thompson.

2.3   THE LEGITIMACY OF REPRESENTATION

The idea of representation is useful because it offers a way out of the scale problem: it may be that people who are not physically present in a given deliberative forum may nonetheless feel they have had their voices heard because their representatives have spoken for them. However, I have also argued above that representatives can only legitimately act for others if they are authorized by and accountable to followers. This insistence on accountability and authorization creates some real problems for policy actors trying to use deliberative techniques, and in this section I explore those tensions, along with issues connected with other ways of thinking about representation.

There are, of course, other ways of holding decision-makers accountable without elections: there are various internal audit mechanisms, which Uhr (1998) describes in some detail, while government agencies are themselves held accountable to their elected masters in various ways, and thus indirectly accountable to the people themselves (see also March and Olsen 1995). However, I am not going to look at these methods: they do not help very much with solving the particular legitimacy problems at hand because they are not quite 'public' enough, focusing on intramural accountability between representatives and agencies rather than accountability to the people themselves. In chapter 5 I consider another possibility the activities of the media, which serve both an accountability function and help transmit communication well beyond the confines of particular micro-deliberative events. For now, however, the question is whether representation can help solve the scale problem.

There is a vast literature on representation, a literature in which descriptive, conceptual, and normative issues intertwine (Frankena 1968). I do not have space here to go through every conception of representation and every institutional permutation: that would be quite a different book, if not several.[3] So, in what follows I by no means exhaust the possibilities. However, one useful starting point is Birch (1971: 15), who offers three main usages of the term 'representation':

---

[3] The classic exposition of the way in which the concept of representation has been used in political theory is Pitkin (1967), while Catt (1999) summarizes the diverse practice. Both Kateb (1992) and Manin (1997) argue for the moral superiority of representation, while Phillips (1995) offers an important feminist response.

1. To denote an agent or spokesman who acts on behalf of his principal;
2. To indicate that a person shares some of the characteristics of a class of persons;
3. To indicate that a person symbolizes the identity or qualities of a class of persons.

Starting at the end of this list and working back, symbolic representation occurs where something or someone comes to symbolize a group of people in the way that, say, the kiwi symbolizes New Zealanders like me, Queen Elizabeth symbolizes Britons in some circumstances, or Nelson Mandela symbolizes the idea of a hopeful and united South Africa. Such symbols can be extremely important for legitimation because people feel they have had an impact on a decision or a regime if they see the symbols they identify with having an impact. Obvious examples include the way people feel a sense of validation and identification when their soldiers perform various missions, peaceful or otherwise; or if a person they feel symbolizes them—a local sport star, a well-loved civic leader—is seen to have had an impact on issues which matter to them. Despite its usefulness for legitimation, however, symbolic representation does not help us with making more substantive or procedural legitimacy claims, because there are no direct ties of accountability between such representatives and the people they represent.

Descriptive representation occurs when a representative embodies some relevant characteristics of the people he or she represents: that a woman represents other women, a Mexican other Mexicans, and so forth. Descriptive representation emphasizes identities, because those identities are politically and normatively significant (Phillips 1995); again, it matters whether specific groups of people speak for themselves or are spoken for. On this account, fair representation is about mirroring: to what extent are the relevant cleavages in society replicated in the deliberating group? This is contrasted with representation which focuses on beliefs and interests, where the identity of the representative is irrelevant, and fairness consists in responsiveness and accountability (Squires 1999).

One major advantage of descriptive representation is that, when the channels of public communication are clear, it allows those who are outside a decision-making forum to see that 'people like me' are in there having an impact—thus, descriptive representation includes aspects of the symbolic. However, there are two major problems associated with descriptive representation. The first is that it essentializes identities, which is the mistake of assuming that all women are the same, all workers vote Labour, or all members of any identifiable group think the same way, feel the same way, and have the same hopes and dreams. Essentializing can add to marginalization: 'the claim that whites cannot understand the needs of blacks, or that men cannot understand the needs of women, can become an excuse for white men not to try to understand or represent the needs of others' (Kymlicka 1995: 139). We can overcome this problem to some extent if assembly memberships are not fixed but gathered on a more ad hoc basis. The salient differences which require representation can vary from issue to issue, and so people will find themselves representing different descriptive characteristics at different deliberative moments: on one topic I may speak as a man, on another as an academic, on another as a taxpayer, and so on. However, it is also true that for many marginalized groups the experience of marginalization transcends policy issues—they are powerless no matter what the issue is—and to that extent there will always need to be some groups who require a seat in any deliberative forum (Williams 1998: 6, 16). The second problem is that, as with symbolic representation, pure description does not come with clear bonds of authorization or accountability, and I take up the practical difficulties this causes in Chapter 4.

The final category concerns the direct relationship between one or more principals and an agent who acts for them. We encounter authorization and accountability again at this point: not only are they necessary for building legitimate bonds between deciders and followers, they also refer to distinct models, of principal–agent representation (Pitkin 1967), often known as the trustee and delegate models, respectively. In cases where there are clear principal-agent links between representatives and the people they represent, principals can either bind their representative to follow instructions to the letter—the delegate model of representation—or give the representative free rein to make decisions and strike agreements as he or she sees fit—the trustee model. On the delegate view, representatives are held to account by their principals, having to be responsive to their wishes; on the trustee model, the representative is authorized by the principal to act as they see fit within a specified field, and within that field his or her actions bind the principal, not the other way around. The argument over which should have more weight has raged for centuries but cannot be resolved in such general terms, the weight depending on the functions expected of representatives at a given decision-making moment: where epistemic considerations dominate, trusteeship tends to be favoured; where 'right answers' are considered to be a function of procedures which guarantee inclusion and a range of views, delegation is favoured (Birch 1971: 15; Catt 1999: 88).

A key tension in deliberative democracy is highlighted by the trustee/ delegate distinction. For authentic deliberation to take place, participants must be open to persuasion, and so we should favour the trustee model and stress acts of authorization. Indeed, the idea that preferences are transformed as they confront others is one of deliberative democracy's core features and major strengths. However, legitimacy also demands bonds of accountability between agents and principals, and so we should favour the delegate model and stress accountability mechanisms. This causes real conflict for deliberators: on the one hand, they are expected to represent their principals' views forcefully; on the other hand, they are meant to change their views in the face of better arguments. The exchange and critical evaluation of reasons can mean that the eventual decision reached by a deliberative body may resemble none of the ideas taken into the forum; or may match an idea held by a minority group, and is in no way 'representative' of the views of the majority (perhaps even the overwhelming majority) of non-participants.

Part of the solution is that there is, of course, no such thing as pure trusteeship or pure delegation: every representative performs a mixed role, wielding authority but being required to account for it (March and Olsen 1995: 59–60; Pennock 1968: 18). Even in liberal democracy, representatives are transmitters of information and instructions in two directions, not just one: ideally, they convey the views of their principals, and convey the arguments of other delegates back to those principals for further consideration, performing what Young (2000: 125) calls 'representation as relationship'. If that is the case, then it may be that the 'better arguments' that persuade representatives within a micro-deliberative forum will also convince people outside it once they have been exposed to those arguments in their own, separate deliberations. This solves the scale problem by turning deliberation into an iterative, macro process in which everyone participates in the *argument*, just not in one room at one time.

Alas, things are not that simple. Political representatives are not like lawyers: they have more than one 'client', and thus more than one set of obligations to multiple principals (Catt 1999: 80, 88; Pennock 1968: 16–18), as well as sometimes conflicting obligations to act in people's best interests versus following people's express wishes. To take the example of representatives in a legislature, should they put more weight on those who actually voted for them; or all those living in their electorate; or their party caucus; or cabinet; or the 'national interest' (however that might be defined); or their ethnic group; or their gender; or some universal rights perspective? The answer to such questions will depend on the institutional setting in which the representative works as well as the dynamics of particular situations (Squires 1999). This complexity means that we cannot take the politics out of politics: a legitimate deliberative democracy will be one in which communication flies thick and fast between decision-makers and followers, speakers and audience, in processes which feature multiple micro-deliberative sites offering ideas and scrutiny.

In such an environment, the opportunity for representatives to manipulate other citizens is greatly enhanced. Given that, if citizens are going to have effective power over their representatives, they need to be autonomous in the sense that they have reasonably full information about the performance of incumbents and the likely actions of competitors; that they are presented with a range of options which reflects the diversity of opinions and interests, and not restricted to trivial qualities only; and that their choices have not been manipulated in any way.[4] To this, Mansbridge (1998) adds the requirement that communication induce reflection on preferences and proposals on the part of both representatives and citizens.

But note that the trustee/delegate tension is not just a problem when representatives have direct agent-principal bonds. It is perhaps more serious where they are selected by lot, or by stratified random sample, or by some other means of generating a deliberative body that is descriptively representative. I will cover arguments for and against lottery and randomness in more detail in Chapter 4, but for now I want to consider briefly the legitimate status of such representatives. It would appear that direct election is the more legitimate way of choosing representatives because the lines of accountability and authorization are clear, although election would have to be by means which are more deliberative than at present to avoid Dryzek's objection to this solution.[5] However, deliberative practice is heading in the opposite direction, with forum organizers choosing participants by stratified random sampling. Participants in deliberative polls and citizens' juries, for example, are chosen by sampling a national telephone directory, postal districts, or electoral rolls, often by market research firms. What is missing from such selection processes is the legitimating bonds of authorization and accountability between participants and non-participants. This problem was clearly an issue for decision-makers in the Leicester case, confronted as they were by the results of a micro-deliberative process recommending one course of action, and a petition of 150,000 signatories demanding another.

The question of methods of choice is bound up with the question of whether different relevant groups should be represented proportionately or not. The argument for proportionality is similar to the argument for descriptive representation: that the deliberative body should mirror the wider population. However, proportionality can conflict with equality of voice, a fundamental procedural requirement of deliberation. So long as group

---

[4] I have drawn on the conditions of autonomy given by Raz (1986: 369–78) to produce this list.

[5] This problem of the non-deliberative character of elections is what Fishkin's (1991) deliberative poll was originally designed to solve.

representatives are present in proportion to their numerical strength, identities and views which command the allegiance of the many will always dominate those of the few, regardless of the reasonableness of those views. On this principle, indigenous Australians, for example, would rarely get a seat at forums that involve fewer than fifty people. On these grounds, some democracy theorists recommend a 'threshold' level of representation which ensures that relevant groups get an effective voice in deliberation regardless of their actual numerical strength in the population (Kymlicka 1995: 147; Phillips 1994: 89n), although precisely at what level the threshold should be set is a matter for debate (Grey 2002).

Based on these considerations alone, it seems that representation by random selection is only legitimate when the aim is information-gathering, or when it is part of a wider deliberative decision-making process that involves the people more generally. Just as experts have a legitimate, derivative role in informing democratic deliberation, so do statistically chosen representatives have a role in informing the deliberations of representatives with formal bonds of accountability and authorization. But only the latter should have collective decision-making power on behalf of everyone else.

The distinction between selected representation and elected representation is often blurred in the literature on deliberative practices, the second either being ignored or being taken as equivalent to the first. Process designers make much of the effort that goes into recruiting a statistically representative sample of participants but rarely consider accountability and authorization.[6] This is often because many deliberative processes seem to be driven by information-gathering imperatives rather than decision-making ones, simply because research is itself a 'currency of institutional power' (Schratz and Walker 1995: 122), the authority to which technocrats appeal to legitimate their programmes (Beetham and Lord 1998: 16–22). There are dangers in such an approach. The relationship between organizers and participants is often a hierarchical one in which the organizer holds the power and manages the agenda, while the participants are subordinate, providing information rather than being active citizens involved in self-government, although there are ways of relaxing such control by handing over some agenda-setting power to participants, while there are cases of participants in real deliberation resisting what they see as limited agendas. This research approach to deliberation can be, I suggest, inimical to the democratic spirit because it conducts debate as if it were an 'inquisition of objects' rather than a 'dialogue between

---

[6] For example, Fishkin (1997: 3–4), Lenaghan (1996: 1591), McIver(1997: 36–7), Smith (2000: 56), Threkeld (1998: 5).

subjects' (Gergen and Gergen 1991). I will discuss how this became problematic in the cases in Chapter 3.

What I have tried to do so far is identify the rules which make exclusion legitimate, to avoid what I see as the impossibility of full inclusion. Let me briefly summarize what has been discovered in this discussion of accountability and representation before moving on to the motivations problem.

First, good representation varies according to context. The memberships that individuals consider relevant, the representatives' roles vis-à-vis their principals, the selection process, and the issue of proportionality all depend on the topic at hand and the aims of the representative body. So, what is legitimate in one context will be illegitimate in another. Legitimacy also depends on the people themselves deciding what is relevant and what it not at any given decision-making moment, not on predetermined divisions set in constitutional stone or public servants alone making that call. How exactly that would work in practice is up for grabs at this stage, but in general it argues in favour of a degree of ad-hockery in decision-making institutions. In the case of a legislative body, for example, this principle might speak in favour of ad hoc committees with members appointed to capture the range of opinion and experience on an issue, rather than standing committees with membership set by party proportionality. It also argues against setting particular group distinctions and proportions in constitutions, as has happened in Switzerland whose institutions reflect the major cleavages current in 1848 and 1959 (when the federal council seat allocation formula was decided) and thus fail to capture significant economic, political, and social changes since then (Kobach 1997).

Second, deliberative representation should either be based on *election*, or it should have just 'recommending power' not decisive power (Fishkin 1997: 162). There is a role for *selection* of participants when the purpose is information-gathering, but only as an input into a wider deliberative democratic process in which representatives are directly accountable to the people affected, not as a substitute for such accountable deliberation. Equally, deliberative bodies should only be proportional when their purpose is information-gathering, not when it is decision-making. This is to protect minorities from being dominated by majorities.

Third, legitimacy demands that representatives act in a dual role. They must be free to be persuaded by better arguments, thus acting as trustees; but they must also communicate with their principals as delegates, meeting the condition of accountability as well as authorization. Thus legitimate representatives have a delicate balancing act to perform; in Chapter 4 I discuss how real representatives in the cases dealt with the conflicts and what solutions present themselves.

Recalling the warning I gave at the start of this chapter about the incompleteness of the principles emerging from the theoretical discussion, all these points would seem to require a broader, macro conception of deliberative democracy rather than putting all one's deliberative hopes in the micro-deliberative basket. The legitimacy criteria push us towards thinking about the different contributions a variety of (imperfect) institutions can make to legitimate deliberative democracy, rather than continuing to hope for perfection in one ideal micro-deliberative moment.

2.4   THE MOTIVATION TO DELIBERATE

The scale problem is only one of the legitimacy problems bedevilling deliberative democracy. The other issue concerns motivations. Readers of Habermas would be familiar with his criticism of the motivational difficulties presented by basing democratic institutions on instrumental rationality: it undermines the values which push people into wanting to debate issues and come to agreements in the first place (Habermas 1995: 116). However, the idea that deliberative democracy also presents motivational problems has only recently been noticed. The fact that it does should not be too surprising: different institutions provide 'opportunity structures' for different kinds of motivation and behaviour (Tilly 1978), and so are likely to present motivational barriers just as much as they are motivational opportunities.

Deliberation's motivational problems can be defined in three main ways. The first issue is that deliberative procedures are said to exclude women and ethnic minorities because they privilege formal, general, dispassionate styles in an agonistic confrontation.[7] This style is said not to allow the experiences of other 'speech cultures' to be expressed adequately, particularly those of women and ethnic minorities within Western settings, and so their claims cannot get a proper hearing in deliberation. This presents motivational difficulties because certain groups of people may come to perceive that they have little chance of being heard in a deliberative forum simply because what they want to say cannot be expressed in such a setting, leading them to stay out of such processes, after a possible initial experiment or two. The obvious solution is to welcome a variety of forms of communication in deliberative

---

[7] Young (1996: 123–4). Note that this claim about agonism is quite different from that of Mouffe (1999) who famously *contrasts* deliberative democracy and 'agonistic' approaches. See Dryzek (2005) for further discussion.

settings (Dryzek 2000: 62–72), and I present some limited evidence from the cases on this point in Chapter 6.

The second issue is a variant of the first, and has been raised by disability activists in Britain. One of their complaints against micro-deliberative processes is that they are unable to give disabled people's concerns due weight because of the narrow agendas and motivations of those who set up a deliberative forum. Clearly, agendas and problem definitions matter a great deal: they limit the kinds of solutions that can be considered, and hence the views and experiences that go with those solutions (Kingdon 1984). Thus, many disability activists are of the view that proposals that follow from their social model of disability will not get a fair hearing at events commissioned and run by people who have an interest in maintaining the primacy of the medical model, such as health authorities and charities. This is not an in-principle objection to micro-deliberative processes: it is an objection to the way they have been used, and I will go into the detail of this problem in Chapter 3. But note that limited agendas can be equally problematic for macro deliberation, because of the way in which problems are socially constructed, and the limited ability of the channels of public communication to transmit certain kinds of information. I will take up this problem in detail in Chapter 5.

The third issue is one of pre-deliberative commitments, and it is raised in several forms. Shapiro (1999) criticizes the ideal that deliberative procedures require people to give up some fixed attachments and act impartially. He argues that this is to wish away the fact that these attachments to specific goals or to other persons are significant in motivating some people to take up political activity in the first place. It also ignores the fact that partiality may be quite justified sometimes, particularly when it comes to commitments to projects which are more than simply personal but are, in various ways, public without being universal, such as commitments to family, friends, to colleagues, and to causes (see also Larmore 1987: 141; Nagel 1991).

This problem is made more complicated by the social-psychological facts of public commitments. Mackie (2002) points out that once we have publicly committed ourselves to a view or position, it can be very difficult to admit a mistake of fact or interpretation, to admit contrary evidence or contrary premises. Instead, many people tend to advocate positions even more forcefully in order to maintain consistency, a consistency which is an important ingredient in maintaining credibility, esteem, and social status. We may not care much about angering 'others', but care very deeply about appearing consistent to those people with whom we share bonds of allegiance. This is particularly problematic for representatives who have bonds of accountability back to principals, as these bonds mean they cannot easily let go of commitments they have made even in the face of 'the better argument'. It is on these grounds that Kuran believes that deliberative democracy is unlikely to deliver the results it promises, because the 'motivation to retain social approval can easily overwhelm the courage to stand alone' even among deliberators within a micro-deliberative setting, let alone between representatives and principals (Kuran 1998: 542).

Existing solutions to the motivations issues are thin on the ground. Chowcat (2000) argues that the simple fact of holding a political view means one has not only a commitment to seeing that view acted on, but also defended against those who hold alternative views. Failure to do so, for Chowcat, undermines any claim that one's own views are best justified (2000: 751). That commitment entails a further commitment to supporting processes in which one's own view may not win; not to do so would undermine any claim to have a right to try to persuade others. Thus, Chowcat argues, to hold a view about political life is to be committed in advance to deliberative procedures regardless of whether one wins or loses.[8]

This is a plausible account of what people's first reaction to a challenge might be in the early stages of a debate, but it is not at all clear that, perceiving they are losing a debate, some people would not simply retreat into silence, to disengage from the wider community, or to pursue their goals by other, non-deliberative means: 'I refuse to dignify that with a response' is an old and highly effective strategy. The key weakness is in Chowcat's claim that views must be defended publicly if they are to count as valid views for the holder of those views. People can just as easily get validation within limited social circles without having to go public at all, and it is to these fellow members of groups that we feel the strongest bonds of commitment, and who place on us the strongest burdens of consistency. The result is that people can easily reinforce their prejudices rather than engage constructively with different views (Cox and Putnam 2002; Sunstein 2001).

Interestingly, where prior commitments do not present such a problem is in private interactions, away from the scrutiny of one's peers. Some people could privately express a wish to come to an amicable agreement but publicly be unable to because of the fact that they are being watched and held accountable by those they represent (Moscovici 1985). Therefore, it may be motivationally easier to get people with pre-deliberative commitments to engage in discussions and negotiation which is not public, and thus not 'deliberative' in the technical sense of the word. We seem to be left with a paradox: for deliberations to have motivational force for at least some of those who we want to include, it may be necessary to conduct them in small, private

---

[8] Shane O'Neill (2000) makes a similar type of argument, but spends more time diagnosing the ailment than recommending a course of treatment.

settings where the demands of prior commitments do not intrude; but to do so is to remove the legitimating power of publicity, and to reintroduce the scale problem.

Because deliberative democrats have given so little attention to the motivational issues, we need to look further afield for possible solutions. Drawing on Schultze (1977), Goodin (1982: 95) notes four broad ways of motivating people to perform desirable behaviour: coercion, self-interest incentives, moral incentives, and social benefits. I leave aside the first one, as coercion has been definitionally excluded from the discussion of legitimacy. That leaves self-interest incentives, moral incentives, and social benefits.

I can cover the social benefits quite quickly. While not everyone is motivated this way, what social psychologists call 'affiliative benefits' (Bandura 1982) rank quite highly with many. That is, lots of people enjoy participating in collective decision-making simply because they enjoy talking and sorting through problems with each other on an equal footing, regardless of substantive outcomes (see also Baumgartner and Leech 1998: 69–71). In principle, deliberative processes offer just such an opportunity, and so would be attractive to many, the more so if the processes are welcoming of other forms of communication than dry committee styles. However, this does not help much with the problem of motivating those whose pre-deliberative commitments override such affiliative benefits.

The self-interest incentive is the least attractive because it is the least effective and efficient means. Goodin (1992: 9) puts it this way: 'Suppose that what makes the act right is one thing, and what makes people do it is quite another. If so, then there will inevitably be some room for slippage between the two', which means that people will sometimes fail to do the right thing if the payoff to them is greater. We therefore need to consider the fact that some people will base their decision to participate on the basis of a rational calculation of expected effectiveness given their power relative to other actors in a given political setting; the 'probability of winning' given ones economic, rhetorical, or charismatic power relative to others (Goodin and Dryzek 1980).[9] The frequency of such occurrences is an empirical question on which I present some limited evidence in later chapters. Normatively, of course, deliberative democrats would prefer that the outcomes of decision-making processes came down to the better argument rather than economic power or charisma, and so deliberative institutions would have to be

---

[9] This is quite a different conception of 'efficacy' from the political psychology view (Almond and Verba 1963; Verba and Nie 1972). According to the latter, efficacy is simply a positive psychological state of general competence which comes with socio-economic status, having little relationship to the actual likelihood of achieving one's goals in the political realm, which seems implausible (Pateman 1971).

organized both so that people's chances of winning depended only on the power of their arguments, and so that the attempt to flex one's muscle in other ways would be unsuccessful. This would mean that other avenues of political influence were closed off, perhaps by rules restricting or publicizing private lobbying activity. This is another reason why deliberation needs to be as inclusive as possible: if one sees that one's social class is never invited, is never questioned, is never listened to, and is never decisive, then one's calculation of one's own likely efficacy, and thus one's motivation, will be dragged down too (Bandura 1982: 143; Koch 1995: 69).

It may be more effective if people engage in deliberation not because they have to but because they want to, although there certainly are cases of reasonably effective deliberation that started as a last resort, including the Leicester debate. If that general claim is true, we need to come back to moral motivations, which involve appealing to a sense that deliberative processes are the right way of going about things. Deliberative procedures may be a right way of doing things because the publicity principle 'works to ensure Golden Rule style outcomes', outcomes which respect the more fundamental moral value of reciprocity, because 'you cannot expect others to buy an argument from you that you would not buy from them' (Goodin 1992: 132–3; see also Elster 1997: 132; Gutmann and Thompson 1996: ch.2). Having to act in this way may make one internalize the reciprocity norm: 'What motivates you, on this model, is not the fear of losing support of others but rather sheer embarrassment at the utter inappropriateness of certain styles of arguments in the public forum', (Goodin 1992: 135) as well as, presumably, the embarrassment caused when one refuses to engage and has that refusal publicly paraded. The implication is that the simple practice of deliberative democracy, in which norms of reciprocity and publicity feature strongly, may be enough to motivate participation by those who are most eager to see their proposals for public action taken seriously, and for whom the problems associated with pre-deliberative commitments are the most severe.

Summing up this section, deliberative democracy faces three main motivational problems to do with its alleged speech culture: limited agendas resulting either from the specific motivations of an event's commissioners; the more general social and political forces which construct 'problems'; and people's pre-deliberative commitments to pursue substantive goals. The first issue may be solvable in a fairly straightforward way—simply broaden the definition of deliberation to include a variety of communicative styles—and in Chapter 6 I show that real deliberators can do precisely that. The second is more obviously a problem in micro-deliberative processes because most macro ones have no 'commissioner' as such. This means that the demands of legitimacy may once again point in the direction of relying more on macro-deliberation than micro, as did the requirements of representation.

The commitments problem has resulted in three somewhat conflicting recommendations: close off, or subject to public scrutiny, non-deliberative channels of influencing decision-makers; institutionalize public deliberation on a broad scale in order to encourage people to internalize norms of reciprocity; but at the same time, encourage some in camera deliberation where the commitments make it difficult for people to deliberate in good faith. This is hardly a satisfactory solution in micro-deliberative processes because it undermines the legitimating power of publicity. Again, however, there may be more hope if we turn away from trying to achieve perfect legitimacy in a single micro-deliberative moment and think more about macro deliberation in which such in camera discussions are simply one input into a larger, society-wide debate. That is, it may be perfectly okay to close the doors to thrash out a knotty problem, if the doors are subsequently thrown open once more and publicity is given to the reasons for and against a decision and its alternatives rather than the minutiae of what each individual or group brought into the room.

2.5 CONCLUSION: THE SHAPE OF A LEGITIMATE DELIBERATIVE DEMOCRACY

What has been discovered in this closer analysis of deliberative democracy's legitimacy problems, and in what institutional direction is all this pointing?

First, legitimacy has three aspects to it: legality, legitimacy-proper, and legitimation. Much political science, including the classic deliberative conception, conflates legitimacy and legitimation, but I have clearly distinguished them to emphasize that legitimacy includes norms which ground the concept: that is, it includes norms about the sources of authority and the substantive ideals and goals of a society. This threefold nature of legitimacy means that there is no 'magic line' which, once crossed, a decision or regime becomes legitimate: it might be considered excellent on one level and poor on another.

Second, the facts of complexity in a large-scale society mean that some specialization and division of labour is inevitable, even in the discursive conception of democracy, and so we require some way of assessing the legitimacy of representation claims made by insiders on behalf of outsiders. This will vary somewhat according to context, but a minimum requirement for legitimate decision-makers is that they can be held accountable, preferably by electoral means, to their principals. If they are also descriptively representative then so much the better, but descriptive representation alone, like expertise, is insufficient grounds for conferring legitimate decision-making authority: such representatives should only have advisory roles. Still, elected representatives have a very difficult balancing act to maintain, having to deal with cross-cutting lines of accountability, and accountability clashing with the requirement that deliberators be free to change their minds.

Third, deliberative democracy may not be legitimate if it fails to treat people and their points of view fairly: this is deliberative democracy's motivations problem. At least in part, the problems are about the transition from one set of institutions to another, and may vanish if fully deliberative institutions are the only game in town. This is because deliberative institutions may help participants internalize the requisite norm of reciprocity and deactivate the strategic ones; these are empirical questions on which I will present some limited evidence in coming chapters. One of my aims, however, is to think about how we shift current institutions in a more deliberative direction, so the pre-deliberative commitments cannot be wished away. This reintroduces strategic calculations of relative power which can both undermine the deliberative spirit and overwhelm affiliative motivations. This may be overcome by holding discussions in private, but that undermines the solution to the scale problem: so, for some participants at least, solving the motivations problem may make the scale problem worse, and vice versa. One aim of Chapter 3 is to get more clarity on exactly how difficult this constructive agenda will be.

All of this points strongly to the idea that legitimacy is a process, not a destination, created iteratively between many different participants and processes. It cannot be the property of any one individual or deliberative site, but could possibly be the property of a deliberative system featuring many different deliberative processes. While it would be an odd deliberative system if none of its components exhibited any deliberative features, each element could draw on a different kind of representation, a different kind of accountability, different motivational imperatives, different status for experts and lay persons, different levels of formality. There may be some permanent institutions which consider all collective decisions, but other elements of the system would form and engage on an issue and then move on or dissolve; and there is a clear legitimacy advantage to some degree of ad-hockery because good descriptive representation varies according to context. While legitimacy is enhanced the more democratic the components are in their internal workings, it to is the degree that those components are open to one another that overall legitimacy is created on a given topic.

Even then, however, the legitimacy problems do not vanish in a puff of smoke. The competing representation claims can be extremely difficult to sort through, and I go into more detail about the nature of the problem and potential solutions in Chapter 4. There are also questions about how deliberative and democratic the 'sum of deliberation' on a given topic would be. On the one hand, if the mass media are used as the means by which conversational threads are transmitted between citizens in different deliberative spaces, we need to be aware that key features of the media may distort communication, thus undermining communicative rationality; this is the main focus of Chapter 5. On the other hand, because some sites in the deliberative system are less powerful than others, they will be less attractive to some participants, who may then seek to participate only in those institutions which seem to them to be worth the effort, especially where pre-deliberative commitments come into play. Thus a competitive element is introduced into macro deliberation, one of the manifestations of which is a competition to define what counts as rational, the subject of Chapter 6.

It seems, then, that to pursue perfect legitimacy is to pursue a chimera: there is no such beast as a perfectly legitimate decision, a perfectly legitimate institution, or a perfectly legitimate regime, because legitimacy's elements cannot all be present at once. Does this mean we should abandon legitimacy as a critical standard, or abandon all hope of institution building? I do not think so. It may simply be a fact of life that all our categories, all our standards, have such tensions within them, that all utopias are contradictory (Hood 1998: 47). Nonetheless, simply because existing institutions cannot be perfect does not mean they cannot be improved, and utopias provide useful critical standards for measuring the improvements. In that spirit I use the critical standard established here to explore the real worlds of deliberative democracy, suggesting reforms in the concluding chapter to move current deliberative institutions in a more legitimate, democratic direction.

3

Health politics and deliberative techniques

When setting out my approach in Chapter 1, I remarked that health politics makes for a tough testing ground of the ability of any deliberative process to handle legitimacy conflicts. In this chapter I set out the relevant features of that context, revealing a great deal about the opportunities and challenges to be faced if we want to move current institutions in a more legitimate, deliberative direction.

My approach to this descriptive task is to explore the impact of ideas, setting out the major points of contact and conflict between deliberative ideals and some of the key motivations behind the deliberative experiments. Thus, underlying this chapter is the thought that ideas matter in political life: that complexes of ideas, values, beliefs, and facts are 'soft' institutions that help shape political action by specifying what counts as natural and unnatural, what agents are or are not recognized, what motivates them, how their interests are perceived, and so on. While hardly the mainstream approach to politics, it has informed numerous strands of political research including discourse analysis, interpretive studies, and frames analysis, and is particularly good at revealing anthropological data about the motivations of subjects themselves rather than the analytic categories of the researcher.[1] For this kind of task a historical narrative works best rather than the application of a supposedly generalizable theory of the policy process (Parsons 1995: 175), and I do this in two stages. In Sections 3.1 and 3.2 I sketch the history of central government initiatives driving the use of deliberative processes, tracing the impact of key ideas and public doctrines. I also consider the influence of 'policy entrepreneurs' in pushing those ideas (Kingdon 1984), and the features of health care institutions which have provided those ideas with fertile ground, although it needs to be kept in mind that deliberative techniques have been just one part of a much larger public involvement 'tool kit'. Step two drops down one level of abstraction to examine the motivations

---

[1] The bible of 'textual' discourse analysis in social sciences is Fairclough (1992), while a more statistically oriented approach is summarized by Brown (1980). For interpretive analysis, see Bevir and Rhodes (2003); for frames analysis, Schon and Rein (1994). John (1998) gives a reasonably balanced summary of the pros and cons of ideational approaches.

which drove the various commissioning bodies in my cases to use deliberative processes, the discussion of which will speak to the agenda-setting problem raised in Chapter 2.

One of the reasons for doing such an analysis is that it is not at all likely that deliberative processes have been taken up 'pure'. We know from policy studies over the last two decades that political practices constitute solutions to problems, problems which are rhetorically constructed (Fischer and Forester 1993: 6; Kingdon 1984: 115); particular solutions are successful only to the degree that they are—or can be made to be—consonant with dominant discourses, consonant with the particular values and understandings of the world which are embodied in those discourses (Hajer 1993: 46). So, one of the outcomes of this chapter will be to identify what gets added to, what gets subtracted from, and what gets left alone in deliberative processes when they are picked up and used by government agencies. The answers to those questions will have significant bearing on the institutional recommendations I make later on.

3.1   CENTRAL INITIATIVES I: PUBLIC INVOLVEMENT TO 1997

One of the problems with describing the health policy context in the UK is that it is highly complex: what counts as a 'health' issue is socially constructed and framed by technical expertise (Moran 1999); the policy community is large and complex; and the institutions vary between members of the Union and are constantly changing. In what follows, therefore, I have been extremely selective, pulling out a few key features which have a direct bearing on the kind of citizen participation practised primarily in England and Northern Ireland at the time of my study, and leaving Wales and Scotland to one side. More comprehensive descriptions are given by Ham (2004), Klein (2000) and Webster (2002).

From the founding of the National Health Service (NHS) in 1948 until 1974, the only real means of channelling public input into the NHS was via general practitioners (GPs), but that was fairly limited given the awe in which medical professionals generally were held. Health was 'professionalized' in the sense that doctors mystified and controlled access to medical knowledge so that people had nothing to contribute but their ailments (Harrison and Pollitt 1994): legitimate authority over health matters rested entirely with the medical profession. While the governing boards of NHS institutions had some lay members, they 'represented the elite of available voluntary effort' rather than having any demographic commonality with the public at large (Webster 1988). GPs were expected to act as the gatekeepers of the whole system, responsible for referrals to hospital-based specialists, a bargain reached with government in return for maintaining their private contractor status (Klein 1990; Moran 1999: 32, 67).

The first major change to this limited public role was the creation of the Community Health Councils (CHCs) in 1974. Governed by a board made up of nominees of the relevant local authority, local voluntary associations, and the Secretary of State for Health, the 186 CHCs were to act as watchdogs over the Health Authorities. However, the CHCs seem to have been created 'almost by accident' (Klein and Lewis 1976: 1). Phillips (1980) argues they were simply created in the image of the now-defunct nationalized industry watchdogs which, even then, were regarded as ineffective by most observers. Interviewees suggested that few people were aware of their existence. As with many other British quangos, they had no formal bonds of accountability to the public (Barker 1982); and, like the NHS boards, were not descriptively representative of the wider community, although they did attract some supporters (Hallas 1976). The CHCs were abolished on 28 November 2003; some of their scrutiny functions were handed over to local government, while their advocacy and complaint handling functions were redistributed to a variety of new local and central bodies.

It was under the Conservative governments of Margaret Thatcher and John Major that public involvement received a boost, but under quite a different model in which groups like the CHCs and their member organizations were no longer lauded as essential to broadening participation in democracy, but damned as 'vested interests' that diverted public resources for their own private ends. The key features of neoliberal government in the UK and its administrative offshoot, the New Public Management (NPM), are fairly familiar.[2] At their core is a view of human activity as the individual pursuit of competitive advantage, but a pursuit that can be made to serve the needs of others by encouraging markets which supply people with goods and services. Thus individual advantage and collective benefits are believed happily to coincide, so long as markets are not 'captured' for private gain by strategic

---

[2] For overviews and analysis of the Conservative reforms, see Gamble (1994), Kavanagh (1987), and Kerr and Marsh (1999). The term 'new public management' gets used for one, or several, or all of a not-always-compatible set of ideas including contractualism (Lane 1987), other public choice or agency theory inspired prescriptions (Hood 1991), and managerialism which draws on (idealized) private sector management (Pollitt 1993). I use the term in its broadest, catch-all sense, which I recognize glosses over many distinctions of intent and content. For critical discussion of NPM in many of its varieties, see Boston et al. (1996), Ferlie et al. (1996), and Hood (1998).

misrepresentation of supply and demand. The purpose of government, on this view, is not to supply goods and services, but to ensure that markets for those goods and services are created where they do not already exist, and are not distorted where they do. Market forces were introduced into the NHS most dramatically in 1990 when an 'internal market' was created such that health service providers were forced to compete with each other and private sector providers for contracts to provide services commissioned by the health authorities—thus creating what was strictly a quasi-market, 'involving choice by the purchasing agency rather than by the patient' (Harrison and Mort 1998: 62; see also Le Grand and Bartlett 1993; Bartlett et al. 1994).

Market discipline was combined, not always happily, with managerialism, a view with a long history that management is a neutral, 'scientific', and hence more noble function which should be kept quite separate from the messiness of politics, and that its methods, developed in business settings, are universally applicable (Dunsire 1973: 87–94). Managerialism includes the doctrine that 'managers should be free to manage'. Given objectives and budgets specified by ministers, managers should be free to develop whatever programmes and services they felt would meet those objectives without further interference. These ideas were first introduced to the health sector following the publication in 1983 of a cabinet-commissioned report by Roy Griffiths, managing director of the Sainsbury's supermarket chain, who recommended the creation of a general management function which would plan, implement, and control services, leading to a dramatic increase in the number and cost of managers in the NHS (DHSS 1983; Milewa, Valentine, and Calnan 1998: 509).[3]

In order for an organization to become a good supplier, however, it needs to know what consumers demand, and whether contracted targets have been met or not. Thus, health agencies in the centre and periphery invested heavily in developing new needs assessment and measurement tools, drawing heavily on 'total quality management' ideas taken from business settings (Besterfield et al. 1995), greatly increasing their management staff to handle the load of that and other changes. They conducted customer satisfaction surveys, designed standards and performance criteria, ranked providers according to how they met those criteria, and published those rankings. This trend was strengthened by a fundamental feature of health services around the world: the fact that demand for health interventions, and medicine's technical ability to meet that demand, greatly outstrip resources available. This has led to a global concern with health care rationing, also known as prioritization. The

---

[3] For an analysis of the impact of the Griffiths reforms on management in the NHS, see Pollitt et al. (1991).

failure of early attempts at priority setting to take full account of public values has led to greater interest in methods, including deliberative methods, of eliciting public values and making difficult trade-offs (Coulter and Ham 2000; Klein, Day, and Redmayne 1996; New 1997).

By the 1990s the focus was not purely on 'consumers': the key 1992 document on involvement matters, *Local Voices* (NHS Management Executive 1992), recognized that citizens more generally had a legitimate interest in the way their health services operated, regardless of whether they were 'users' of those services. Although it did not mention any of the techniques under study here, *Local Voices* has been credited with sparking the interest in deliberative methods in the health sector (McIver 1997: 3), leading directly to the six experiments with citizens' juries conducted by the Kings' Fund and the Institute of Public Policy Research (IPPR) between June 1996 and March 1997. However, the purpose of this involvement was quite different from that advocated by the IPPR and Kings' Fund: it was very much focused on research (NHS Management Executive 1992: 5, 9) rather than decision-making (Stewart, Kendall, and Coote 1994: iii). It was to research opinions, not to enhance collective decision-making (Pollitt 1993: 183–4). This is because, at root, public involvement initiatives were extensions of tools by which central government controlled local agencies, not tools for local people to control central government. *Local Voices* makes this explicit: involvement was to help health authorities build strength based on better information, making them more powerful in their negotiations with service providers (NHS Management Executive 1992: 3), a topic to which I will return at the end of Section 3.2.

Why is this problematic? In one respect, the problem is not that the processes were purely advisory, because they should not be anything else, recalling the legitimate role of randomly selected representatives discussed earlier. Rather, one problem is that deliberative techniques are used to advise the wrong level of the hierarchy, using citizens to answer quite limited questions on behalf of relatively powerless agencies (Pickard 1998: 237). This became an issue in the Leicester jury when it became clear that one of the reasons why the health authority was pushing for changes was because of a lack of trained medical staff: the jurors recognized that staff increases were very important, but training, employing, and paying for extra staff was not within the authority's capabilities, and therefore not on the agenda, which undermined the process's legitimacy in the jurors' eyes. In such processes, citizens make recommendations within boundaries that are quite narrow, and determined at levels of power to which they do not have access. Of course, the higher the body is in the bureaucratic hierarchy, the less this is a problem; but central bodies hold fewer deliberative processes, and almost none that are rigorously deliberative, for reasons to be explored in Section 3.3.

In another respect, however, I wonder whether part of the issue might not be a fundamental contradiction in the design of citizens' juries and other deliberative processes: that they combine incompatible selection methods with deliberation. These processes go to enormous lengths to inform lay participants and give them power to question experts and come to their own conclusions. This has a powerful effect on the participants: once they too have become 'experts', exposed to an even broader range of arguments than many specialists, they may come to feel that *they* should have the only legitimate voice, that their voice should be decisive, not merely advisory, as one of the journalists covering the Leicester case pointed out to me:

One of the good things about after the jury, some of these jurors got a little power hungry! I'm mean this is my personal opinion, I found it quite amusing, because I spoke to them afterwards, and some of them were like, 'Well I think we should ask about this next time it comes up.' They wanted to follow the process all the way to the first building being built, they wanted to be the ones that were asked and decided almost, so they got a bit power hungry, I think, by the end of it. But I suppose you would, wouldn't you? You'd get so into it, spending a week [deliberating] . . . 'Right, we've got a right to know now, we should be asked, at every step, which way they should go'.

Putting aside the question of why the journalist should frame this as 'power hunger', the more important issue here is an apparent selection/deliberation conflict. Participants are chosen according to research imperatives, the urge to generate a representative sample, but then are put through a process which empowers them as one would decision-makers, without having the legitimating principal-agent bonds required to make any decisions binding. Like the Black Knight in Monty Python's *The Holy Grail*, participants in such exercises could be highly motivated and well armed but lack legs. Conferring responsibility without authority is the classic way to create frustration, undermining the motivation to participate in the future (Czikszentmihalyi and LeFevre 1989). I will come back to this point in Chapter 4 when I address representation issues in more detail.

The research orientation was most explicit in the Belfast citizens' jury, which was conducted as a learning experience for the organizers themselves: to learn about 'ordinary' citizens' capacities, and to elicit values and recommendations which would form part of the Board and Councils' submission to the government on Northern Ireland's version of the 1998 white paper:

It was to see if there were other ways other than we had been using to talk to people, and so it was just one in many of the different approaches that would have been used at the time, because we were operating in other ways, like various focus groups or public meetings or questionnaire type things, or whatever. So this was, what were the pros and cons of a citizens' jury approach. And particularly because this was a policy which was going to restructure the whole of the health and social care, and we were trying to get a way of looking at the citizen without representative groups representing the citizen. You know, what could you do with 'the citizen' rather than some proxy for citizen about policy areas in the health field.

... We were wanting to see to what extent people taken off the street would have knowledge, interest, structured information, how one would have to present, how one would have to deal with presenting technical material to people who were not experienced in the field.... It was a case of trying to find ways of talking to people about what their values were about these things in a situation where we weren't coming to threaten, so that we could develop the agenda along with them. (NHS manager, Belfast)

Interestingly, the research orientation was connected with a key aspect of the jury design, namely, the question setting. The topic was deliberately chosen to be a 'low stakes' one, because the Board feared that in an atmosphere of extreme financial pressure the jury would come up with recommendations that were beyond the Board's resources; but, because the jury would be seen to carry a great deal of weight, it would put pressure on the Board to deliver something they could not. Essentially, the Board used the question to ensure that the citizens' jury had only advisory, not decisive, power. One Board member described it as an accountability issue: because the jury was not formally accountable to anyone else, they would 'leave us to carry the can for a decision they made' (NHS board member, Belfast). As an aside, it is worth noting that the 'low stakes' nature of the question meant that it would not normally be considered a 'good' one for a citizens' jury to consider: it was too broad, unfocused, and not directed towards a particular decision that needed to be taken (Jury manager, London).

In summary, then, the push to improve participation in health policy-making until 1997 was strongly influenced by the rhetoric of the Conservative government and its new public managers about controlling supposedly wayward public service providers, especially local agencies, by using a limited range of research tools, applied to a limited range of questions, to find out some of what people wanted and needed, and to make sure that providers gave it to them. As for doctors, the reforms left their power relatively untouched: the agency problem addressed by the Conservatives was more how to control local NHS organizations, less the medical profession, although Cairney (2002) argues that the doctors hardly emerged unscathed. While deliberative techniques like citizens' juries were first used late in this period, only six were run in the health sector before the 1997 general election, and all of them by a think tank and an NGO on behalf of fairly low level agencies; central government's involvement was minimal. Even where deliberative techniques were mentioned, they were simply lumped in with research tools like focus groups, surveys, and interviews. Thus, while the techniques were being promoted as a solution to one problem—the lack of responsiveness of *central* government—they were picked up by public managers to address problems of responsiveness of *local* government to central commands.

3.2   CENTRAL INITIATIVES II: THE BLAIR GOVERNMENT AND PUBLIC INVOLVEMENT

While experimentation with deliberative techniques began at the local level under the Conservatives, a degree of institutionalization was encouraged only once the Labour government came to power. Senior Labour figures, including Prime Minister Tony Blair, were well aware of the citizens' jury model: the present Health Secretary, Patricia Hewitt, is a former IPPR deputy director who would have been familiar not just with the model but with deliberative ideals; and they were promoted by Labour before the 1997 election when they made a promise (as yet unfulfilled) to use citizens' juries to examine the provision of electricity, water, and gas services (Elliott 1996). Thus, deliberative democratic ideals certainly had 'traction' with senior members of the government right from the start (DoH manager, London).

The change was partly due to the influence in the Labour Party of 'Third Way' ideas. According to Blair (1998: 2), the Third Way is about the social justice goals of social democracy, but is 'flexible, innovative and forward-looking in the means to achieve them' (see also Giddens 1998). It combines this with a somewhat conservative brand of communitarianism which stresses reciprocal duties to the state in exchange for welfare, and group membership above individualism. Thus, the Third Way has both egalitarian and collectivist tendencies: adherents believe both in decentralization of power to local communities and the encouragement of individual drive and ambition; but also in duty, cohesion, and norm-reinforcing institutions like the family and the nation, with which individual ambition does not necessarily sit comfortably (Driver and Martell 2000: 157).

Therefore, despite some claims of a clear break with the past (Gray 1996), public administration under New Labour shares some features with managerialism and with the strong government of Thatcherism. Like managerialists, Blairites are more concerned about outcomes than the means of achieving them; they claim to have a more pragmatic view about public versus private provision of services, but nonetheless admire 'entrepreneurial zeal' (Blair 1998: 4). They are interested in devolving power and working in 'partnership' with local communities, but still expect uniform quality across the land, enforced using performance measurement tools even more sophisticated than those developed in the days of 'distrust' (Klein 2000: 208).

These ideas were first applied to health in the government's white paper, *The New NHS: Modern, Dependable* (Secretary of State for Health 1997). Reflecting the mix of old and new in the government's approach, it became clear that some things had changed while others had not. The internal market was abolished in name, to be replaced by initiatives which aimed to devolve power and work in 'partnership' with local communities, but GPs still effectively act as purchasers choosing among competing providers, just not on the basis of price. The purchaser/provider split was still in effect in other ways: the Department of Health (DoH) in London managed policy advice and target setting, while the NHS Executive in Leeds managed service planning and delivery to meet those objectives through its nine regional offices, health authorities, hundreds of NHS Trusts running hospitals, and a variety of primary and specialist services. While the government abolished an unpopular Conservative policy known as 'GP fundholding' by which some purchasing power passed to some GPs, it still aimed to devolve up to 75 per cent of the health budget to Primary Care Trusts and, in October 2002, consolidated the ninety-five health authorities into twenty-eight 'Strategic Health Authorities', responsible for needs assessment and planning for an average of 1.5 million people each. There is still much uncertainty about precisely what differentiates 'strategic planning' from trust-level planning; how the health authorities' role differs from the regional offices; or how conflicts with local trusts are to be managed. Thus the tensions between forces of centralization and forces of decentralization, always inherent in the NHS, continue under the new regime (Klein 2000: 96).

While continuing experimentation was encouraged, neither patient participation nor specifically deliberative techniques were key features of the 1997 reforms, which were about re-empowering GPs and nurses as the patients' proxies (Secretary of State for Health 1997), strengthening rather than challenging medical professionals' authority. What put direct public participation in the spotlight was the publication in July 2000 of *The NHS Plan* (Secretary of State for Health 2000*b*). The plan was the government's response to a growing sense of crisis after the 1997 reforms, reforms which were supposed to 'fix' the NHS. This was partly of the government's own making: it made waiting lists the key measure of performance, but the length of those lists was neither entirely under its control, nor an unambiguous measure (Klein 2000: 213). When the lists continued to grow, the government was blamed. The sense of crisis was exacerbated by several well-publicized cases of medical mismanagement, the Harold Shipman murders,[4] and the failure of 'lean' hospitals to cope with a major outbreak of influenza in early 2000.

For my purposes, *The NHS Plan* is interesting for two reasons: because of the conscious use of deliberative principles to create it; and because, in 'Changes for Patients', (ch. 10) it promised a dramatic increase in patient and general citizen involvement throughout the health service. The creation process, and the importance of key policy entrepreneurs advancing deliberative ideas, has already been outlined in the introduction (pp. 15–16), so here I just describe the involvement initiatives themselves. Chapter 10 had eight sections which dealt with both new and familiar initiatives like improving informed consent and new complaint handling procedures. It also proposed a series of measures which were aimed at creating 'a system whereby the patient voice is stitched right throughout the healthcare system',[5] including patient satisfaction surveys, but also bodies designed on the citizens' jury model attached to every NHS Trust, every health authority, and several central organizations including the National Institute for Clinical Excellence (NICE), whose Citizens' Council is a modified jury writ large. All this was to be complemented by having local authorities take over CHC scrutiny powers.

In the context of the previous Conservative initiatives, these proposals were evolutionary more than revolutionary. First, they did not so much create new functions as redistribute the functions of the CHCs, although not without a fight, as I discuss further in Chapter 5. Second, survey research still featured strongly, becoming a significant means of performance measurement, standardization, and centralized control. Third, just as in 1974, the increase in the public's voice went hand in hand with further strengthening of medical authority: again, this was all about controlling local agencies, not so much the front-line doctors. Fourth, there was very little detail, which left much room for the reforms to become a new way of doing old things. For example, there was little specification of what 'lay' meant or in what sense they would represent others, which left open the possibility that the new forums would simply be made up of the same people who staffed the CHCs, people who were thought unrepresentative. This was deliberate: the aim was not to impose a single model on localities but to allow those local practices which were working to flourish (Milburn 2001). The risk associated with this approach is, of course, that the vision is implemented patchily, with key elements given inadequate attention or left out altogether, although the

---

[4] Harold Shipman was a Greater Manchester GP who was convicted in January 2000 of the murders of 15 patients; in July 2002 an inquiry found him responsible for 215 deaths.

[5] DoH manager, London. A similar phrase was used by two other interviewees.

Modernization Action Teams (MATs) set up following the chapter 10 consultation process were supposed to share ideas and to ensure some consistency across the country. Nonetheless, anecdotal evidence from interviewees suggested wide variation in the kind of person appointed as a lay member on NHS bodies, ranging from genuine attempts to involve a variety of non-specialist opinion to a continuation of involving only the 'great and the good'.

While 'deliberation' was not specifically mentioned in chapter 10 of *the NHS Plan*, experimentation with variants on the citizens' jury and panel theme was encouraged by the department, by some managers inside the NHS, and by an increasing number of consultation entrepreneurs in the private and public sectors. It was estimated by one interviewee that around 200 citizens' juries had been run in the UK, of which around half were in the health sector (although there is no definitive list—I was unable to confirm either the number or the relative frequency). However, all were conducted by health authorities, at a relatively low level of the hierarchy, and the numbers were steadily tailing off: authorities seemed to have begun experimenting with shorter, cheaper, and less complex variants rather than take the large amount of time and expense required to run a jury.

In part, this situation was allowed to develop thanks to a model of deliberation held by health policy actors which is simpler than the full deliberative democratic model I advanced in Chapter 1. As Jo Lenaghan of the DoH Strategy Unit explained it, the criteria for a deliberative event were that it include information for participants, discussion between them, and adequate time for points to be raised, questioned, and agreed on. Even health policy academics have set forth a stripped down account of deliberation: Harrison and Mort (1998: 63) write that deliberation only 'occurs where members of the panel have the opportunity to discuss/interact with others about the question(s) under consideration', criteria which can be met by processes much simpler than the citizens' jury model. Harrison and Mort include focus groups, but such groups have fundamentally different purposes: they are not oriented towards making decisions but towards uncovering the attitudes and beliefs of participants; the time frame is short and participants homogeneous to facilitate easy rather than lengthy discussion, and stratified to facilitate the confrontation of difference; they are ideal for brainstorming, less for the critical analysis of facts and values (Berg 2001: 112–13); and they include none of the democratic elements, such as prescriptions for who the participants should be, whether the deliberations are decisive or not, what the scope of deliberation should be, and so on.

Thus, it is important not to overstate the impact of deliberative ideals in the British health policy context even under the Labour government. The word 'deliberative' is used in a stripped-down sense excluding key democratic elements, despite the democratic rhetoric used to promote the processes; even that limited model has not been imposed by central government, which has preferred to allow local agencies to choose their own methods; and the processes have been run almost entirely by local organizations well down the hierarchy, not by the large central agencies with the real decision-making power. They continue to be categorized as part of a 'research' tool kit, not as part of an agenda to hand over authentic decision-making power; and they continue to stress involvement of 'patients' and 'service users' rather than citizens. Given those facts, the Blair government may be said to be encouraging some *deliberation*, but it is not implementing deliberative *democracy*.

What does all this history mean for our questions about legitimacy in deliberative democracy? Beyond the specifics of a given case, any democratic deliberation on health policy happens in the context of a three-way tussle for legitimate authority over health decisions between medical professionals, local managers, and central government. At the micro level, this means that it is likely that citizens will need to fight to have their voice accepted as a legitimate source of authority in health cases rather than merely 'contributors of ailments'. There are other implications at the macro level. Historically, public and patient involvement has been used by the UK central government as a stick with which to beat local agencies, not so much to give citizens control over central government and certainly not to empower patients over medical professionals, let alone health care industries like large pharmaceutical or insurance companies. And yet some of the most pressing problems of health policy are related to the political economy of health care, particularly the fact that the demand for and cost of health services is driven ever upwards by technical advances which are largely in private hands, and the fact that the users of health services pay almost none of the cost directly. As medicine's technical capacity to intervene in a range of conditions has dramatically increased, so people have begun to demand those interventions as a matter of right. As more can be done, demand has grown that it should be done (Davis 1992; Marmor 1994; Moran 1999). These costs are borne by governments, and thus by citizens generally, yet people-as-citizens rarely get to deliberate on such matters; most of the deliberative voice is given to people-as-users, who have few incentives to exercise restraint.

It is certainly the case that deliberation on these topics is not made any easier by the fact that the NHS in its current form is something of a sacred icon in British politics, unquestionable and untouchable. But equally, deliberative experiments in UK health policy have barely engaged with that broad level of generality, instead addressing relatively small issues for agencies which have little power to change things. Furthermore, the control motivation has allowed a kind of deliberative experiment from which many of the democratic elements have been stripped away, and some of the deliberative ones too. As for what this means for instituting deliberative democracy, it seems clear that legitimacy will require citizens retaking control of agenda-setting and deliberating on things which matter. But this would mean battling enormously powerful private interests, governmental, professional, and industrial, who have an interest in keeping citizens deliberating on the little stuff. I will have more to say about this in the conclusion.

3.3   LOCAL MOTIVATIONS FOR DELIBERATING

In Sections 3.1 and 3.2 I have concentrated on some of the broad ideas driving central government's increased promotion of public and patient involvement generally. But why have lower-level managers chosen specifically deliberative methods of involving the public? The answers my interviewees gave to that question come in two broad categories: rationalization and legitimation.

3.3.1   Rationalization and 'the usual suspects'

The new public management continues a long-standing tradition of 'deep-seated animosity' (Fischer 1990: 21) towards standard, pluralist democratic politics, seen as open to strategic manipulation for private gain and thus irrational in the sense that it leads to suboptimal results. This view of politics is based on the assumption that people are motivated by self-interest, and thus are subject to the pre-deliberative commitments problem (see Section 2.4). But this concern is shared with deliberative democracy, which is also concerned with eliminating manipulation of political processes for private or sectional gain. As noted above, the NPM way of dealing with such distortions has generally been through centralized controls like contracts, markets, and central agency preview and review. For local agencies following the introduction of Third Way rhetoric, however, deliberative techniques promise both some input from 'local communities' while still meeting the bureaucratic demand for rationalization of that public voice; that is, 'the informed view' of the public (NHS manager, Leicester; see also Dolan, Cookson, and Ferguson 1999: 916).

   This is not rationalization of critical theory, the inherently democratic communicative rationalization which results from free, inclusive debate oriented towards understanding between communicatively competent and reflective equals (Dryzek 1990: 14; Habermas 1996: 27). Rather, it is means-ends rationality which lacks an inherent democratic component, a rationality which is more about providing inputs which serve the needs of an 'active management' than facilitating the creation of an 'active citizenship' (Milewa, Valentine, and Calnan 1999: 463). Thus, while many advocates of deliberative techniques stress the promise of democratic legitimation, it is the promise of rationalization of both participants and outcomes that has resonated more clearly with public managers using the processes.

Several interviewees repeated the NPM line that the main obstacle to rationalization was the tendency of usual political processes to be dominated by particular patient and medical interests which would then degenerate into polarized 'shouting'; which is ironic, given that the rise of health consumer groups is directly attributable to the neoliberal revolution (Hunter and Harrison 1997). One phrase cropped up often when interviewees described the ideal participants in deliberation: 'Not the usual suspects'. The phrase means, 'Not the same members of the same charities and pressure groups we always have to deal with', and it is often said with a tone of exasperation and a wry smile which suggests that public servants and others are most grateful not to have to deal with these people in deliberation. While the remarks apply equally to professional societies and commercial lobby groups as consumer groups, it was the consumer groups which interviewees discussed the most, as in the following example:

Someone came to my surgery and her husband had died of cancer, and she had this recent experience of what she regarded as absolutely excellent clinical care, but the way it was being delivered, the way she was told about radiotherapy [was poor]. And she quite consciously knew that trying to feed that back would be part of her grieving process, so she would only want to be involved in this for say, six months, and then there would come an end, and then she would want to move on. Now her experience . . . was the kind of experience which was extremely valuable because it is current, it is extremely relevant, it doesn't have a hidden agenda, and it moves on. So it is those kind of recent users of the system . . . The proposal we've put in for replacing [the CHCs] will give that kind of turnover of membership, and will bring that continuously. You know, people who . . . wouldn't be professional patients. (Politician, Birmingham)

This contrast between 'professional patient' and some kind of 'real' person was made over and over again in my interviews; indeed, only two of the thirty interviewees questioned the dichotomy or offered a more positive view of the role of activists. What is interesting from a legitimacy point of view is that it implies that managers using deliberative processes assumed that the motivations problem of pre-deliberative commitments was a serious one, and hence the appeal of processes which confine those with such problems to secondary roles, either sitting on the steering groups which oversee the process and/or as witnesses and panellists. In citizens' juries, those with expertise in a policy field do not get the chance to interact, to change *each others'* preferences in light of the better argument. They only get to offer those arguments to an audience of 'innocent' lay people who then go away and do the deliberating behind closed doors—and I discuss the nature of the 'lay participant' category in more detail in the Chapter 4 on representation and representativeness. This separation of lay participants and interest groups is seen to be crucial in cutting through polarized debate and reaching rational outcomes:

You could look at it as being a way out for us in a particular messy situation. . . . We almost got the point where there was an impasse. . . . It was the single biggest factor that freed up the next steps in the service review. I don't think, if we hadn't done that jury, we would not have got through. Well, we could have got through, we'd have got through, but with losing huge public confidence because it may have been in the end that we would have bowed to particular stakeholders, in other words those clinicians who shout the most. (NHS manager, Leicester)

Despite its benefits, the role separation can be frustrating for some of the expert participants in deliberative moments. One of the organizers of the Belfast jury felt this particularly keenly:

You are a witness, you make a statement, to some extent you get cross-examined a bit, but you don't get an opinion as it were from the jury. . . . And therefore I found it a bit frustrating, like, 'Am I making the point here, is this a point that has been understood, am I misunderstanding them?' And I found it was a case of—I mean not disparaging it, I found it a very positive process—but it was a bit like giving blood. You go, you give, and you don't know where it goes after that, it just goes (*laughs*). They're doing the deliberation and they're doing among themselves and that is fine, but it is not the most normal human interaction because I would normally have an opportunity to say, 'But I didn't actually mean that,' or, 'Where are you coming from on that?' In the normal course of events I would expect to transact with you for a bit longer until we came to some understanding, or I said, 'Well, you can think that if you like and I think this'.

The lack of dialogue between those active in a debate is also a feature of the deliberative poll process: panellists are questioned by the chair and by a few members of the audience, and give short answers before moving on to the next question. In the NHS poll, none of the five plenary sessions involved dialogue between the panellists; in only one plenary, that with then-Opposition Health Spokesman Ann Widdecombe, were people able to ask follow-up questions; and only once, during the session with then-Health Secretary Frank Dobson, did anyone other than the chair make a statement back to the panellists rather than asking a question of them. While I lack evidence on how they felt in the NHS poll, one panellist in an Australian example clearly felt the same frustration that troubled the Belfast witness, calling the process a 'quiz show format' in which genuine dialogue did not get the chance to develop outside the fairly restricted confines of the small-group sessions.

This is quite a different kind of deliberation from that put forward by most deliberative theorists: deliberative democracy has been advanced as a model in which people who disagree can debate *with each other*, either directly or through representatives: it is explicitly thus for Gutmann and Thompson (1996: 346; 2004) and implicitly thus for Bohman and Rehg (1997: ix), Cohen (1989: 146) and Elster (1998: 1). The great disadvantage of this strategy is that the active do not necessarily have *their* motivations or preferences transformed by such processes because they do not get to test their arguments against the counterarguments of their opponents, nor have to face the motive-transforming power of the reciprocity norm. In addition, undermining the active may in some cases, be undermining the legitimate representatives of the inactive citizenry who do not have the time or inclination to participate directly, a topic I will take up in more detail in Chapter 4.

3.3.2   Legitimation up and down

The other key motivation for running a deliberative process which came up in the cases is legitimation, but legitimation aimed both up and down. The first kind is to legitimate the actions of the organizing agency with those to whom it is accountable, usually their political masters or supervisory bodies in the bureaucracy. The second kind is directed at those subject to a decision of, or action by, the organizing agency: it involves legitimation to the public, users of services, their activist representatives, or subordinate organizations within the public service, such as service providers like NHS trusts. It is also possible that organizations aim to legitimate actions to peer groups or those with equal status in the hierarchy, such as fellow managers in the NHS, in local government, or other members of one's own policy community, but I mention this only as a logical possibility: I found no direct evidence of this kind of legitimation taking place in the cases I examined.

The use of public involvement to legitimate downwards is specifically mentioned in *Local Voices* (NHS Management Executive 1992: 3), which advises, '...as health authorities seek to bring about changes in services and make explicit decisions about priorities they are likely to be more persuasive and successful in their negotiations with providers if they secure public support'. In the case of *The NHS Plan* deliberations, the DoH designed them to achieve not only high quality and rationalized inputs, but also to make sure that potential critics were 'inside the tent', in Lyndon Johnson's words. It was what Jo Lenaghan of the DoH Strategy Unit called an exercise in 'big tent politics' in which the legitimating effects on participants were at least as important as the quality of information and decision-making. It was designed to bind people to the process and to the outcomes by making them feel part of something significant, something with power, and the attention of the Secretary of State.

Of the four elements of *The NHS Plan* process (see Section 1.4.4), the postcard technique was clearly more symbolic than substantive. The primary aim was not to get information from a sample of British households, although Lenaghan expressed surprise at how useful they actually turned out to be in that regard. That job was done better by the focus groups and public meetings, information which was then dealt with by the stakeholder working groups. The primary purpose of the postcards was legitimation: to show the British people that something was being done. So, even though the million households which received the cards were just a fraction of the 21 million households in England, Scotland, and Wales, the publicity surrounding the cards ensured that the message 'we're listening' was transmitted loud and clear.

The stakeholder groups were both better informed and more substantive, although some felt that there was no clear link between their inputs and the final product; while some felt that they were not being involved in decision-making so much as being the objects of a research exercise themselves. For example, one NHS manager made this comment:

There's an academic approach to involvement that's . . . the gold standard in terms of a process. You have to be clear about what your expectations are, what you're involving people in, what you're asking them to do, give them sufficient information and sufficient support to be able to do that, effectively take on board what they say even if it perhaps challenges your own perceptions of the way things ought to be, your own model of the way things ought to be, and then you need to feed back to people how you've actually arrived at your decision. Now in terms of *The NHS Plan* it was very crude as a process, I think. Very quick and dirty, there was no feedback mechanism necessarily. The man in the street, I don't think they really care, but if you were to take your more informed lay membership, people who feel they have a stake in the NHS, I don't know that it altogether satisfies their need to feel involved and listened to.

Thus, the process made for an interesting change from the usual power relationships, in which the technical experts make the decisions and the public simply provide input, a role reversal some managers were not comfortable with. But even then the process had the desired effect: one of the remarkable things I noted during my interviews was that there was no criticism of the aims or ideals of *The NHS Plan*. People in the health service were busy trying to figure out exactly how they were going to implement the changes; and while they felt some discomfort about the process, they were not spending their time criticizing the vision. The same goes for subsequent reviews (Audit Commission 2003) and for the wider public: while there may have been criticism about the pace of change or the specific way things were being done, there was almost no criticism of the plan itself. It was agreed to be a good thing.

The Leicester case also featured downwards legitimation. Clearly the original decision to devote Glenfield Hospital to planned care services lacked legitimacy with the people subject to it both on substantive and procedural grounds—it did not accord with their views on Glenfield and was reached using a process which excluded their voices—and the jury was part of an effort to correct that initial mistake both because it involved citizens more directly, meeting the legitimate source criterion at least in part, and because the process met the rational deliberation criteria by hearing all sides of the argument, giving equal time to opposing voices, and reaching a consensus decision. The fact that a subsequent effort to mount a defence of the General Hospital failed dismally was cited as evidence of consensus by two interviewees, although that could have been simply because the attempt was made after the issue had ceased to be salient for most people.

Legitimation upwards was clearly a feature of the Belfast jury. While one of the motivations was to research citizen capabilities, another aim was to strengthen the persuasive force of the Eastern Health & Social Services Board (EHSSB)'s and Eastern Health & Social Services Council (EHSSC)'s joint submission to the Northern Ireland department, using the citizens' jury as a 'technology of legitimation' (Harrison and Mort 1998). Upwards legitimation was also a feature of the Leicester jury, but only as a pleasant, unintended consequence, not as a result of intentional planning. According to one of the journalists covering the jury, their decision allowed the health authority to put in a stronger, and eventually successful, bid for Private Finance Initiative (PFI) funding since changes to Glenfield would not have been as likely to attract PFI money; upgrading the old and somewhat dilapidated General was a stronger proposition.[6] While this was speculation, the journalist wondered whether it was not just the outcome, however, which made the bid stronger, but the process as well, since it allowed the health authority to go to the DoH and say, effectively, 'This is the will of people, and we know that because we've used a good process, a process you recommend'.

---

[6] For details of the PFI in the context of the NHS see www.dh.gov.uk/ProcurementAndPropo-sals/PublicPrivatePartnership/PrivateFinanceInitiative/fs/en (accessed 16 August 2005). Dawson (2001) offers a critical review.

The remark 'we've used a good process' suggests another possible angle on the legitimation imperative: that battles over public policy and political influence are in part a matter of whether or not one used a good decision technology or not. This is more than 'playing the user card' (Mort, Harrison, and Wistow 1996): different user cards can be stronger or weaker. This seems to have been the case in the Leicester example, in which the battle to have a decisive voice was at least in part a battle between different methods of getting at public opinion. I have already mentioned the key elements: the initial stakeholder consultations, the variously appointed spokespeople for different interests in the debate, the petition, the research conducted by the CHC, and the citizens' jury itself. The stakeholder consultations were flawed simply because they were exclusive: they only included key medical interests and not the service users or wider public. The interest group representatives, on their own, could not claim to speak for the wider public and, given the views about 'the usual suspects', were not seen by decision-makers, or even other interest groups, as representative in any sense. By launching the petition, they increased their legitimacy by securing acts of consent from 150,000 or more citizens, but the petition was attacked by the CHC on the grounds that it represented only the unreflective, uninformed views of the public. The CHC's own strategy was to commission survey and focus group research from De Montfort University (Wilcox 2000), appealing to the 'science' of the method to legitimate its claims, but the research once again drew on the uninformed voice of the public, not the informed view wanted by the health authority (NHS manager, Leicester). All these technologies were trumped, in media discourse, for the campaigners and for the health authority, by the citizens' jury for which more legitimation claims could be made: the scientific rigour of its design, the multi-level political support, the fact that it used ordinary citizens who became informed about the issues, and the attempt to include all sides of the argument (Burns 2000*a*, 2000*b*). While I have no direct evidence that this is generally true, the fact that such a technology contest occurred in this case suggests it may be possible that public officials, when presented with competing claims in a policy argument, take more seriously those whose claims are based on a more sophisticated technology than a lesser one, regardless of the substance or justice of the claims.

The advocates of other deliberative processes make similar claims, especially focusing on the science of the method. This is most clearly the case with the deliberative poll: the NHS poll presenter did five segments in which the academic credentials were stressed, including interviewing the process's inventor, James Fishkin, and focusing especially on the selection and resulting 'representativeness' of the deliberative group. It is the science of the process which is the basis for claiming legitimate 'recommending force' (Fishkin 1997: 162).

Beyond the specifics of the individual cases, however, there are legitimation imperatives to do with the nature of the organization doing the consultation. It has already been remarked that the vast majority of deliberative processes in health have been run by health authorities. Along with other quangos, health authorities have been repeatedly criticized for their lack of accountability either directly to the people or, in many cases, to elected representatives (Barker 1982: 7; see also Flinders 1999). Harrison and Mort (1998: 67) suggest that it is this unauthorized, unaccountable status which has led health authorities to use citizens' juries and other tools to increase the degree to which they can claim responsiveness to the public. To that I would add that the motivation to do so is not just an internal recognition by health authorities of a lack of accountability, but is a reaction to pressure applied by central agencies and ministers over the last two decades to demonstrate responsiveness to customers.

This discussion of the motivations behind specific deliberative cases has added to our understanding of the legitimacy challenges in two ways. First of all, the rationalization concern has meant that public managers have been particularly attracted to processes which quarantine those who are most likely to face motivational problems to do with pre-deliberative commitments, commitments which undermine the deliberative quality of a decision-making process. Thus, in practice, and contrary to the expectations of deliberative democracy theorists, those who are actively engaged in advancing political views do not get to deliberate together; deliberation is reserved for the inactive. While this may have rationalizing benefits for a given micro-deliberative process, it is not clear that it rationalizes the macro-deliberative environment, because those who are most active in that environment do not necessarily have *their* preferences or motivations transformed by participation. Second, the legitimation drivers have added another reason why we should think of some cases of actual deliberation as things which help empower not lay participants, but government agencies themselves. In the Belfast case, local agencies 'played the user card' in order to win resources from their political masters, as well as to gain support for their actions from the public.

3.4 CONCLUSION

The analysis leads to four conclusions regarding my goal of taking the next steps towards a legitimate deliberative democracy. First of all, the motivations of those who commission micro deliberation matter a great deal. They can affect not just the agenda of a specific deliberative event—which is a serious enough problem, given the frustration caused to the Leicester jurors—but also the very procedures themselves. Recall that the initial pressure to experiment with deliberative processes came from central government in the form of imperatives to conduct needs assessments and customer satisfaction research, in the name of providing better services to the consumers of those services. Specifically deliberative techniques had some appeal for central government because of their fit with the rhetoric of devolving power to local communities, although this clashed somewhat with the continuing emphasis on consistent national standards and quality control. For health authority managers, the appeal was the rationalizing and legitimating promise of such techniques. Combined with a limited conception of deliberation and a certain laissez-faire approach to how the techniques were to be applied, these motivations meant that when deliberative democracy was picked up by the bureaucracy it was not picked up whole: some of the democratic elements were left behind, while in some cases the deliberative elements survived in only a minimalist version. Where they are used at all—and remember that deliberation has been very much a side issue—they are seen as another tool of research, albeit a sophisticated one which could be useful when one wants to claim greater legitimacy for one's views.

Second, it matters a great deal at what level of the hierarchy micro-deliberative techniques are used. The more rigorously deliberative processes have been used lower down the hierarchy because their legitimation needs are stronger and because of the pressure on them to be responsive. Deliberation at this level tends to be about relatively small problems and does not address the big issues which frame those local problems.[7] The rigorous techniques are not used further up the hierarchy, where the bigger issues can at least be addressed, if not solved. This could have serious consequences on the motivation of citizens to participate in deliberation: if they feel that they are spending a lot of time on things which do not matter very much, the incentive to turn up diminishes rapidly. This problem may actually be exacerbated by a feature of many micro-deliberative techniques, namely the random selection methods which rob the participants of legitimate, binding decision-making power.

One exception is the case of *The NHS Plan* process which was conducted by a fairly high level of government, although only a few elements could be described as deliberative, even given the minimalist definition of deliberation used by the DoH, because legitimation concerns were at least as important as the substantive inputs. This led to a need to involve large numbers of people

---

[7] A problem described in a US case study by Gutmann and Thompson (2004).

which came at the cost of less rigour, there being an implied trade-off between quality and quantity. The other exception is the deliberative poll which also confronted large questions at the national level. As I shall discuss at length in Chapter 5, the problem is that it was not connected to any particular decision-making moment or attended to by any of the key policymakers, and thus had no effect.

It is for these reasons that one should treat with caution claims that deliberative democracy was being trialled in UK health policy (Barnes 1999; see Pickard 1998): some partially deliberative *techniques*, yes; but not deliberative *democracy*. The key questions confronting the health system were still in the hands of senior politicians and policymakers; the people only got to deliberate on little details, or in forums like the deliberative poll which was disconnected from real policymaking. Even those micro deliberations result in recommendations or research inputs into other decision-making forums; they are not decisive, and therefore show little of the popular control necessary to make a process democratic.

Third, and despite the worries expressed so far, even micro-deliberative techniques can have clear legitimation benefits: *The NHS Plan* vision has been accepted almost without question despite some confusion about implementation, while the Leicester case showed that a citizens' jury can cut through a bitter public debate to help managers, interest groups, and citizens reach a legitimate public agreement. However, this is achieved in part by assigning active citizens to a role in which they are quarantined from the deliberations, the deliberation itself being done by 'pure', uninvolved, lay persons, leaving the views of the active relatively untouched by the exchange of reasons. This is something that contrasts starkly with the expectations of many deliberative theorists. The advantage is that it helps deal with the motivations problem to do with pre-deliberative commitments; the disadvantage is that it might transform the character of activist engagement in public discourse less than theorists would think desirable.

Finally, it seems we are presented with an instance of an old joke, for which I credit the late Irish comedian Dave Allen:

Stranger: Tell me, how do I get to Dublin?
Local: Well now, I wouldn't start from here.

Just like the stranger, if one was trying to build a deliberative democracy, one might think twice about starting from here. There are serious difficulties to be overcome with establishing a political regime based on free public reasoning between equals if one starts from a position in which the political agenda is dominated by enormously powerful private interests like the medical profession, the health care industry in all its guises, central government trying to exert its control over local government, and local government using the public to extract resources from the centre (Fung 2005). Certainly it seems that one should not just recommend the general implementation of thousands of micro-deliberative processes: although that might be an advance on present dabbling, if one relied solely on such methods, the risk is that citizens would be allowed to deliberate only on small matters, constrained by forces over which they have no control, leaving them as 'creature[s] of great means devoted to small ends', as Barber (1984: 22) bewailed.

In addition, perhaps we should look to two other sources. First, the state can have a role in counteracting private power, and it should use that power to open up the deliberative agenda so that people get to discuss the big issues as well as the small, and in more than just micro-deliberative processes but in macro deliberation throughout the public sphere. For instance, rather than concentrating on letting people discuss which therapies should be funded in the Citizens' Council of the NICE (www.nice.org.uk), perhaps it would be more democratic, more useful, and motivationally easier, if the DoH organized a series of deliberative events on how best to control demand for health services so that money is not simply transferred from taxpayers into the hands of doctors, insurers, and pharmaceutical companies, as the authorities in the US state of Oregon attempted in one well-known but often misunderstood case (Jacobs, Marmor, and Oberlander 1999). I will offer some further ideas on how to do that in Chapter 7. Second, however, it may be that the liberal state as currently constituted is simply not up to the task alone—Dryzek (2000) certainly thinks so—in which case the role of activists like the disabled people's movement would be essential, challenging state and private action by means of 'insurgent' activity in the public sphere, provoking protests like those that were seen in Leicester. I will have more to say on that in Chapter 5.

That concludes the more abstract discussion of deliberative democracy and its legitimacy problems in theory and practice. It is now time for a change of focus. In Chapters 4, 5, and 6, I dive more deeply into the case material to see how the theoretical concerns discussed so far are grappled with by real policy actors. I explore in detail the three answers which my interviewees gave, explicitly or implicitly, to the question, 'What makes deliberative democracy legitimate?' Those answers were when insiders represent outsiders; when communication is open and public; and when the inputs and outputs of a deliberative process are rational. The first of those is the subject of Chapter 4.

4

Representation and Representativeness

Making good representation claims is one of the most important ways of establishing the legitimacy of having one particular set of participants and not another at any given decision-making moment (Judge 1999: 19). I ask two major questions in this chapter: What are the representation claims made in deliberative processes, and how do the different claims interact in a deliberative system? That is, do different representation claims conflict with or complement each other?

To address the representation issues, I have taken a similar approach to Saward (2003*b*) who points out that before one can ask about the basis of a representative claim, one needs to ask who or what is being represented. This is important because the way in which constituencies are constructed by representative claims can have significant political impacts. Take, for example, the way in which a limited construction of 'the Swiss' as German-speaking mountain dwellers is used to define and limit the rights of immigrants in Switzerland (Parkinson 2001*a*); or supposedly universal ideals of rough-humoured 'mateship' have been used in Australia to advance conservative social and immigration policies (Stokes 1997). I follow up this 'who' question by asking what kinds of representation claims are made; and what normative strength each claim has, both from the perspective of my respondents and my own normative framework.

I have outlined the key elements of my methodology in Chapter 1, and will not go over all that ground again here, but the bulk of the argument derives from an analysis of 108 mentions of representation issues in the thirty interview transcripts, identifying the answers that participants offered to each of the questions above, and the normative valuations they gave the various claims. Sometimes the answers were explicit; often they were not. Indeed, claims of representation were most often stated as fact without the grounds of the claim being made explicit or the statement being challenged which, as will be seen in later chapters, was the case with many such claims in the cases. It was not difficult for me to infer the grounds of the claim from other things the interviewee said, although there were six occasions where the nature of the claim was indeterminate. However, it is important to recognize that it was very rare for the interviewees themselves to discuss the grounds for representation claims or make them explicit in any way: only four interviewees directly commented on conflicts between different kinds of representation, and two of them were academics, familiar with the idea that there are different models. The remaining twenty-six wielded 'representation' as an unproblematic category without drawing attention to the tensions in the ways they used the term. In what follows, therefore, the claims have been inferred by me from the context, unless specifically noted otherwise.

4.1   WHO IS REPRESENTED?

In much of the democracy literature, the answer to this first question is considered unproblematic and is assumed to be 'the people' or 'citizens'; in the deliberative democracy literature, it is 'all those affected', although precisely how political actors determine who is affected and who is not is left as an open question. I have already noted that these categories can be constructed in fairly limited ways. Phillips (1993: 26–7) makes the point that these kinds of exclusions are an ever-present part of group identity formation; when a group is identified as 'the people', it is only done by reference, often hostile, to another group that can be labelled *not* the people. The people means 'us', but only with reference to a 'them'. In such ways, 'the people' can range from pretty much everyone on the planet, to those present in a given state, to citizens of that state, to a bare majority of participating voters of that state (Sartori 1987: 22), to 'people like me', and so on.

4.1.1   Ordinary people and excluded groups

As already emphasized, in the UK's involvement initiatives the people being represented are usually defined in opposition to 'the usual suspects', excluding people who belong to organized groups, or who have specialist training or socialization in medicine by which they would 'acquire new norms, assumptions, values and ways of behaving' (Hogg and Williamson 2001: 3). What is left is the concept of 'ordinariness', stressed by many interviewees using terms such as:

'Joe Public' (NHS manager, Leeds)

'the bloke in the street' (Journalist, Leicester)

'ordinary members of the public' (City councillor, Leicester)

'we don't want the usual suspects, let's get some real people.... They were real, ordinary people' (CHC officer, Bradford)

'we were trying to get a way of looking at the citizen without representative groups representing the citizen; you know, what could you do with 'the citizen' without some proxy for citizen' (NHS manager, Belfast)

This emphasis on ordinary people was for a good reason when seen from the public manager's point of view: it was to ensure some kind of equity in the representation of different groups in decision-making, to make sure that all kinds of voices get heard in the decision-making process, a need identified well before this particular phase of deliberative experimentation began (Richardson and Jordan 1979: 173). Indeed, five interviewees stressed the importance of representing excluded groups, and those who did not usually have a voice in public decision-making. The same point was made in the press release calling for applications to join the Citizens Council of the National Institute for Clinical Excellence (NICE), one of the citizen bodies proposed in *The NHS Plan* (see Section 3.2). While several interviewees expressed the view, two put it this way:

I suppose part of our problem always as a public servant is that you don't know to whom you are talking, and what weight to put on anybody's opinion, because anybody is only one of 650,000 bodies, and so always at the back of your mind . . . you felt it was those who talked loud, the people who speak often, the doers in the community who get heard, and I suppose the citizens' jury in a sense was us trying to move away from that. (NHS manager, Belfast)

You've got the same people with the same axe to grind all the time, and they're not representative of the wider public, because inevitably you ask people who are representing [mental health interest group] Mind or cancer where they want to see resources and you know what the answer is going to be. (NHS manager, Leeds)

The Q&A (questions and answers) attached to the NICE press release said this:

Because groups such as NHS employees, suppliers to the NHS, or patient groups already have a strong voice in making their opinions known in the decisions NICE makes, we would decline applications from anyone in those groups. In addition we would decline applications from those who work in lobbying organizations. We are anxious to give a voice to people who normally find it difficult to have their opinions heard. (NICE 2002)

Thus, the concern is to express the deliberative principle of inclusiveness (Webler 1995). The claim is not that the bureaucracy is excluding the usual suspects—they already have channels of communication—but is creating new channels for those who normally lack them.

There are three main problems with how the category gets used, one to do with the representation role that activists can play; one to do with a tendency to individualize the concept of representation; and one to do with motivations. I will postpone discussion of the first issue as it has much to do with conflicts between types of representation which I deal with in Section 4.2. The second problem is to do with the way in which the category 'ordinary' is used to try to find representative individuals. Interviewees reported that this causes problems in many situations, but it was most starkly illustrated in the Belfast jury. On the final day, the jurors asked to hear from a 'service user', which posed the organizers a problem: how were they to find a 'typical' service user, when everyone had such different experiences of the health service, different needs, different levels of involvement, let alone persuade them to come to the jury on a day's notice? The solution was to bring in a woman who cared for a disabled child, but that person was herself a member of a carers' organization and therefore, by definition, not 'ordinary'. Another interviewee, a National Health Service (NHS) manager and academic, almost put his finger on the problem when speaking of trying to find lay representatives for Primary Care Trust boards:

> ... how do you actually ensure fair, adequate, representation? By its very nature it is almost impossible, isn't it? It is like somebody saying, 'How do you get a representative GP?' As somebody said to me the other day, 'If you've met one GP, you've met one GP!' It is very, very difficult to get somebody representative of that wide community.

The important point is that it is not 'very, very difficult', it is impossible. There is no such thing as a typical individual, because it is an empty concept, resting on a fundamentally mistaken idea of representativeness in statistics: it is to claim that the middle point (whether mean, median, or mode) of a distribution curve is 'representative' of all the points on the curve, no matter how far away from the middle those points are, the skew of the curve, or how wide the variance in the data. One can only have statistically representative samples, within certain confidence limits, not statistically representative individuals. So, if representing the population in this statistical sense is important—and I will explore whether it is or not later—it makes more sense for the organizers of deliberative events to select random samples of participants than it does for them to attempt to select representative, 'ordinary' individuals.

The next problem is that even if we could simply distinguish ordinary people, it was commonly suggested that it may be difficult to motivate them to participate. Perceptions of efficacy come into this, but just as important for interviewees was the concern that deliberation, like socialism for Oscar Wilde, would take up too many evenings:

I think the concern of many patients' organizations is the structure [in *The NHS Plan*] is great in theory, but where are all these people who are going to be the foot soldiers representing patients? Life is busy these days: where there are couples, both people are working. I know myself from my own political experience . . . people don't want to go to meetings in the evening. It is like, 'I'm busy, I've done my work for the day, what about me?' (Interest group officer)

Given the problem of time, four interviewees speculated that the new 'lay' representatives on the various health boards were more than likely to be the same individuals who had served on the Community Health Councils (CHCs), the same individuals criticized by the bureaucracy as being 'unrepresentative' because they were generally retired, upper-middle class, white, and male. While one-off deliberative events might attempt to solve this by randomly selecting participants, as deliberative poll and citizens' jury organizers do, they would not escape similar problems if such methods became generally used: legal academics are becoming increasingly concerned about the demographic skew of legal juries towards those who have the time to participate (Abramson 1994: 143). A one-off event has novelty value, and may attract all sorts of participants; if it is one among thousands, novelty is a much less compelling motivation.

Disability activists have identified another problem with the view that public servants are simply adding channels for the otherwise excluded. As the bureaucracy has moved away from a reliance on interest groups and towards direct research and engagement with the public, some have felt that it is not so much a matter of creating additional channels but of changing channels, closing down the old ones while installing the new. This could lead to the exclusion of the disabled voice entirely, because the very nature of disability tends to mean disabled people are only given voice through advocacy networks (Beresford and Campbell 1994: 321). This is beyond the complaint by activists in the disability movement that citizens' juries and other deliberative techniques are a 'top-down' means by which the 'abled society', especially the health bureaucracy, engages with disabled people on abled people's terms, rather than a grass-roots approach which allows disabled people to set the terms, set the agenda, and develop and implement solutions.

This applies to more groups than just the disabled: the Leicester CHC chief officer pointed out the importance of representing the socially excluded, especially the working poor. Thus he placed more value on the social research commissioned by the CHC from De Montfort University which targeted those groups (Wilcox 2000). One could argue with his valuation: the jury selection process also tried to balance the jury on the basis of disability, employment, income, and housing tenure and, from a new public manager's point of view, was more successful at doing so since the CHC's research only talked to interest groups for the excluded, not the excluded themselves. However, the general point still stands: an important legitimating factor for some interviewees was the degree to which a process included those whose voices are not normally heard.

An alternative approach, mentioned by two interviewees and used in tandem with random selection by the developers of *The NHS Plan*, was not to represent people so much as views. This resonates with the more discursive approach to legitimacy in deliberation (Dryzek 2001), in which the important thing is not to make sure that all individuals are represented, but to make sure that all the points of view surrounding a particular issue are represented and get the chance to engage with each other in the deliberative moment. However, this was very much a minority response, and since the issues it raises are closely tied in with problems of how representatives are selected, I will postpone further discussion of this until Section 4.2.

4.1.2   Localities

One other important answer was given to the question, 'Who is represented?', and that was localities. In government documents and in the interviews surrounding the two citizens' jury cases, the people whose involvement was being sought were local people, local communities. Again, this ties in well with the Third Way emphasis on 'strengthening communities' (Blair 1998). One general advantage of an emphasis on locality is that it allows a community to have ongoing involvement in all sorts of initiatives which affect them. Of course, randomly selected citizens would not *individually* have an ongoing involvement, and much would rest on how one defined 'community' (Kukathas 1996). The local committee model, trailed in the West Midlands town of Walsall and taken up by the UK government for use by former coal mining communities (ODPM 1999), addresses the challenge by having 100 neighbouring households elect a representative to a committee to decide on local development budget allocation and monitor council performance, a model that was replicated in the Health Action Zone initiative, now apparently defunct.

Locality was used in an interesting way by citizens' jury managers: they tended to de-emphasize external factors and emphasize the locality not just of the participants but of the process itself, even to the extent of changing its name. It was called a 'citizens' panel' in Leicester to create a sense of local ownership. Speaking of a Scottish jury run for a local council on public health issues, one jury manager said, 'I got the feeling they didn't much like us coming up from England and doing this process'. Equally, in Belfast the organizers went to much effort to stress the originality of the concept in Northern Ireland and the involvement of a local think tank, Democratic Dialogue, which only had a secondary role to that of the London-based Institute of Public Policy Research (IPPR); the latter was almost invisible in documents and media coverage, and deliberately so. This was part of an effort to legitimate not only the process with the local public, but also to legitimate the commissioning agencies with central government, particularly in the face of pressure on local agencies to be more responsive to their constituents (DETR 1998). But it also attracted the attention of local media—a process that appeared to be 'home grown' held more interest than the application of something designed in Germany or the United States—which is important if one is trying to build communicative links between participants and non-participants, as discussed in Chapter 5.

Given the new public management concern with controlling local agencies, and the Blair government's concern with universal benchmarks and centralized performance measurement, one might think that this perspective is reversed for those in central organizations: that there would be a suspicion of locality and a positive valuation of people or processes which emphasized a national perspective, representing all the people of the UK (or whatever the relevant unit is for a given policymaking moment). However, suspicion of locality was not obvious in my cases. Instead, there is a view that local issues are best dealt with by local people, and that national issues require national perspectives; but that the latter are generated by creating debate between lots of different local voices so that a genuinely 'national' perspective emerges. The key to this is inclusion of a range of people with different perspectives. So, while the deliberative poll presenter stressed the idea that participants represented 'the whole of Britain' and 'the country at large' (Channel 4 1998: Episode 1, 20:00:30), the role of those people was to contribute their *different* perspectives (Fishkin 1997: 40–1) so that a national view could emerge from the debate. In *The NHS Plan* process, the organizer and participants stressed the importance of including a range of locality and interest-based perspectives in order to generate a national consensus.

The major disadvantage of the emphasis on locality, however, is that it exacerbates the agenda-setting problem, unduly restricting the scope of democratic deliberation to issues which are decidable at the local level. While I cannot make any firm claims on this point based on my case material, I would be willing to bet that where local people decided to operate in ways which diverged significantly from central standards, they would quickly be brought back into line.

So, the major answers to 'who is represented' are ordinary people and localities. In terms of legitimacy, ordinariness is valued for reasons of inclusion, giving excluded groups access to decision-making; but it is a category without much content which causes problems when organizers try to find 'representative individuals' and when they definitionally exclude the active; it may also cause problems for time-poor citizens. Locality has legitimacy advantages in that it gives local people the chance to develop ongoing rather than one-off relationships with decision-makers, and gives them a sense of ownership of the process; its downside is that it can restrict the scope of deliberations to local issues only.

4.2 TYPES OF REPRESENTATION

Having explored some issues to do with who is represented, we now need to consider how they are represented, exploring issues of type, composition, and role. Before doing so, it is worth reiterating where we got to with the theoretical discussion in Chapter 2. There I argued that good representation varies according to the purpose of the deliberative body: if it is research and opinion formation, then descriptive representation seems particularly important; if decision-making, then principal-agent bonds are also required, along with requirements that representatives communicate back and forth with each other and their principals. When considering legitimacy, however, we are fundamentally asking questions about decision-making, not opinion formation: legitimacy is the grounds for obedience to decisions, not the grounds for agreeing with a point of view. Therefore, I place more normative weight on the accountability and authorization requirements than the descriptive ones, without discounting the value of the latter for bringing a range of voices into a particular decision-making moment.

How do ideas about representation appear in the cases? To answer this, I look at the means by which a representative deliberative body is composed, connecting the method with one or more of the types of representation discussion above, and highlighting the advantages and disadvantages of the various processes. The major methods are random selection, self-selection, and election.

4.2.1 Random selection: mirroring the population

Among micro-deliberative techniques, random selection is by far the dominant means of choosing participants (Ryfe 2002). It was the way lay participants were chosen for both the citizens' juries, the deliberative poll, and for one of the consultation exercises in *The NHS Plan* process.

As well as being a relatively cheap way of choosing representatives (Broome 1984: 41–2), random selection, or lottery, has the virtue of fairness: given the democratic value placed on the political equality of all citizens, it is a just means of choosing which citizens will rule and which will be ruled at any one moment because no one with an interest in the outcome can control the result (Goodwin 1992). Random selection has a venerable history: it was one of the means by which the Athenians selected many office holders, the Florentines and Venetians selected magistrates, which early republicans recommended as an essential element of good government (Manin 1997), and which recent participatory democrats including feminist groups and workers' co-operatives have used to apportion roles (Catt 1999). Indeed, lottery was regarded as the defining feature of democracy by Aristotle, with election characteristic of oligarchy and aristocracy (Aristotle 1997: VI, 9, 1294b6). Manin (1997: 41) argues that this was because alternating rulership and obedience, facilitated by lot, was seen as essential to the development of good citizens by giving everyone lessons in both leadership and obedience; because it helped avoid the undue concentration of power in professionalized political classes encouraged by elections; and because it protected equal rights to speak in assemblies.

The other major virtue of random selection, and the one that receives more modern attention, is descriptive accuracy. For example, Carson and Martin (1999) criticize existing representative and bureaucratic institutions for being dominated by a limited set of powerful interests who then manipulate the public policy process and institutional arrangements for private ends. Random selection is said to solve these problems by comprising a decision-making body of a variety of interests. The same point is made by Burnheim (1985: 195, n. 10), for whom the point of randomness in his proposed 'demarchy' is to create a body 'that is sensitive to the interests of those affected'. From a deliberative point of view, therefore, randomness seems to encourage inclusiveness, and thus seems a promising way of making up an assembly.

It should be noted, however, that what some modern advocates are talking about is not strictly random. Rather, it is random stratified sampling, or quota sampling, in which those selecting the sample have predetermined quotas of certain characteristics to fill, proportional to their observed frequency in the population. This is quite a different concern from that of the Greeks: they aimed to give all citizens, regardless of their identity, an equal chance of exercising power, and 'representation' in the modern sense was not the issue. For modern advocates, however, two new considerations arise. First, identity is important, following the calls for a politics of presence (Phillips 1995), and so the descriptive characteristics of the people in the forum matter in ways they once did not. Second, the research paradigm (see, Section 3.1) dominates to the extent that randomly selected bodies are used to research what the people think, or *would* think given the time and information (Park, Jowell, and McPherson 1998). Given that, it is important that the membership of the forum is descriptively representative of the population in order to give results which 'accurately' describe what the rest of the population thinks (Carson and Martin 1999: 26). A pure random sample can be descriptively representative if large enough, but a stratified sample can be much smaller, because it does not leave the selection of key characteristics to chance. The upside is that relatively small groups can be said to be statistically representative of a large population on the criteria chosen; the downside is that such small groups are representative *only* on those criteria, leaving the risk of missing important differences which have not been selected for. This concern with stratification has interesting consequences for the legitimacy of deliberative bodies, as I shall show shortly.

Returning to the cases, both the fairness and rationality benefits were mentioned by those interviewees who noted random selection. One of the journalists covering the Leicester debate stressed the incompleteness of perspectives coming from well-organized interest groups and the 'suits'—that is, the health authority managers—by implication hailing the jury's random selection for generating a more complete view of what should be done:

> ... because everyone's got an opinion based on their own experience, and some people are more outspoken than others, so it was felt that perhaps either the charities had a bigger voice than they should have got compared to other people, for example kidney patients.... So what we need [is] to get a group of people together who represent the whole of Leicestershire as best we can, in geography and age and class and everything else, and see what they think, and take it from what they think. I think everyone felt that meant there needs to be somebody else making the decision other than the suits.

An interest group leader in Leicester linked randomness with rationality. He suggested that randomly selected 'ordinary' people did not have specific interests which clouded their judgement about the benefits of alternative proposals. The implication was that they were able to weigh arguments free of emotional attachments to specific outcomes, and thus look at the information they were given in a rational manner. Thus it seems randomness can have a circuit-breaker role, helping move debates on when politics as usual, conducted between competing interests and networks, has broken down.

The US originators of citizens' juries and deliberative polls make much of representativeness based on random selection. For example, the Jefferson

Center (1998: 9) claims that 'a random and scientific method is a critical step towards creating a jury that truly reflects the public as a whole', although those who have taken up the method in Britain have been careful to tone down the claim that a sample of sixteen people can be 'truly' representative in this way (Lenaghan 1999: 54–5). Participants in a deliberative poll are said to be a 'microcosm' of the nation, the word being repeated like a mantra by the NHS poll presenter and in the various reports and briefing documents produced before and after the event (Channel 4 1998; Park, Jowell, and McPherson 1998). Indeed, the ability of a deliberative poll to gather together a random sample of people in one place is an aspect many participants remark on, in words like this: 'I've selected thousands of national random samples, but I've never *seen* one—no one has' (Fishkin 1997: 163). The importance of this was further stressed to the field staff who recruited participants:

In order for the event to be successful, it is important that the people who turn up can be seen as representative of the British population. We appreciate that certain groups of the population will be less likely to agree to take part than others (e.g. the very elderly) but we must try as far as possible to get a balanced sample of participants. Therefore, when necessary, stress that it is important that we represent everyone so that we can get a true cross-section—the old as well as the young, the less well-educated as well as the well-educated, those who know little about the subject as well as those who know a great deal. (SCPR 1998: 8)

This is clearly representation in the descriptive sense. The groups are selected as random stratified samples, either by telephone or by door knocking, filling specific quotas from national census data on the basis of age, gender, and geographic location. Further, the claim is made that the groups so selected are representative of wider opinions, not just physical characteristics: according to deliberative poll developer Fishkin (1997: 205–6), there were no significant attitudinal or demographic differences between those 300 people who participated in the first UK poll and the 869 people who responded to the initial survey. That may not be quite true, however: if there were any distortions in the sample they would have occurred at the stage before the one Fishkin uses as his baseline; that is, those unwilling to participate even in the initial survey may be in some important way different from those who did participate.

The importance of this descriptive, statistical representativeness was expressed by Fishkin in an interview in the NHS poll broadcast:

They are in effect a microcosm, not only of the nation's attitudes, but of the nation's health vulnerabilities: its future cancer victims, its future heart attacks, its future diabetics. And so to make hard choices, in effect they have to choose among themselves, face to face. (Channel 4 1998: Episode 3, 19:20:40)

The idea is that people must confront uncomfortable facts, and have their views challenged because they are sitting with and engaging with those who have different experiences, sometimes experiences of oppression or deprivation.

There are several remarks to be made about representation in a deliberative poll, and about random selection more generally. First, it appears that Fishkin overstates claims to statistical representativeness. Even if we accept that, with appropriate stratification techniques, a sample of 300 can represent the British population on their stated criteria of locality, age, gender, working status, and social class—and that is by no means assured[1]—those 300 never actually get to deliberate *together*. The deliberative poll process only brings the entire sample together during the plenary sessions, sessions which are in a question-and-answer format rather than a mutual giving, weighing, and acceptance or rejection of reasons. The participants only get close to the deliberative ideal in their small groups, but these groups number just fifteen to twenty people. With a group of twenty it is impossible that all the relevant differences between people will be present, and so unlikely that participants will confront anything other than the most dramatic, dominant cleavages in the personal, face-to-face way Fishkin envisages. That is beyond the problem that the small groups' deliberative quality is moderate at best: They spend only four hours in those groups, of which at least one hour is spent on settling in, introductions, setting ground rules, and choosing questions to ask in the plenaries (Gibson and Miskin 2002). This is not enough time to go through all the stages of breaking down barriers, expressing emotions freely, and searching for mutual understanding that occur in longer, more intensive processes like a citizens' jury.

The second remark is about a problem created by selecting samples which are stratified proportionally to the presence of relevant characteristics in the wider population. As I have already argued, if a body is to have any moral force for winners and losers alike it is more appropriate to represent relevant characteristics equally: equal numbers from different classes, regions, educational backgrounds, and so forth. If one's sample is proportional, there will only be a few people with particular minority characteristics to go around:

---

[1] To get to the 95 per cent confidence level one would need a sample of 399 people just to accurately 'represent' the observed gender proportions in the population, let alone all the other factors. The details of the NHS poll's stratification are as follows. The localities were broken down into 50 clusters of postcodes used for the British Social Attitudes survey, also run by Social and Community Planning Research (SCPR), managers of the deliberative poll. There were four age categories: 18–29; 30–44; 45–64, and 65+. The five working status categories were working full-time or part-time; unemployed; retired; looking after home/family; and other. The five social class categories were based on the standards used in British statistics, namely professional/managerial (classes A and B); junior manager/other non-manual (class C1); skilled manual (class C2); Semi- or unskilled manual/unemployed/dependant on state (classes D and E); and not known/can't classify.

not every group will have a black member, not every group will have someone from an isolated rural community, not every group will have a young mother on welfare. Without direct observation of the groups, I am unable to say how this affected the NHS poll: the broadcasts included only 9 minutes 41 seconds of small group activity in 2 hours 45 minutes of broadcast, almost all of which featured single speakers relating stories without much engagement from other participants. However, the potential is clearly there for any process which relies on such 'mirror' representation: it may exclude minority perspectives from elements of the debate entirely, as was the case with the Belfast jury which included no non-Europeans because they make up only 1 per cent of the Northern Ireland population; and, where a minority is given a presence that is less than the effective threshold, those perspectives may not be heard or taken seriously. Being present is not enough; those voices also need to be heard, recognized, and effective.

However, even if it were possible to create a body with effective quotas, it is not at all clear that such purely descriptive representation is desirable because of its inherent essentialist problems. By selecting participants by quotas (as opposed to a more purely random system), the selectors, consciously or otherwise, set an expectation that, for example, the women will represent the views and experiences of all other women, without having had any contact let alone received any instructions or mandate from those other women. My evidence on this is limited, but two citizens' jury managers noted that people who are chosen to represent certain sectors of society in such ways strongly resist attempts to label them 'representatives', while an indigenous woman participant in the Australian deliberative poll I attended made a point of specifying that nothing she was about to say could be taken as applying to or binding other indigenous women. She was there to present *her* perspective, no one else's.

What seems to be at stake here is some slippage between 'representative-ness' in a statistical or descriptive sense and 'representation' in the principal-agent sense. Lotteries produce representativeness but not representation, and so lack a fundamental legitimating element, but it is a major criticism in the literature (Manin 1997), and one raised by four of my interviewees, that decision-makers will nonetheless feel pressure to act on the recommendations of such bodies, even though their participants have no direct bonds of accountability to non-participants who are still subject to their decisions. The concern is that without the discipline such bonds provide, representatives will make unjust, inefficient, or otherwise irrational decisions: witness the worries expressed by two members of the Belfast steering committee that jurors would make financially irresponsible recommendations for which they were unaccountable.

However, the lack of formal controls did not seem to have dire consequences in practice. 'People were actually quite astounded at the recommendations and how sensible they were, that they weren't outrageous', said
one of the commissioners of the Belfast jury. A consultant who had run
several juries reported that this is common experience, that jurors generally
do feel a sense of responsibility to the wider public interest, take that responsibility seriously, and so act *as if* they were being held to account. This raises
an important potential divergence from theory: if deliberators feel accountable to others thanks to other mechanisms, then perhaps my insistence so far
on principal-agent bonds is overstated. I am speculating now, as I have no
direct evidence on this, but I wonder if the simple fact of being placed in a
position where one's decision will *matter* means that one takes one's role
more seriously, an argument Burnheim (1985: 167–8) runs, although he too
does so without direct empirical support. This effect would be enhanced to
the degree that the deliberative event is subject to public scrutiny by the
media, which I take up in Chapter 5. It is certainly consistent with Goodin's
idea (2000) that participants in any democratic process imagine what it is like
to be in others' shoes, and what impacts their decisions will have on those
others, which in turn generates some limited democratization of their internal
reasoning processes. As Goodin himself argues, however, such processes
cannot be a complete replacement for more 'external', public deliberation
and decision-making because of how accountability appears to the outsiders
themselves. Legitimacy still depends, in the final analysis, on a public act of
consent, while confronting difference face-to-face may still be necessary
before people can make the 'imaginative leap' needed to fully take another's
interests and point of view into account. Therefore I still insist on either direct
public involvement or directly accountable representatives when it comes
to decision-making; I am less dogmatic when it comes to informing those
decision-making processes.

Unlike Burnhein, other modern partisans of processes which rely on
randomness, such as Lenaghan (1999: 50) and Fishkin (1997: 162), accept
the 'unaccountable' criticism and suggest that randomly selected representative groups should only have the power to make recommendations, not
decisions; that is, they should be restricted to opinion formation as in
Habermas's model (1996). Fishkin agrees, although in his typically enthusi-
astic style he does seem to be suggesting something more binding:

A deliberative poll is not meant to describe or predict public opinion. Rather it
prescribes. It has a recommending force: these are the conclusions people would
come to, were they better informed on the issues and had the opportunity and
motivation to examine those issues seriously. It allows a microcosm of the country

to make recommendations to us all after it has had the chance to think through the issues. If such a poll were broadcast before an election or a referendum, it could dramatically affect the outcome. (Fishkin 1997: 162)

As I suggested in Chapter 2, this is fine if there are many other deliberative processes which *are* decisive and into which randomly selected bodies feed information, but if this is the only purpose to which deliberative principles are put, then deliberation has not deepened democracy very much.

The final problem of 'representativeness' is one that is peculiar to deliberative democratic ideals. It is what I call the Grandview problem, from a story related by Fishkin (1997) about the 1947 movie *Magic Town*. In a nutshell, the Grandview problem is that deliberation destroys the representativeness of descriptive representatives. As I noted earlier, deliberative poll and citizens' jury members are chosen to be representative not just of physical characteristics but of the attitudes, beliefs, and values of the population too; but as they deliberate, those facts and values are challenged and, to the extent they are found wanting, undergo transformation in the face of more persuasive arguments. Thus, if the deliberative moment is working as it should, by the end of the event the members are *no longer representative* of the attitudes, beliefs, and values of the population. Fishkin himself suggests this is a likely outcome of deliberation when he discusses the effect that becoming the polling microcosm of the whole nation had on the town of Grandview:

With this new sense of responsibility, and their heightened interest in the issues, the townspeople's views soon diverge from those of the rest of the country. The climax comes when the town announces the result that 79 per cent of them would be willing to 'vote for a woman for president'! This is taken as such a preposterous departure from conventional opinion that they become a source of national ridicule. (Fishkin 1997: 1–2)

However, Fishkin does not draw the lesson from his own example. The moment that a group's opinions start to depart from the distribution found in the general population, they cease to be 'representative' in a descriptive sense on anything other than physical characteristics. Because the deliberative poll is representative in no other sense (authorization or accountability) it loses even its weaker, descriptive legitimating element between the first and second survey, and so it is not clear, from Fishkin's own account, what 'recommending force' a deliberative poll retains. This is not just a problem for deliberative polls: it is a problem for citizens juries too, as Smith and Wales (1999: 300) point out; for citizens' panels (Pretty, Hine, and Deighton 1999), as a student in a public policy class once pointed out to me; indeed, for any process which transforms the preferences of the citizens on the inside, but not those on the outside.

It is a problem which did not escape the notice of interviewees. A health policy academic who was a panellist on the NHS poll directly challenged Fishkin's 'recommending force' claim by reference to the usefulness of deliberative events as a guide for policymakers:

Q: Do you think these processes have a place in policy making?
A: Nope! I don't. Because they're utterly unrepresentative. I mean, it is useful for me as an educator and as a general concerned citizen to know that if a cross-section of the general public is given a lot of information about a topic they will... respond to the information and deal with the topic in a much more sensible and well-informed way.... When policy makers make policy, though, they are dealing with the public who is not in this highly artificial jury-type situation. And actually the citizens' jury responses might be totally misleading as far as the response of the general public are concerned when the policy maker is trying to convince them of the merits of the policy.

As well as the lack of correspondence between deliberators and non-deliberators, some interviewees were concerned about the effects of deliberation on the representativeness of the jurors themselves. One of the Belfast jury commissioners used some of the jurors as a reference group well after the event, but worried about their usefulness in these terms:

...this is a group of informed people now, these are not recruited off the street anymore, these are people who had this concentrated time together and who learned the structure of health and social services. So you can't regard them as ordinary people, you have to accept that they're now educated, informed individuals.

Another jury manager reported that in a series run near Brighton a woman who had been on the first jury was selected again in the pool for the second:

...you're looking for a fresh public voice, and you wonder, having gone through the jury process, are you ending up with someone who's essentially like an activist, although you could say that the whole point of the jury is to create a nation full of activists, if you like.

In other words, some managers worried that deliberation transforms the 'ordinary' person into a 'usual suspect', something which was clearly problematic, concerned as they were with the attempt to find some mythical ordinary person, unsullied by knowledge or interests:

[t]he definition [of ordinariness] can seem to imply that as lay people become more knowledgeable and develop more understanding of the professions, health services and clinical issues, they lose their amateur status and, thus, their value. Like the wise fool of mythology lay people's innocence and naiveté are considered useful by professionals, managers and health service commentators. Knowledgeable individuals are considered unrepresentative of other lay people. In particular, activist members of

voluntary lay groups are liable to be regarded as unrepresentative (atypical) and, therefore, unable to represent (voice) the views of their peers. (Hogg and Williamson 2001: 4)

This may well be an unfounded fear. There is no reason to connect being 'informed' with the bias which is thought to come with membership in a particular interest group, no reason to think that informed jurors will behave anything like activists. However, there is an alternative normative standpoint which positively values activism and involvement, which would suggest that even the fear of interests is overstated, and it is to this kind of activist representation that I turn next.

Before I do so, let me briefly sum up the main points about random selection identified so far. Pure random selection seems to have legitimacy benefits in terms of promoting fair access to decision-making positions, and in terms of promoting rationality. It curtails the ability of the powerful to influence the selection of the deliberators and thus influence the arguments which come up, diminishing the chances that they can protect poor arguments from scrutiny. However, modern deliberative designs are not purely random. Thanks to the impact of the politics of presence and research imperatives, deliberative moments have been stratified to ensure the inclusion of various groups. Again, from a legitimacy point of view, this inclusion is a positive thing if different voices are represented equally; and equal representation may mean that only some kinds of people are invited into particular deliberative events if others have alternative channels of communication. However, if there are no other channels, or if an important group is numerically small, or simply is not captured by the categories used by those who conduct the sampling, then important voices may be left out or be ineffective in processes which rely on randomness. In addition, randomly chosen participants resist the implied essentialism that comes with stratification: they have no formal bonds with any principals, so any decisions they make cannot bind non-participants, and they resist any implication that their recommendations 'represent' what others would have said. That is to say nothing of the Grandview problem, which is that participants are not 'representative' post-deliberation, and so offer no guide as to how arguments from decision-makers will be received by the wider population, and no strong reason for those non-participants to go along with the recommendations. On top of all that, face-to-face deliberation tends to happen in small groups which cannot be strictly representative in this statistical sense. That may have an unintended benefit: the designers of small groups like citizens' juries, by not being able to deliver strict proportionality, may in fact improve equality, and thus the deliberative quality, of their events.

All this is additional to the major problem that randomly selected participants have no direct bonds of accountability to non-participants, and so their
agreements should not be binding. While the fears about 'unaccountable',
randomly selected participants were not borne out in the cases I looked at—
such people did feel a sense of responsibility to others, despite the lack of
formal electoral sanctions—nonetheless, principal-agent links are essential
when it comes to legitimate decision-making. This is important because the
designers of some deliberative processes have got a little hung up on representativeness, confusing it with representation, and making claims about the
former which only apply to the latter. The real value of random selection lies
elsewhere: not in representation per se, but in its ability to promote fairness,
inclusiveness, and political equality. In order to do that, quotas must be used
with caution to avoid exclusion based on the use of over-broad categories,
and must be filled equally, or at least to some threshold level.

4.2.2   Self-selection: activists representing the inactive

The next idea to explore is the representation of inactive citizens by the active.
At one level this too involves a kind of descriptive representation, in which
activists claim shared experience, shared interests, and sometimes shared
physical characteristics as the basis of their representation claims, although
these last claims must surely be weak for the essentialism reasons already
discussed. Sometimes there can be direct principal-agent linkages through
some form of democracy within activist groups, but rarely do activists hold
positions in organizations thanks to an election conducted among all the
constituents they claim to represent. Generally they are the self-selected, and
for public managers this makes a great deal of difference in their normative
scheme: indeed, it is perceptions of the unrepresentativeness of the self-
selected that has driven public managers to embrace the possibilities offered
by stratified random selection.

The idea that activists have a role in democracy to represent, and on
occasion mobilize, inactive citizens is associated most obviously with pluralism (Dahl 1961, 1967; Truman 1955). Pluralists saw activism, particularly
through forming voluntary associations, as a means by which citizens secured
various rights from the state, and thought that those who faced problems
would form a group to seek its redress. For many, the pluralist vision was dealt
a fatal blow by scholars like Olson (1965), who exposed the collective action
problems involved; Verba (1972), who revealed low actual participation rates;
and the accusations of bias and 'capture' of public services for private gain
emerging from the neoliberal tradition, noted in Chapter 3, which greatly

thinned the ranks of 'legitimized' interest groups (Kogan and Bowden 1975). However, Wood (2000) shows that obituaries for interest groups are premature, especially in the health sector, and especially following moves to involve the third sector directly in the delivery of public services. Wood is certainly cautious enough not to claim that every interest group has the same capacities and track records—some are clearly more 'insular' than others (2000: 175)—but the tendency to write off interest groups is certainly, in his view, unwarranted.

The early pluralists assumed that the state was relatively passive, presenting few barriers to citizen engagement; since then, critics from numerous camps have highlighted the range of barriers that face groups attempting to engage with the state, and, for some, the role that interest groups play in challenging the status quo, breaking down the barriers. From that starting point, the relationship of groups to inactive citizens has been discussed most clearly by Christiano (1996) and Mansbridge (1992) who defend interest groups in very similar terms to Truman but stress what I call a deliberative facilitation role. Given the need to 'devote time, resources and energy to acquire knowledge' (Christiano 1996: 257), and given interest groups' ability to marshal such resources, they emphasize the role groups can have in providing the entire deliberative system with information that would not otherwise be available, facilitating debate at all levels of the public sphere, including between other interest groups, between citizens, and within the state; although Christiano puts this forward as a normative ideal, while Mansbridge offers it as a description as well. Thus, interest groups need not have direct principal-agent links with the relatively inactive citizenry to have a legitimate role in a deliberative democracy: they are the essential facilitators who *do* have the time, resources, and expertise to facilitate communication throughout the macro-deliberative system.

One can find this kind of facilitation happening most clearly in the Leicester debate. While the announcement of the imminent reconfiguration was the triggering event, it was attentive interest groups like Heart Link and Bosom Buddies who acted to focus a vague and general public fear of NHS service degradation into a specific and actionable fear. It was they who set up the petition and solicited signatures, went to the media and encouraged letters to the editor, mobilized local councillors and MPs, and lobbied the CHC; who provoked the dispersal of a discussion which, until then, had been conducted by a much smaller group of specialists and managers. One can also find it in *The NHS Plan* case, in which the CHCs' national body, the Association of Community Health Councils of England and Wales (ACHCEW), provoked a wider debate on the future of patient involvement in the NHS in response to the Plan's proposals to abolish the councils, a case I will take up in more detail in Chapter 5. At the micro level, interest group officers also acted as witnesses and steering group members for both citizens' juries, providing information to the jurors and to the organizers right from the agenda-setting stage.

Deliberative facilitation of this kind is not necessarily about representation. Christiano and Mansbridge advance it for reasons of efficiency and effectiveness; they do not make claims about direct principal-agent linkages or even descriptive representativeness between the active and inactive. However, interest groups in my cases did not confine themselves in this way: they linked facilitation and representation claims. Specifically, they made a trustee type of claim: facilitation was talked about in terms of 'championing' those who could not speak for themselves. Several interest group representatives argued that people from excluded groups were at a power disadvantage to others in society, and so needed 'professional' representatives in interest groups with greater power to make their case for them. One took this a step further and stressed that their knowledge and expertise made them both more effective advocates and more effective at holding the powerful to account (see March and Olsen 1995: 152):

[i]t is not about lay people because lay people can get marginalized and sidelined [by a] sharp manager who can just wipe the floor with [them]. They're very dedicated people, but to keep up with the changes in health: [even] I nod and make out I know sometimes when I haven't a clue what they're on about. It needs to be more professional, and then you can really hold these people to account. (CHC chief officer)

While it is too early to assess this view of lay people's capabilities in the post-*NHS Plan* context, it does receive some support in other domains. Farrell and Jones's (2000: 256) report that many parents on school boards 'feel they lack the expertise and experience to challenge professional expertise', while others struggle with workload. As a result they are marginalized by head teachers and board chairs. Foley and Martin (2000: 486) report similar results in the case of local development initiatives. However, such results may well be process-specific: my interviewees reported significant improvements in citizens' jury participants' sense of efficacy and willingness to get involved in future collective decision-making, whether deliberative or not. Every jury manager I spoke to had anecdotes about people being transformed from passive shut-ins into active citizens by participation in the jury, and of people becoming much more willing to engage in other political and civic activities beyond the jury itself. This has clear resonance with earlier studies on the effects of workplace participation on political efficacy (see Pateman 1970: ch. 3).

However, even micro-deliberative processes emphasize facilitation in another way: by the use of professional moderators to guide small group discussions. Moderators help those with low efficacy gain both the confidence and space in which to speak (Carson and Martin 1999: 55; Dryzek 1987). From the discussion of motivations in Chapter 2, one would expect that the decisiveness of the event would have an impact as well: a well-moderated research exercise on an issue with low salience is likely to have less effect on efficacy than a well-moderated decision-making exercise on an important public issue. Nonetheless, it may be that the concern about lay people being marginalized is only valid in non-deliberative events without skilled moderators; when moderators are involved, anecdotal evidence suggests that the concerns are less well founded. It seems, therefore, that champions are useful, with interest groups performing the champion role in macro-deliberative settings, moderators performing it in micro deliberations.

Interestingly, exactly the same 'champion' claims are made by, and on behalf of, other political actors. While stressing the value of direct involvement of ordinary people, one Leicester City councillor argued that lay participants need guidance from professionals and councillors who could act as 'champions of the community', vested as they were with powers to hold health authorities accountable, and accountable themselves to the people at election time. The Department of Health (DoH)'s *Local Voices* paper made mention of the aspiration of health authorities to become a 'champion of the people' (NHS Management Executive 1992: 3); the cross-departmental Age Positive programme looks for individuals and organizations to 'champion' the cause of elderly people within various social services, including health; at the time of writing, the word 'champion' appeared in 182 documents on the DoH's website, including speeches by the Secretary of State calling doctors and nurses the 'patients' champions'. The concept originates in management consultancy approaches to change management, in which successful projects are pushed through by enrolling people in positions of power and influence to champion the project at various decision-making forums, from the board down; it is a concept not dissimilar from the policy entrepreneur 'softening up' a policy community to accept a problem definition and take specific action (Kingdon 1984: 134–7).

There is another way in which the 'champion' idea is applicable, and that is that public managers may champion ordinary people simply by deciding to run a deliberative process. This can happen in two ways. Jo Lenaghan of the DoH highlighted the normal way that the department made decisions, 'particularly in the creation of a white paper ... which would traditionally have been drafted by Ministers and officials, perhaps sent out to a few stakeholders to read and comment on and then published' (personal correspondence). Indeed, she was eager that this usual approach, rather than ideal theory, be the comparator in my study.[2] For Lenaghan, the point was that she and others within the NHS broadened debate beyond the normally limited circles, devising means of involving non-traditional participants directly in the decision-making process, thus 'championing' their right to be involved directly in decisions which affect them.

The other way this can happen is as an unintended consequence of the concern with statistical representativeness. Because process managers have been focused on achieving a statistically representative sample of participants, they have been active in approaching people from excluded groups, investing considerable time and effort in persuading them to join a jury or deliberative poll. This means that managers do not give up on people who would normally face great motivational problems to do with low efficacy. Rather than sending out an invitation and hoping for the best, they actively 'shoulder tap' such people and encourage them to attend, helping them with payment for time and expenses, child care arrangements, transport, and so on. Thus the high-level concern to encourage public and patient involvement, combined with a local concern for representativeness, can help overcome the motivational barriers which many people would otherwise face in deliberative democracy.

The facilitation claims made by various actors went largely unremarked and unchallenged; but the representation claims made by interest groups were attacked strongly by public managers. Indeed, the perceived weakness of those claims, plus a new public management view of interest groups as bleeding the deliberative system rather than feeding it, was a key ground used to justify the sidelining of activists in deliberative processes. Managers dismissed the representation claims on both principal-agent and descriptive grounds, suggesting that many interest group officers do not get elected; or match the demographic features of the people they claim to represent; or even share their experiences; or, in the case of the CHCs, all three.

Activists sometimes try to firm up their ground by claiming descriptive representation based on shared experience. For example, the disability movement suggests that the only difference between those active in a movement and 'ordinary' others is not their experiences or the content of their views but their willingness to formulate political aims on the basis of those views and take action to achieve them (Beresford and Campbell 1994: 319). This may be as firm as disability activists' footing gets: some can claim principal–agent links between themselves and their members (BCODP 2002), but they have not yet gone as far as many environmental, anti-globalization or women's

---

[2] Which would indeed be appropriate if this book were about evaluating the government's programme. Even then, ideals play an important role in evaluative work: they tell us how far we have yet to go, and whether we are using the right yardsticks to measure progress.

groups in using participatory democratic practices for their internal structures (Catt 1999: 43–4), while elections legitimate their position as leaders only of their particular group, not disabled people as a whole.

The difference between the ideal expressed by the disability movement and the health interest group leaders I interviewed was that the latter claimed shared experience and emphasized their expertise in the policy field, but could make no stronger claims of connection with the grass roots, by means of internal democracy or anything else. One recognized that merely talking to a lot of people 'out there in the community' was an inadequate representation claim, and felt that deliberative techniques, or even social research, gave more solid ground for claiming to know what the people thought on a given issue. The lack of clear representative links between interest groups and those they claimed to represent seriously undermined their claims to be decisive in public deliberation.

Thus, the actual role of interest groups in these deliberative events contrasts somewhat with Christiano and Mansbridge's ideal. While they certainly performed a deliberative facilitation role, they were *confined* to that role by the various event managers. Their information-gathering skills and expertise was recognized to an extent, and thus they were found useful in informing the deliberations of others, but their representation claims were not generally taken seriously and so were not allowed to be decisive in any way. In one way this is rightly so: it has the benefit of not allowing those with weak representation claims to be decisive within deliberative moments. As I noted in Chapter 3, however, this leaves the preferences of those interest groups unchallenged and untransformed, which may undermine the rationality of the deliberative system as a whole, particularly if these groups are, as Mansbridge suggests, important providers of information and stimulators of debate in the deliberative system. It may be that restricting the role of interest groups in micro-level deliberations may damage rationality at the macro level.

Nonetheless, it seems clear that self-selected representatives have only weak claims to make about speaking for non-participants. Interest groups' positions are strengthened when they successfully claim shared experience; but they are strongest when they can claim direct principal–agent linkages, and it is to that kind of representation that I now turn.

4.2.3 Elected representation

The final type of claim to be explored here is elected representation, the direct choice of a principal by one or more agents. I have already spent considerable time exploring the normative status of elected representation, so this subsection will be fairly brief. I have argued that the bonds of accountability created by election is a significant legitimator of the division between those inside a forum and those outside it; the lack of those bonds undermines legitimacy. However, the lines of accountability between elected representatives and their principals can cut across each other, so in this section I want to look at what elected representation claims are made and how they conflict.

As noted in chapter 3, it was frequently suggested by interviewees that the reason health policy suffers from legitimacy problems in the UK is that it is under the control of unelected managers in quangos, as opposed to managers in departments with direct accountability to ministers (Commons Select Committee on Health 2000: q.62). When making this claim, respondents linked legitimacy with elections, so that the people responsible for health care could be re-elected or replaced depending on public evaluations of the outcomes. Health authority managers were unelected, and could not be held accountable in this way. While they certainly face an increasingly sophisticated barrage of scrutiny from a variety of agencies and the media (Day and Klein 1987), most of these are only indirectly 'public', and so do not help much with the democratic legitimacy problems. Deliberative techniques have been implemented by local agencies in part to try to remedy this accountability deficit (Harrison and Mort 1998), but we have already seen how randomly selected deliberators lack clear bonds with those left outside the forum, which means they should not be used to reach binding collective decisions.

However, the claims of different elected representatives can conflict, and it was in the period immediately following *The NHS Plan* that relations between various representatives became most fraught with tension.

Underlying all the NHS reforms was a general, background representation claim which is fairly familiar: essentially the government claimed legitimacy for its actions on the basis of the free choice by the electorate for them and their programme, a programme which specifically included devolving power to doctors and removing the NHS internal market, but which did not make special mention of the public and patient involvement initiatives.[3] This is the 'mandate' claim which contains both trustee and delegate elements: the government claims it has been elected both on the basis of electors' judgements about its fitness to do whatever needs to be done in the course of a parliament, and its promises to deliver specific outcomes, for which it will be held accountable at subsequent elections.[4] This is not to say that the mandate

[3] A plain text version of the 1997 Labour Party manifesto, along with the major political party manifestos for all UK general elections since 1945, is available from http://www.psr.keele.ac.uk/area/uk/man.htm.

[4] The classic account of the development of the mandate doctrine is Emden (1956). See also Klingemann, Hofferbert, and Budge (1994).

view is unproblematic: recent scholarship undermines mandate-based legit-imacy claims, partly because elections do not provide clear, uncomplicated signals about the details of voters' intentions and preferences (Catt 1996), partly because legitimacy derives from more than just a vote. Saying that, however, does not mean the vote is unimportant: legitimacy is enhanced by elections simply by virtue of the fact that politicians can be thrown out of office by the public. They can be held electorally accountable, which is quite a different kind of moral force than public servants or interest group leaders lay claim to (Kateb 1992: 37).

Given that background representation claim, all *The NHS Plan* consulta-tions only had advisory force: the Secretary of State for Health, as the person directly accountable the people, would be the one to make the final decisions. In practice, this meant that the status of representatives in the various consultative processes could safely be left somewhat vague: even with the Modernization Action Teams (MATs), the explicit goal was to get them to react to and refine ideas for specific reforms of the health system developed by the DoH, given the broad principles of devolution and patient involvement set out by the Secretary of State for Health (DoH manager, London). Whether the participants were elected to their positions, whether they had prior instructions from their principals, or whether they were left to their own devices did not enter the department's calculations; nor did it seem to cause problems for any of the participants afterwards. One NHS manager in Leeds wondered whether this was as it should be, although she posed it as a question which troubled her rather than as a firm, thought-out position:

Preserving that line [between decisive and advisory roles] is legitimate, because Alan Milburn, whoever's the incoming secretary at the time, is actually accountable to parliament and therefore to the people for the planning and expenditure in the NHS. So, if you've got individuals who are accountable to a parliamentary process, what further value and legitimacy can be added by asking individuals, lay people to get involved in this process? Shouldn't it just be left to the people who are [elected] to do it?

However, the Secretary is not just accountable to the people at election time: he or she is also accountable to parliament, which is the deliberative body which explores his arguments, both in committees and in full sessions of the Commons and the Lords (Uhr 1998: 159). In the case of *The NHS Plan*, the issue that caused particular problems was one which was not part of the consultation process, the decision to replace the CHCs with a series of local organizations with more or less democratic control. This decision was strongly resisted by the ACHCEW, which decided to fight by exploiting other channels of influence. While ACHCEW lobbied extensively in a variety of ways, its most fruitful channel was the Commons select committee which scrutinized the Health and Social Care Bill, whose chairman was also chair of a CHC; another committee member also sat on a CHC board. The committee worked to ensure that the sections of the bill relating to CHCs were removed, although they did so by also claiming the legitimating mantle of elected representation.

However, the government did not simply accept *that* as the legitimate outcome of a legitimate process. The criticisms can easily be guessed: the decision's legitimacy was attacked on content grounds, that it was the 'wrong' decision in the context of the rest of the reforms and that CHCs were ineffective at representing the public anyway;[5] and on consent grounds, because the reforms were necessary to achieve what the people had said they wanted in consultations (Commons Select Committee on Health 2000: q.317). Privately, one interviewee suggested that it was on source grounds as well, that the committee was 'tainted' by its associations with CHCs. While the government did a deal to get other reforms passed before the May 2001 dissolution of parliament, it returned to a consultative process and built support among other interest groups and other members of the Health Select Committee for the new structure, bolstered by claims that 'this is what the people want'. The abolition of the CHCs was reintroduced to parliament as part of the National Health Service Reform and Health Care Professions Bill, which passed its final reading in July 2002.

In the UK case there is little in the way of the descriptive/elective blend which is so desirable for legitimate representation, but this is due to the plurality voting system and the limited pool from which potential parliamentarians are recruited in Britain (Catt 1999: 98; Norris 1997: 158). Legitimacy would be enhanced if elected representatives were themselves more descriptively representative, at threshold levels, of the people they represent, but even without those descriptive elements, elected representation offers clear legitimacy benefits in that there are bonds of accountability between participants and non-participants in any given deliberations. In practice, however, the claims of different elected representatives can cut across each other, with some representatives claiming a mandate for a specific programme while others claim the right to scrutinize and, if necessary, change that programme on behalf of the public between elections. Mandate claims are not particularly sound when voters are being asked to vote on more than just a specific

---

[5] A point was made by the Secretary of State thus: 'I genuinely think that if my hon. Friend were to ask most members of the public whether they had heard of their CHC—let alone contacted it—he would find that the answer would be a resounding no' (House of Commons 2000: vol. 357, col. 160).

programme: only a referendum can deliver that kind of legitimacy. In an election of representatives, voters are rarely choosing on the basis of one preferred programme, or even a basketful of them. As a result, elected representatives are on safer ground when all they claim is the obligation to engage in the mutual giving and weighing of reasons; their ground is more slippery when they try to claim legitimacy for a specific plan of action.

4.3 REPRESENTATION COMPLEMENTS AND CONFLICTS

How do all these different claims by different kinds of representatives interact when they come together in a deliberative system? As I noted right at the start of this chapter, very few interviewees noted conflicts of representation directly. However, for some there is clearly a conflict between elected and randomly selected representation. Some elected representatives feel that deliberative events usurp their role. In the Belfast example, the Eastern Health and Social Services Council (EHSSC) was hauled over the coals by the members of the North Down Borough Council Health Committee in a resolution which stated, 'That the Committee write and advise the organizing authorities that it reject the concept of the Citizens Jury and would have nothing more to do with it on the grounds that it was merely a window dressing exercise' (North Down Borough Council 1998).

Although not formally accountable to any borough council, the chairman and chief officer of the EHSSC went to North Down to try to explain the citizens' jury concept, putting it in the context of the enormous cost of market research:

Their stance was that we didn't need to go out and ask people. That they're elected by the people to speak on their behalf and we didn't need to go out and spend £25,000 engaging sixteen people. We could have engaged them and they would have told us what their opinion was. And I don't know that we actually convinced them that that wasn't quite right.... We have a council ... and we wouldn't dream of presuming to know what all the people are thinking, and that's why we constantly engage in consultation and public participation.... But their stance was, they're elected representatives, they could have told us, and we wasted public money. (Jury commissioner, Belfast)

This kind of reaction by no means reflected the attitudes of all. In Leicester, for example, the two (Labour) city councillors most closely involved in the fight for Glenfield could understand the reaction of the North Down councillors, but saw themselves more as facilitators than trustees:

But, at the end of the day, you've got to put your personal feelings aside, and it is what is best for the community, what is best taking it forward, what is best for the resources; and I feel, so what if our power is diminished, if it is for the benefit of the people?

The response of the Leicester councillors suggests a way out of the apparent conflict between elected and selected representatives. That is, elected representatives like those in North Down are simply wrong if they claim that they know what the people want on the grounds of having been elected with a mandate. Given that, consultative events are useful means of probing beneath the vague signals that an election sends and as means of sorting through new issues and the details of existing ones. Nonetheless, final decision-making power should rest with representatives who can be held electorally accountable.

Other kinds of conflict and complementarity can arise between different kinds of representatives in a deliberative system. It is useful to look at the Leicester case to highlight these dynamics since all of the actors and processes in the case were aligned with different concepts of representation and different kinds of legitimacy claim. The initial decision had little legitimacy because it was based on an exclusive process in which only a limited range of experts' facts and values were represented; and the decision was dramatically at odds with popular values and the popular understanding of what the 'right' decision was. Activists opposing the changes had fairly limited legitimacy on their own. There was no agent-principal relationship between them and those they claimed to represent, but they could claim shared interest on the grounds of shared health experiences. However, the petition device allowed them to solicit and win consent from the people of Leicester, which boosted their representative claims. The legitimacy of the petition was contested by the CHC on the grounds that it had only 150,000 signatures, 'Which,' said the CHC Chief Officer, 'is a tenth of the population I have to represent'. The CHC's representation claim was partly a mandate claim—'this is what we've been appointed to do'—and partly based on the representativeness of the sample used to generate a series of focus groups and survey research commissioned from De Montfort University (Wilcox 2000), but that 'scientific doctrine' claim weighed less heavily in the public discourse than the direct public voice claim of the petitioners. Further, it was the petition and protest which opened the doors of previously limited deliberations conducted by the health authority. The local city councillors claimed representative status and legitimacy on the grounds of their election to public office, but they also backed that up with a claim that they were representing the specific wishes of the people when they took the petition to the DoH in London. Having forced the doors open, however, mere rhetoric was not legitimately decisive: rather than depending on involving just those who 'shout the most', legitimacy was further enhanced by the citizens' jury whose random selection ensured that no interested actor could influence the outcome by influencing the selection of decision-makers.

There were, of course, clear imperfections in the process, some of which enhanced and some of which undermined legitimacy. For one, the statistical selection of jurors had an advantage in that they were seen to be independent of the various sides in the argument; but this also meant that their recommendations could not be binding on representatives who had clear bonds of accountability to the public. Thus there was room for the legitimacy claims of different kinds of representatives to conflict. This can be most clearly seen if one considers what would have happened if the citizens' jury had *not* reached broadly the same conclusion as the protestors. The CHC Chief Officer speculated in this way:

Q: What do you think would have happened?
A: Wisdom of Solomon, that would have been. I think we, the CHC, would have agreed with the citizens' jury, and you can imagine the flak that we would have got from the Save Glenfield campaigners.
Q: Who do you think would have won?
A: They were very, very organized. They got powerful. [There was] Patricia Hewitt[6] behind the scenes. They had a lot of contacts with the Department of Health. It would have been a political decision, it wouldn't have been our decision. 150,000 petitioners, Labour government, three Labour seats in the city, we had councillors putting pressure on, we had a CHC councillor, he never turned up for CHC meetings, [but] when the Glenfield issue [came along you] couldn't get him off the papers. So politically I think [the Health Authority] would have been forced to change that decision.

In other words, the jury recommendations may have given way to the petitioners' demands, simply because they had many other political channels through which they could apply pressure, particularly through their elected representatives. The jury was not the only game in town, just one element among several, each with more or less power. Overall legitimacy would have been enhanced even further had those other 'games' operated according to deliberative principles, and to the extent that the protestors, the health authority, and the CHC themselves were democratic in their internal workings. Still, this is speculation: without a real case of fundamental disagreement between a deliberative process and wider public opinion it is hard to draw any concrete conclusions.

---

[6] In her capacity as the MP for Leicester West, the constituency in which Glenfield Hospital is sited.

Summing up this section, then, there can be some conflict between elected and non-elected representation, but that conflict is minimized if elected representatives give up any tenacious adherence to the mandate model and realize the contributions consultative processes can make to deliberative democracy; and if elected bodies are themselves more descriptively representative of the population at large. Interest groups too play a vital role in opening up deliberative systems to new voices, but without principal-agent bonds they have limited legitimate decision-making power: they enhance their legitimacy by democratizing their procedures for appointing office holders and spokespeople, so that they have more well-founded claims to speak for those they descriptively represent. Finally, randomly selected participants—I hesitate to call them 'representatives' for reasons already explained—can play a vital role where politics between elected representatives and interest groups has led to an impasse. Random selection, if genuinely random, means greater fairness because it stops any one interest from influencing the outcome. However, it remains unclear whether the losers in such processes would go along with the outcomes: there may be good normative grounds for asking them to, but whether their substantive interests overwhelm those grounds is a question I have not been able to answer beyond a speculative 'yes'.

4.4   CONCLUSIONS

What have we discovered, then, about how legitimacy questions in deliberative democracy are managed in practice, and how has this added to the theoretical understanding reached at the end of Chapter 2?

To begin with, who is being represented matters a great deal as it can have an effect on the scope of deliberation, and thus its motivational attractiveness and democratic character. If, as has happened so far in Britain, deliberative democracy is all about local communities, then this exacerbates the scope and motivation problems noted in Chapter 3. Where micro-deliberative processes focus on involving 'ordinary people' then this is positive for the deliberative system as a whole, since it gives those people a channel of direct influence over policy which they have never had before; where other channels of influence are closed off, however, then deliberative techniques simply become a legitimating mask for exclusion in macro deliberation, hiding the degree to which those who have a legitimate facilitation role are silenced.

Next, principal-agent claims seem to have the most strength not only in my normative scheme, but in practical politics as well. It is not a matter of having a 'mandate'—such claims are shaky—but rather is a matter of such representatives being subject to electoral accountability. Exactly to whom such agents are accountable can be hard to sort through, a problem which goes beyond the constituency definition issues noted at the beginning of this chapter. A representative like the Secretary of State for Health has multiple constituencies which at least include his own electorate, those who voted for his party, parliament, the Commons Health Committee (CHC), patients, the medical professions, and so on, all of whose interests can and do conflict. Furthermore, some of those constituencies will be more powerful than others, which means that the minister need only pay attention to a subset of them if he is to retain support. Given that, the use of inclusive consultation processes, preferably of a deliberative kind, is essential to balance out the range of opinion and interests of which elected representatives take heed.

No matter how difficult that balancing act and how constrained they should be to consult widely, electoral accountability gives such representatives greater authority than those who do not face such discipline at all. One example of the latter is interest groups who, I have argued, should not have decision-making power because they are frequently self-appointed, lacking even descriptive features in common with those they claim to represent. This does not mean that interest groups should have no role at all in the deliberative system. In both macro- and micro-deliberative processes they can play a valuable facilitation role, acting as 'champions' for others who, for whatever reason, are not so active. Championing should be two-way, however: there should be some mechanism by which citizens are able to state publicly, 'On this issue and at this moment, these people speak for me'. The Leicester petition was one such mechanism.

Championing happens in another way. By running micro-deliberative processes, managers shoulder-tap citizens who might otherwise lack the efficacy required to get them to participate directly in the deliberative system. This clearly has legitimacy benefits by giving the citizens involved the confidence and skills needed to engage in other political environments, and by giving 'ordinary' people a direct role in macro deliberations which they would otherwise lack. The wider spread deliberative practice becomes, the more people and politics would benefit from this increased efficacy. Random selection processes have some serious theoretical flaws, however: the lack of principal-agent links which mean their decisions cannot be binding on others; the essentialism problem created by quota sampling; and the fixation on proportionality which marginalizes minority voices. The worry among some interviewees was that the lack of principal-agent (or any other) accountability would mean that citizens would make irresponsible recommendations which would be difficult to ignore given the democratic value placed on listening to ones' citizens, but this fear proved unfounded. None-theless, I argue that this does not lead to the conclusion that one can dispense with the insistence on principal-agent bonds. One needs to keep in mind the distinction between deliberation as opinion formation and deliberation as decision-making: randomly selected participants have valuable roles in the former, but should not be relied on solely in the latter.

What is the overall lesson? No one representative can claim perfect legit-imacy because every kind has flaws. Legitimacy depends on a variety of representatives, activating a variety of constituencies, coming together at a decision-making moment. The Leicester debate had a legitimate outcome for exactly this reason: the interest groups opened up the debate in the first place and acted as critical information brokers throughout; politicians acted as facilitators, championing the people's right to be consulted; the petition provided an act of consent to the interest groups' and politicians' claims; while the jury acted as neutral arbiters, helping cut through the sloganeering which had dominated up until that point, although their flaw was a lack of effective accountability which means that had serious opposition remained, the outcome might have been very different. The NHS poll was weakened because it was unclear whether any of the participants were 'speaking for' anyone else, undermining the claim that such events have 'recommending force' for non-participants.

However, establishing strong representation claims is not all there is to legitimacy. Another significant means of developing bonds between insiders and outsiders is by means of the publicity condition, and the way that plays out in my cases is the subject of Chapter 5.

5

Deliberation as drama:
publicity and accountability

Witenagemote,[1] old Parliament, was a great thing. The affairs of the
nation were there deliberated and decided; what we were to do as a
nation. But does not, though the name Parliament subsists, the parliamentary debate go on now, everywhere and at all times, in a far more
comprehensive way, out of Parliament altogether? Burke said there were
Three Estates in Parliament; but, in the Reporters' Gallery yonder, there
sat a Fourth Estate more important far than they all.... Literature is our
Parliament too. Printing, which comes necessarily out of Writing,
I say often, is equivalent to Democracy: invent Writing, Democracy is
inevitable.... Whoever can speak, speaking now to the whole nation,
becomes a power, a branch of government, with inalienable weight in
law-making, in all acts of authority. It matters not what rank he has, what
revenues or garnitures: the requisite thing is, that he have a tongue which
others will listen to.... The nation is governed by all that has tongue in
the nation: Democracy is virtually there.

—Thomas Carlyle (1840)

So far we have seen that representation, while an important legitimating
factor for any group of decision-makers, is a complex, partial, and sometimes
contradictory solution to deliberative democracy's scale problem. The other
solution that I want to consider is using publicity, establishing communicative links between insiders and outsiders such that those outside are exposed
to the arguments that are made inside a deliberative forum.

In deliberative theory the publicity condition is the requirement that only
those arguments which can be made in public should have any force. In some
ways, publicity is the essence of deliberative democracy: it is its procedural
foundation, the means by which information is brought into a deliberative

---

[1] *Witenagemote* was the assembly of the Anglo-Saxons. The word means, roughly, 'assembly
of the wise'.

moment and by which claims and counterclaims are weighed and sorted; and it is its ethical foundation, the yardstick by which one judges the rightness or wrongness of political action, and one of the means by which the powerful are restrained (Gutmann and Thompson 1996: 95; Luban 2002: 296). Thus it has, in Habermas's words (1996: 171), the function both of 'monitoring' and 'feeding' deliberation. However, as I have argued before, accountability also depends on those who hold decision-makers to account having the power to make their displeasure effective, which is one of the functions of elections.

The idea of accountability through publicity can hold both in micro and macro accounts of deliberation. In the micro account, all the participants are in one forum together, and exchange reasons face-to-face; in the macro account, citizens participate in all sorts of debates, conversations, forums, and assemblies, each of which must give account for its actions and decisions to the others. The troublesome nature of the micro account should be fairly familiar by now: not all those affected can be in any given forum, so account-ability in this sense is only generated between participants, not between participants and non-participants. As I suggested in Chapter 2, one solution is to abandon the micro account in favour of the macro: think of publicity operating between rather than within different forums in a deliberative system, and then legitimacy is created to the extent that people in different forums or conversational threads give account to each other by sharing reasons throughout the system, typically through the news media but also through the myriad of ways human beings interact every day. This is precisely the point that Thomas Carlyle (1993) made in the fifth of his London lectures in May 1840, quoted above: democracy exists to the extent that citizens engage with each other in debate in the public sphere, well beyond the four walls of parliament or any other deliberative forum.

But is accountability in the macro sense unproblematic? I have already suggested a reason for thinking it might not be: there may be problems to do with intervening institutions, of the same kind encountered in Chapter 3. Both formal institutions like the news media or informal social structures like discourses are likely to shape communication in various ways, ways that may alter the content and nature of that communication. What is lost and what is gained when we rely on various media to bear the weight of responsibility for generating insider-outsider links? These questions of mediated deliberation are the central concerns of this chapter, and I explore them primarily by focusing on the nature and use of the news media, and the distinction between speakers and audiences which this kind of large-scale deliberation presupposes. The news media are notorious for their distorting effects on communication, yet those deliberative institutions which rely on the media do not take those distortions into account. These effects can undermine the very deliberative values such processes strive to uphold.

Of course, there is much more to the public sphere than the news media; indeed, there is much more to the media than news. The various media produce drama, comedies, satire, documentaries, talk shows, even sports coverage which are permeated by political discourses: think not just of obviously political comedies like *Yes, Minister* but of films or even soap operas which tackle issues like criminal justice or HIV/AIDS. Beyond the formal media, people engage in political discourses at work, through membership in or affiliation with interest groups, through all sorts of everyday talk (Mansbridge 1999). Furthermore, the advent of the internet may expand dramatically the means by which people can engage in democratic dialogue, although emerging scholarship suggests that the democratic claims of early 'internet futurists' were wildly overstated (Norris 2000: 278). So, a thorough analysis of publicity would need to look right across the public sphere, not just at the news media; Chambers and Costain (2000) sketch some of the terrain. To pursue all these elements, however, would be a book in itself, and so I focus on the traditional news media because it is considered the most important part of the public sphere by many deliberative democrats, and was one of two key sites in the public sphere that interviewees consistently identified and took into account in their planning; and because the media has an important influence on what issues become defined as 'problems' that require public action (Cohen 1973; Edelman 1988). The other site that attracted the attention of interviewees was interest groups, whose media-related activity I deal with later.

The chapter begins by setting out the place of the media in democratic theory, and surveys the reasons why the media may be considered to play their democratic role poorly, concentrating especially on the structural features of news. I then examine how these features influenced what the television audience saw of the National Health Service (NHS) deliberative poll, asking whether certain arguments made it through the media to reach non-participants.[2] Attention then shifts to those events that were more successful in generating media coverage, asking what it was about those cases that made a difference, before concluding with some general implications for the quest to establish legitimating links between participants and non-participants in deliberative democracy.

---

[2] For a discussion of the effects of the media on the deliberators themselves, see Gibson and Miskin (2002).

5.1   DEMOCRACY AND THE CONSTRUCTION OF NEWS

That the news media are central to democracy in all its variants is an old and well-known idea. For J. S. Mill (1974: 75), for example, the media encourage self-government by exposing people to different ideas, increasing people's capacity to exercize citizenship and judgement, as well as scrutinizing the powerful. For other theorists of democracy, the media are essential to ensure that all voters possess adequate and equal information about the choices confronting them (Manin 1997: 228–9; Page 1996: 2). In these accounts the mere presence of the media is not enough: the information they provide must also be undistorted, free from domination or interference by powerful interests. Thus media freedom is part of what defines democracy (Beetham 1994; Dahl 1971).

The news media are central to deliberative democracy for much the same reasons. For Habermas (1996), the media have a two-way role: to make the public sphere more inclusive by spreading political communication among a broader public, and to provide means by which public opinion is transmitted to the state for action. The principles are applied by Fishkin in the deliberative poll: indeed, it was specifically designed by him to be televised, so that deliberation among a few would be brought to 'an audience of millions', acting as a 'catalyst' to change the nature of discussion on a topic in a broader community (Fishkin 1997: 130, 175).

That the news media fulfil their 'fourth estate' function poorly is as venerable an idea as their indispensability. Two main kinds of criticism tend to be made, which I call input complaints and structural complaints. Input complaints concern the nature of the information which goes into the media pipeline for transmission to the public: for example, that media debate is ill-informed and based on 'rickety opinions' (Luskin, Fishkin, and Jowell 2002: 456); that the media focuses on the 'horse race' of electoral politics rather than issues, institutions, and ideas (Anderson 1998); or that powerful interests can dominate and distort the media's agenda (Habermas 1989). The concern here for deliberative democracy is clear: its rationalizing quality depends on the free exchange of ideas and arguments, something that would be undermined if the media were only transmitting a limited range of issues and ideas. This would be the case regardless of where one stands on questions of the relative influence of the media on the content of public opinion.[3]

If inputs are the problem, then the solution is to change the nature of those inputs, and this is precisely the concern behind Fishkin's deliberative poll

---

[3] For a summary of the literature on media influence on voting behaviour, and a presentation of new evidence in the British context, see Gavin and Sanders (2003).

method (Fishkin 1997: 13). In a deliberative poll, survey questions on a given topic are put to a random sample of the population, who are then brought together to a conference venue where they get the chance to debate the topic with each other and with panels of experts, including partisans of the various positions. Finally, the participants are polled again to see how their opinions have changed. The results are then said to have 'recommending force' for others because they are televised—the audience can see the debate, be exposed to the arguments, and thus have their opinions transformed (Luskin, Fishkin, and Jowell 2002: n. 20).

However, from another viewpoint it would be odd to characterize the problem simply as one of poor inputs. Of at least equal concern is the fact that the media 'frames' those inputs in certain ways (Capella and Jamieson 1996; Iyengar 1996). Like any institution, the media are not neutral transmitters of whatever is put into them, so changing what goes in may not have a straightforward influence on what comes out.

This structural concern about the media's role in democracy comes in two variants. The first is the idea that journalists and editorial teams themselves are biased because they are self-interested, ill-trained, inexperienced, or in-attentive, or are just under so much pressure that they do not have the time to get things right (Gutmann and Thompson 1996: 124; Stokes 1998). This complaint can be based on some dubious presumptions: it is often framed in such a way as to presume that authoritative knowledge is possible on every topic, or that there is a deliberate conspiracy to deceive (Langer 1998). Such failures are also relatively minor. Even if we fix them through training and regulation, and guard against conspiracies, there are still features of news— news values, physical limits, and organizational features—which systematic-ally favour some kinds of information and filter out others, features which are less tractable to incremental policy solutions. This is the second variant of the structural complaint: it is not that the media *do not* transmit some kinds of information, but that they *cannot*. If that is the case, then we need to know what kinds of information are filtered out, and the impact that has on the exchange of reasons between deliberators and audiences.

5.1.1 News values

What makes something newsworthy? This is something widely taught to journalism students but rarely understood elsewhere. Overall, the media is looking for something significant, but significance is defined not so much in terms of any intrinsic value of the issue at hand, but in terms of salience to a given audience (Negrine 1989: 141)

One way of grabbing an audience's attention is to focus on the unusual rather than the commonplace: as the old journalistic adage has it, 'dog bites man' is not news, but 'man bites dog' is. While the media does report on some routine things, such as court reports or the stock market, it does so by focusing on the unusual: the murder, not the bag-snatching, unless there is something unusual about the perpetrator or the victim. Another way is to focus on what triggers peoples' emotions: sex and protective instincts towards children and other loved ones are the prime examples.

News is narrative, with a plot and actors. There needs to be a tale to tell, with a beginning, middle, and ending, and that tale needs to be in one of the classic narrative forms of tragedy or comedy, each with its own subgenre (e.g. soap opera, sitcom, and satire). As Street (2001: 36) emphasizes: 'This is not a metaphor; this is how news is told.' As narrative, people are central: there needs to be a central character or characters who interact with each other to make a news story. This is why popularizations of great science tend also to be popularizations of great scientists, as much about the person as the idea: everyone knows the name Einstein but few could explain why he was important. In news, it helps if those people are themselves in some way significant; indeed, an insignificant thing done by a significant person is news: 'Princess Di's haircut can become front page news, mine passes unnoticed' (Tiffen 1989: 52). Some argue that the fascination with celebrity is starting to override all other news concerns, such that an issue is not considered significant *unless* it involves a famous person in some way (Langer 1998: 45).

Thus news values tend to emphasize contrast and conflict rather than harmonious working relationships, except of course where such relationships are themselves exceptional; to emphasize the atypical features of public life rather than its norms; to overstate the role that individuals play in events rather than groups; to emphasize celebrities at the expense of everyday experience and solutions to problems; and to marginalize accounts which 'draw attention to the social forces or structures that drive change' (Street 2001: 49–50)—studies of media narratives which personalized the 1991 Gulf War (Kellner 1995; Neuman 1996) are particularly instructive here, as will be, no doubt, studies of the War on Terror.

5.1.2   Physical limitations

Different media have different physical constraints which limit what they can and cannot cover. At the broadest, this is an issue of space: newspapers have a limited number of column inches, although the amount of space available depends in part on how much advertising can be sold to pay for it, which raises issues I will cover shortly. This means that there is a relatively small 'news hole' in which a story can appear. This hole is made smaller by the deadlines imposed by daily production processes and competitive pressures between media. Because of their reliance on speech in real time, and because they cannot add more hours in the day like newspapers can add pages, television and radio shrink that hole even further, such that 'the text of a half-hour news service would not fill the front page of a broadsheet news-paper' (Tiffen 1989: 22). However, this can also work in the opposite way: even on a day when there is not much of significance to report, broadcast media still have to fill a news slot. What they tend to fill that with is not more in-depth analysis of 'olds' as much as less significant 'news'.

Different media also emphasize different aspects of stories. This is a par-ticularly complex topic, but take one example to illustrate. As a visual medium, television is said to be the most powerful simply because of the way that the emotional content of a story can be conveyed so quickly with well-chosen pictures (McLuhan 1987). The fact that those pictures are *chosen* means that they are chosen to support a particular narrative line and not another: frame the picture in one way, and one story is told; frame it another way, and quite a different story emerges (MacGregor 1997). This also influences which stories get covered: a story which interests a newspaper may not get television coverage simply because it cannot easily be told in pictures.

5.1.3   Organizational and economic imperatives

The media in modern democracies are embedded in a political economy in which information and cultural production are more or less marketized. Even those media which are largely state supported still face some kind of market discipline thanks to changes in public sector accountability regimes since the mid-1980s. The main form of marketization is that many media outlets rely on advertising, directly or indirectly, to fund their activities. However, organ-izations buy advertising in order to reach a given audience, not any audience: they may be more interested in high-income earners, or main household shoppers, or teenagers, or 30-something single women, because those are the people for whom their specific messages are salient. Therefore, organizations buy advertising with media that reach their target audiences; which means that outlets work hard to reach some audiences and not others, again by considering what is salient to those audiences and not others.

In Britain, half of television broadcasting, almost all narrow-cast television services, most radio, and all national and regional newspapers are in private ownership, and advertising is their major source of income. The need to improve advertising revenues, and thus returns for shareholders, dominates. This leads to aggressive competition to attract audiences with 'popular' content which favours entertainment and narrative at the expense of thought and analysis: the so-called 'dumbing down' of political information (Street 2001: 150–2). This is not to say that all media coverage is 'dumb'; rather, that what might be termed 'smart' coverage only appeals to a small (but often influential) audience and so tends to be restricted to small-circulation, often state-supported, media, while the large audiences receive 'infotainment'. Even then, highbrow and state-run media are not immune from such pressures. For example, in Britain the state-run BBC and the non-profit Channel 4 must still compete with the commercial media for audience share in order to justify the owners' investment—spending has been explicitly tied to success in attracting an audience by the Chancellor of the Exchequer (House of Commons 2002: 15 July 2002, col. 22)—and so must still offer content which attracts a mass audience in addition to its more narrowly targeted programming, despite their public service remits. The same influences on public service media have been noted in the USA (Kerbel, Apee, and Ross 2000).

Competition means that every outlet is looking for an 'exclusive', preferably being the first to publish a story at all, but at least to have an exclusive angle on a story, such as exclusive access to a given interviewee. This has two effects on the likelihood of a political story getting coverage. For run-of-the-mill stories, it means that only one outlet will cover it: as soon as a television station, for example, learns that a competitor is also airing the story, it loses interest. However, if the story is newsworthy enough, no news outlet will want to be left out: this means that once a significant story is broken, news organizations will jump on the bandwagon.

5.1.4   Effects and implications

These features of news and media organizations have effects on the kinds of information which dominate the public sphere, and thus the kinds of facts and values that can reasonably be expected to be transmitted in that sphere, and the kinds that cannot. First, physical limitations on the coverage of political stories mean that only some of what will inevitably be a complex tale can be told. Second, the choice as to whether to tell a particular story or not depends on whether it can be made consonant with news values, particularly whether it is out of the ordinary, can be personalized, polarized, and easily narrated. Third, the choice also depends on whether it is, or can be made to be, salient to a given target audience, an audience which is in turn partly defined by the financial imperatives of the media organization concerned. Each story must compete with many other stories in order to make it into the media in the first place, unless it is so significant that the media themselves compete to cover it first. These pressures face every medium to some extent, no matter how highbrow or lowbrow; while there are many differences between *The Guardian* and *The Sun*, for example, they have much in common as well.

The implication of these three points for any given deliberative moment is that in order to get *their* story told rather than someone else's, the advocates of a particular issue, event, or viewpoint must jockey hard for the media's attention, largely on the basis of news values and salience to organizationally significant audiences. One of the most important means of doing this is to use specifically dramaturgical modes of communication to attract attention to problems, such as using a 'colourful phrase' or sound bite (Tiffen 1989: 81), or setting up 'staged' events in which conflict is maximized and played out symbolically (McAdam 2000; Scalmer 2002). Another means is to personalize a story by focusing on leaders to the exclusion of their sometimes-vast organizations (Street 2001: 49) or by using celebrities to advocate a cause in public, since a famous person is more newsworthy than you or me. What gets left out by doing so, as already noted, are the grey zones between black and white, right and wrong, good guys and bad guys—that is, the technical and moral complexities of issues—as well as the material and discursive forces at work.

Now, a possible response to all this is to argue that patchy coverage by particular media does not, in practice, matter all that much, so long as someone, somewhere, is paying attention. On this view, the role of the media is to alert attentive citizens to an issue, who then alert and mobilize others (Zaller 2003; see also Schudson 1999). Thus Page (1996: 7–8) argues that democracy theorists should concern themselves more with the range of information that is available to citizens rather than the balance or otherwise of particular media outlets taken in isolation. The problem with this view is that it assumes two unlikely conditions: that the range of facts and values available through the media is a fairly complete set; and that people pay attention to the range of views available. I have already suggested that the former may not be the case. With respect to the latter, Peterson (1992) has demonstrated that while people from high-status groups (connected with income, education, occupation, gender, and ethnicity) tend to be 'omnivorous' in their media consumption, people from low-status groups tend to be 'univorous' and thus hear a more limited range of views on a given topic, rendering them unable to take those views into account in their own deliberations (see also van Eijck and van Rees 2000). The univores' political agenda is therefore set by a much more limited range of problems, facts, and values than that of the omnivores. Given that, it is not at all obvious that elite-led deliberation has the rationalizing effect on the rest of the public sphere that Page claims, and so may not go terribly far in solving the scale problem.

What is not at issue here is arguments about whether the media has a direct influence over what people think, or whether people pick and choose more critically, accepting some information and rejecting other information on the basis of validity tests against their own experience, other conversations, and so on (Habermas 1996: 377; Street 2001). My point is prior to this kind of controversy: that it matters whether certain kinds of arguments are absent from the news media if we rely on those media to build publicity between deliberative sites, regardless of where we stand on questions of the relative strength of influence of the media on opinions. Without a full range of facts and values to weigh and sift, non-participants in a deliberative moment may well come to quite different conclusions from participants, leaving us with the problem of whose judgement should be decisive for participants and non-participants alike.

Let us now return to the cases to find out what effects the media had on deliberation, and what claims did and did not make it through the media filter.

5.2   NARRATING A DELIBERATIVE MOMENT

The organizers of the NHS poll chose the topic in part because they thought it would make good television : the 50th anniversary of the creation of the NHS was approaching. Indeed, the whole event was timed to coincide with that anniversary on 5 July 1998. That was not the only reason, though. The topic was also felt to be a good one given the aim of deliberative polls:

I feel quite strongly that these things work best when you've got topics that are quite complicated, and that in some ways force people to go against views they might hold superficially but haven't really challenged. Something like health rationing is a good example where, certainly in this country, the NHS is a sacred thing and people wouldn't really question their right to it.... I think all the topics picked in Britain have been good for deliberative polling in the sense that they've all been things that people have quite strong views on, but its unclear what exactly they're rooted in. To me that's an ideal topic. (Event manager, London)

However, it would be misleading to suggest that the NHS poll was an independent entity with an internal, academic logic, which just happened to attract the attention of a television crew; rather, media and academic imperatives were intertwined right from the start, a fact which caused some conflict in the early planning stages:

To a certain extent there's always a tension. The sort of research we do is primarily aimed at producing variables which are useful for analysing for detail later on, whereas from the telly point of view, they want a nice, snappy question which will give them the frequencies, and they're not really interested in whether it's 'strongly agree' or just 'agree'. (Event manager, London)

One can see the way these imperatives intertwined by comparing the broadcast version of the poll, *The Prescription* (Channel 4 1998), with the elements of news noted in Section 5.1. To begin with, television imposed a dramatic narrative structure on the event, a point stressed by a Channel 4 interviewee. It was divided into scenes or chapters, each of which ended with a 'teaser' pointing out what was coming next so that the television audience would stay tuned. It had a plot—the transformation that the participants went through—with a beginning, middle, and end. The beginning was to stress the fact that these people were complete strangers to each other; then showed them getting to know each other casually; then getting down to business in the small groups; progressing to asking questions of and reacting to the panellists; gaining confidence to tackle the politicians; and finally a small group of eight sharing their considered opinions and reactions to the event.

To see the effects of trying to impose a narrative structure, compare how different the experience of the deliberative poll is for those who watched it on television versus those who participated in the Manchester studios. As can be seen in the chart of time allocation during the poll event (Figure 5.1),[4] the participants spent a great deal of time with each other listening, checking, debating, and forming opinions in their small group sessions, during meals and coffee breaks; from the Friday evening to the Sunday afternoon they spent at least twenty hours together, of which only four hours forty-five minutes, or 22 per cent, was spent in plenary sessions of one kind or another. However, as can be seen from the chart of talktime given to different groups in the broadcast (Figure 5.2), very little of what the participants went through made it into the broadcast: group discussion, for example, made up only 15:26 minutes, or 9.5 per cent of the total programme. Of that fifteen minutes, a third was edited highlights from the first day, and all but fifty seconds of the rest was of one small group out of twenty. Even the remaining ten minutes featured *individuals* making points to each other; it featured little *discussion*.

What the programme did do to show changing minds was a series of 'vox pops' (short for *vox populi*, voice of the people, which are five to ten second,

---

[4] Time allocations in Figure 1 are based on the agenda given to group facilitators. Time in both figures is credited to a group where their opinions are the primary focus. 'All plenaries' equals expert and politician sessions; 'all public' equals moderated small groups, informal sessions and public interviews. The facilitators' agenda may undertake the amount of informal discussion.

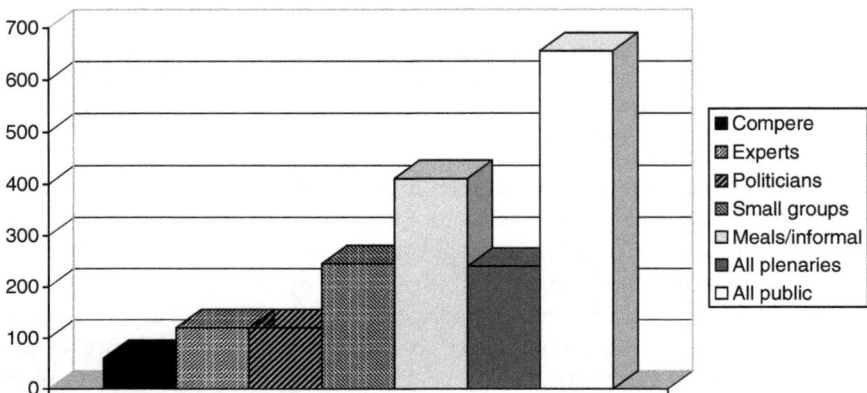

Figure 5.1. NHS deliberative poll talktime (in minutes) by participant

'person on the street' comments about a news topic) giving some top-of-mind reactions to the various plenary sessions; and an interview with eight participants at the end of the whole event who talked a little about their reactions to the issues. Again, however, in none of this was there any discussion; they were simple, brief answers to questions.

The influence of the narrative form is further demonstrated by showing what the programme did focus on, rather than what it did not. Referring once again to Figures 5.1 and 5.2, while the plenary sessions took up relatively little time in the main event, the television programme devoted more time to this aspect of the deliberative poll than any other, one hour fifteen minutes, or 46 per cent of the total. This is because the plenaries are consonant with another

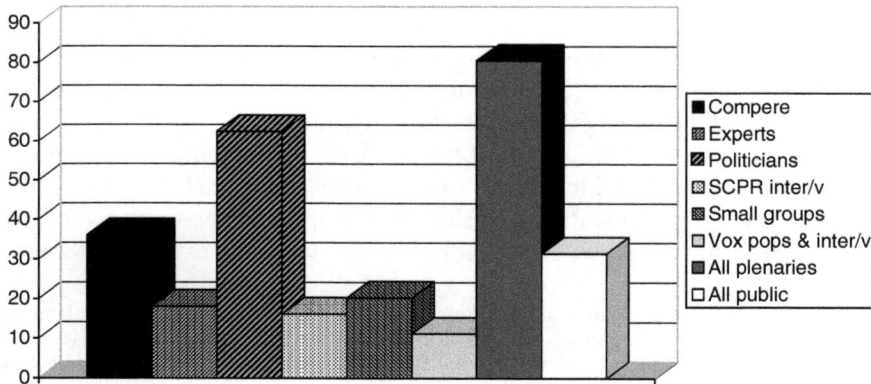

Figure 5.2. *The Prescription* (broadcast version) talktime by participant

element of news, namely the focus on conflict. While the deliberative role of panellists is to provide a range of views and information for the participants and the external audience, their narrative role is to provide clearly contrasting, polarized views, generating the element of conflict. In this respect, the health professionals and academics seem to have been disappointingly in agreement with each other. Although they spent two hours with the participants in the event itself, the programme only showed 12:49 minutes of their session in episode 1 (11 per cent of their real time allocation) plus another 5:36 minutes of highlights in episode 3. By contrast, the sessions with the health spokespeople from the three main political parties generated more conflict, and, of course, they were considered by the media to be much more significant people by virtue of their powerful positions. They took the same amount of time, two hours, as the experts did in the event itself, but gained three and a half times more coverage in the broadcast, 40:52 minutes in episode 2 (34 per cent of their real time allocation), plus another 21:32 of edited highlights in episode 3.

While the politicians provided views and styles which contrasted nicely with each other, the Conservative spokesperson, Ann Widdecombe, conflicted directly with a questioner and the compere, journalist Sheena Macdonald, in a somewhat testy exchange which lasted for several minutes. The exchange finished like this:

Macdonald: Is the logic of your utopia that everybody should have private health insurance?
Widdecombe: No, I haven't said that. I'm really rather saddened that this is the way the debate is going. What I have said I want, and I'll say it again (*looks pointedly* at *Macdonald*), and I'm amazed that with all this time in the studio I have to keep saying the same thing again (*audible muttering from the audience*), I want a National Health Service that is available to all regardless of means.... Now I could say that another six times and you would not necessarily choose to hear it.

(Channel 4 1998: episode 2, 15:07:36)

This exchange was, in the context of the rest of the show, television gold. In episode 3, which included edited highlights of the previous two shows, this exchange was the only segment of any length that was included unabridged. None of the other elements made it into the final episode unedited, be they small group discussions, interviews, or vox pops.

The final element of news which impacted on the poll was the presence of a strong central character in the shape of Sheena Macdonald, a reporter who enjoys celebrity status and who thus enhanced the event's significance by being significant herself. The television show feels more like a documentary in which the lead character does a great deal of direct-to-camera presentation and one-on-one interviewing, rather than a broadcast of parliament, say, where the television crew is invisible. Compare the proportion of talk time taken by Macdonald with the time devoted to others, including panellists, the Social & Community Planning Research (SCPR) team, and the lay participants. Over the three episodes,[5] Macdonald spoke direct to camera, did voice-overs, or ran interviews for more than 37 per cent of the 2:42:39 total running time, almost as much time as was devoted to the plenary sessions. Even in the rest of the broadcast, Macdonald was a dominant presence, introducing panellists, asking questions at least as often as the lay participants, and directing the interviews with James Fishkin and the SCPR staff. Thus, even though the lay participants and their experiences were the putative subjects of the programme, more than 80 per cent of the actual airtime was dominated by the 'significant' people, Macdonald and the politicians.

So, the version that was televized differed from the version experienced by the participants in some important respects. The issue here is not that the television crew failed to capture the vast majority of the actual deliberating; it is that they *could not* do so using the medium of television in an environment where the needs of the audience are a significant factor. While participant development may have been the 'plot' around which the programme was organized, it would have been a struggle for the editorial team to maintain a narrative just by focusing on that. There was not enough drama, not enough conflict, not enough black and white statements, not enough ups and downs and highs and lows in those small group and informal deliberations to capture an audience's attention and hold it over a sustained period of time. So, they needed to use two key elements of news, significant people and polarization, to carry the narrative burden.

Interestingly, Fishkin actually cites such dramatization as a benefit in terms of overcoming problems of sample attrition in deliberative polls, because 'the media could be expected to dramatize the process so much that most citizens would be glad of the opportunity to play a serious role in important historical events' (1991: 9). While Denver, Hands, and Jones (1995) question how attractive that lure really is, the issue I am more interested in is that media dramatization limits the access viewers have to any reason-giving that went on between participants over the three days, which gives viewers little basis on which to judge the quality of the conclusions to which the participants come. Television does not show an audience 'what went on': it shows just one of many possible new things constructed from pieces of what went on, and thus can leave audiences and participants with quite different impressions of

---

[5] Note that just under half of episode 3 consisted of edited material from the first two; only twenty-five minutes out of forty-nine was new material.

events. In the case of the NHS poll, the audience was exposed to some of the information provided by the panels, but not much of it: 11 per cent in the case of the expert panels, 34 per cent in the case of the politicians. They got a taste of what went on in the small groups and informal discussions during breaks, but again, not much: just over 5 per cent of the total, and most of that was from a few individuals in just one group.

Despite Channel 4's best efforts, however, the deliberative poll is difficult to turn into successful narrative for television, which is one of the reasons that, after doing five of them, Channel 4 decided that the NHS poll would be the last. They sponsored the development of a Europe-wide deliberative poll for nearly two years, but never went into production, for reasons undisclosed. One interviewee stressed that it was not that they thought that the polls were bad things in themselves, nor even that they thought the ratings were too low at the time, just that:

> ...one just has to ask whether here, now, that's the amount of time one wishes to devote to this sort of process, whether it actually gets you back the reward in television terms or not. ...I remember points at which the watchability of it was debated even in here by people outside the [commissioning] department, because it is a slow thing. Television works in narrative terms and often better in hour bites than it does in two hour bites. So something like a deliberative poll is difficult. Now, I think we're in a multi-channel environment, we're having to make sure our schedule is one that will be watched when people are surfing with a zapper.

Not only that, but other media found it unattractive too. Channel 4 could cover the event in part because of its unusual funding structure. It is run by a trust which ploughs all advertising revenues back into programming, which gives it more leeway than fully commercial channels to run risky or 'niche' programmes that might attract a small but influential audience, thus 'activating the active' (Schudson 1996). However, in the case of the NHS poll it is hard to find any impact on those opinion leaders let alone the rest of the public sphere. The only reaction SCPR received was 'a few phone calls and e-mails'; it was not considered significant enough by other media to overcome the urge to avoid giving publicity to a competitor's event, and so generated no other media coverage; even the four expert panellists I was able to speak to could not recall having been involved without prompting. So, simply broadcasting something does not mean it will have an influence on the wider public sphere.[6]

---

[6] It has been my experience that event promoters overestimate the impact of media activity on their audiences, because they judge the coverage they receive out of context. They look at

5.3   CONDITIONS OF SUCCESSFUL PUBLICITY:
SALIENCE AND THE LIMITS OF NEWSWORTHINESS

By contrast with the NHS poll, both citizens' juries generated significantly more media coverage in their localities: anecdotal evidence reported by the process organizer suggests that people in Leicester still recalled their jury some months later. Why was that, and what does that say about the likelihood of generating legitimating bonds with non-participants through the media?

The Belfast media coverage was the more limited of the two, comprising a small number of short newspaper articles and some television news coverage from Ulster Television (the private competitor to the BBC). The coverage focused almost exclusively on the process: in the pre-jury clippings only five sentences out of thirty-five mention anything about health service reorganization. The single post-jury item summarized the recommendations, but a third of the article focused on the process.

This emphasis on process can partly be explained by the wider political concerns of the time. The Belfast jury took place just a few months after the signing of the Good Friday Agreement which re-established home rule for Northern Ireland. Various sections of the enabling legislation, the Northern Ireland Act (*Northern Ireland Act* 1998), especially Section 75, included an array of measures for consulting all of the province's 'communities' on every major piece of policy administered by every one of the province's government agencies. In such an environment, there was intense public and media interest in processes which promised to make such cross-community consultation possible without degenerating into name calling or even violence. The citizens' jury process seemed to offer such hope, and so received some (but still limited) coverage. However, the topic was unusual in that the commissioners were using it to prepare a response to the Westminster government's NHS White Paper (Secretary of State for Health 1997). Service restructuring was not highly salient in the sense that it had not been debated in the Northern Irish media, no specific decision was being taken, nor was it likely that the participants would see much in the way of concrete outcomes. These features made it a 'bad question' according to the jury moderator because:

clippings from newspapers and measure the column inches, or collect video and count the seconds, without considering detail such as favorability, length, and prominence; the circulation and readership of the media concerned; and whether the coverage was brief or sustained. A few articles over time in the right place can make more impact than hundreds of different outlets covering an issue only once (Lindenmann 1997).

... it also has to be something that's quite 'live'. This sounds obvious, but because it's quite a long process, and because quite a lot happens in it, it's obvious quite soon if the [health] authority is not asking about something that's a real issue still, or a live issue, or a real thing they're trying to make a decision on. So it's the specificity, the realness, the liveness of the question which is important. (Jury moderator, London)

Interviewees suggested that this general pattern is repeated wherever citizens' juries are held for the first time in a locality: consonant with news values, the first one is news simply because it *is* the first one, not the usual way of doing things; subsequent ones are not news, unless they deal with a significant and pressing public issue and are part of, and have an influence over, a bigger decision-making process. Thus, in Belfast, the actual substance of the discussion came a distant second in terms of media interest to the process itself. This is not at all unusual: think of something far more dramatic such as space flight. The first moon landing held the television-watching world spellbound in 1969; the Apollo 13 mission was captivating because of the inherent dramatic tension of not knowing whether the crew would make it back alive; by 1972, the missions on which most of the useful science was conducted were 'boring' (Lewis 1974: 172). More recently, NASA made feverish attempts to make each space shuttle flight a 'first' or 'most', or to highlight some other arbitrary milestone—first Japanese astronaut, for example, or the 100th mission, heaviest payload, longest, highest, fastest, cheapest—anything to attract media attention and thus to maintain public interest and support long after the shuttle itself was 'news', until the disasters of 1986 and 2003 made news for all the wrong reasons.

By contrast, the Leicester citizens' jury generated significant coverage focused on the substantive issue, not just on the process, although as another 'first', interest in the process itself was also high. It was run in the context of a specific decision that needed to be taken, involving numerous powerful stakeholders both within and outside the local, regional, and central governments, about an issue that had very high salience thanks not only to the deliberate efforts of the 'save Glenfield' campaigners to make it salient, but also to the regular coverage given to the plans by the local newspaper, the *Leicester Mercury*, over a period of at least six months between October 1999 and April 2000. Furthermore, there was likely to be a practical outcome: the jury recommendations were presented to the Health Authority which was expected to act on them. As a result, publicity focused not just on the process, but on the substantive issues being debated.

Given that there was much more publicity surrounding the Leicester jury, it is in this case that we can explore whether arguments were reliably transmitted between deliberative sites by the media, and the answer, at first, was 'depends'. The agenda for public debate, including the problem definition, was set early on by the protestors, not by the health authority, because the latter had conducted its four-year consultation with a very limited circle of medical interests and behind closed doors. While the authority thought that what they were doing was improving service efficiency across all three hospitals, the protestors focused on the changes at Glenfield in isolation. They believed that the authority's plan would downgrade Glenfield to the extent that it would make it easier to close in the future:

> Unless the users' and future users' voices are heard and listened to, this friendly and successful hospital, 'a friend in need', will be downgraded to the position of a rehabilitation unit which, over a short period of time will be found to be uneconomic and those driving daily round the New Parks Estate island will see a for sale notice— 'Apply to the LHA for details and price'. (Letters to the editor, 1999)

Thus the media coverage up until December 1999 focused on 'plans to turn Glenfield into a rehabilitation unit', entirely reflecting the protestor's problem definition, a definition which was only partially borne out by the available evidence. From January 2000, the phrase changed to 'planned care and rehabilitation site', suggesting that the authority's communication machine had finally started to work to get its version of events heard, although headlines still ran the 'save Glenfield' line right up until the jury convened at the end of March 2000.[7] The coverage only dropped the 'rehabilitation unit' description, opting instead for the more accurate 'centre for planned care', from 1 April, after the *Mercury*'s health reporter sat in on the jury deliberations over the four days and heard the various arguments. Indeed, the newspaper carried extensive coverage of the various claims and counterclaims of the protagonists during the jury itself, reporting on each of the presentations the morning after, summarizing them all on the final day, and providing a detailed outline of arguments and recommendations.

So, we can say that in the Leicester case, the media did successfully transmit the various arguments, although this was facilitated by the citizens' jury which provided a forum in which those claims could be aired. Before the jury, the protestors' problem definition dominated the media coverage, even after the health authority got its communication act together. Regarding the concern with the transmission of arguments through the public sphere, it seems this is more likely to be undistorted if those claims are made in a well-designed deliberative moment like a citizens' jury, at which others like the media are

---

[7] Journalists do not generally write their own headlines; they are written by sub-editors who edit the journalists' copy into its final form. Thus it is often not surprising that the headline of a story and the body can give quite a different impression.

present, than if they are allowed to percolate through the media without such a deliberative focal point.

We can also say that the salience of the issue at hand, and its connection to a decision-making moment, are also important. This, I suggest, is what made the difference between the Leicester citizens' jury on the one hand and the Belfast jury and deliberative poll on the other. Clearly, the lack of a decision-making setting had interesting consequences for the NHS deliberative poll. While the impending 50th anniversary gave it some sense of timeliness, it was not as if anyone else could *do* much with the results. There was no upcoming vote, nor was there a specific government process into which the results were fed, a point made to me by an interviewee at the Department of Health (DoH). This meant that not only did it receive little media coverage, it had little impact even on the experts, policymakers, and politicians who were part of it, generating pretty much no debate in policy circles.

Other features of the news media are important. In the NHS poll case, competing television stations were not going to cover a Channel 4 event unless it was a great deal more significant, and newspapers found relatively little in the results worthy of reporting (and by the time of the fifth poll, the process itself was no longer news). Similarly with the Belfast jury, the BBC would not cover it because Ulster Television had, the story not having enough salience to override that desire for exclusivity in a competitive environment. These points have important implications for those who would attempt to create links between participants and non-participants in deliberative process by means of the news media: most deliberative processes are simply not newsworthy, and will fail to generate bonds between participants and non-participants. Something is interesting the first time, but not the second or third, so long as it deals with issues which are outside the fairly limited parameters of newsworthiness.

5.4   CONDITIONS OF SUCCESSFUL PUBLICITY: POLITICAL THEATRE

I noted above that the 'save Glenfield' campaigners made the issue salient in the first place, and thus their problem definition set the terms of debate for most of the nine months in which the public controversy raged. This emphasizes the point that while it is true that, as suggested in the previous discussion, an attempt to generate media publicity will be unsuccessful if the issue is not salient, salience can be manufactured, and that issues—or, more correctly, problem definitions (Edelman 1988)—can be put on the public agenda. As already suggested, the means of doing this are dramaturgical rather than strictly communicative in the Habermasian sense (Habermas 1984: 93). In this section, I want to explore how two groups in the cases under study tried to get their problem definition accepted in the media, and the implications of that for publicity in the wider public sphere. I do so by concentrating on issues of scripting and performance rather than the setting.[8]

5.4.1   ACHCEW and the NHS Plan

The first place to see such dramaturgy in action is in *The NHS Plan* case. Recall that when the plan was launched in July 2000 (following pre-announcements in late May), a central plank of NHS chapter 10, *Changes for Patients*, was to boost what the DoH saw as the key functions of the Community Health Councils (CHCs)—namely complaint handling, service quality monitoring, and providing a patient voice on service changes—by redesigning and redistributing those functions amongst elected local governments and new patient advisory boards, new patient advocacy services at NHS trusts and various government agencies. The CHCs saw it a little differently: what they focused on was Part 1, clauses 14 and 15 of the Health & Social Care Bill which concerned the 'abolition of the Community Health Councils', rather than clauses 7–13, which redistributed their functions. The months of consultation had focused on the principles that should guide the design of the new 'patient-centred' NHS; the precise institutions that should embody those principles were designed by a much smaller group comprising the Secretary of State and his small circle of advisers. The abolition of the CHCs was thought by the designers to fall logically out of the principles, and so the abolition decision was made very quickly without further consultation (DoH manager, London).

Opposition was organized quickly by the Association of Community Health Councils of England and Wales (ACHCEW). ACHCEW ran a 'very, very good campaign', according to one interviewee, by selecting one clear message and hammering it home to their members, the media, the Health Select Committee, and a network of other organizations like Age Concern, the Royal College of Nursing, the Royal College of Obstetricians and Gynaecologists, the Patients Association, even the Local Government Association, whose members were gaining new powers under the Bill. The key message was that the government was trying to abolish patients' only independent watchdog, using the slogan 'Watchdog, not lapdog', implying that the new patient advocates, as employees of the various health trusts, would not have

---

[8] For another example of such analysis, see Benford and Hunt (1992); also Edelman (1976). See Hajer (2005) for a case study of the effects that setting can have on a policy debate.

the independence to fulfil their scrutiny function. Its media 'hook' was to connect the existence of CHCs with two cases of medical malpractice which had already caused significant scandal:

CHCs, which represent patients' interests, played an important role in bringing the case of disgraced gynaecologist Rodney Ledward to light, and supported the relatives of the victims of Harold Shipman, the killer GP. (Staff reporter, 2000)

By comparison, the new systems' designers were on the back foot in publicity terms because they had neither a simple message (DoH manager, London) nor an emotional hook. Indeed, they were held to be partly responsible in both the cases used by ACHCEW as hooks, not having had proper mechanisms in place to catch Shipman in particular. Having framed the issue in the way it did, ACHCEW ensured that the government could not win that particular battle.

The overall point is that this example shows how the publicity function can be used to subvert as well as enhance the deliberative process where specific strategic goals are at stake. On the one hand, ACHCEW had a legitimate gripe: just as the Leicester patients' bodies had been left out of a decision-making process which clearly affected them and took action to force the deliberative doors open, so ACHCEW had been left out of a process which affected their interests and took similar protest action. But where the Leicester case resulted in the campaigners being given a role in putting their cases to the citizens jury, agreeing to leave the decision to them, ACHCEW never asked to be included in some future debate, nor was it offered to them. Instead it pursued a specific outcome using deliberately dramaturgical rather than communicative means, setting the terms of the debate by positioning themselves as the good guys in two scandals in which the government was seen as culpable, terms which could only come out in their favour.[9] Thus they used the real features of the media (i.e., its affinity for simplicity, scandal, and sound bites) not so much to open public debate, but to foreclose it, staking out a position in advance and not entertaining changes to it.

5.4.2   Disability activist campaigning

The second case where dramaturgy is important is in the activities of the disability movement. As noted in Chapter 1, the movement engages with the rest of the public sphere in ways which try to ensure that it does not get

---

[9] At least in the short term: the government gave way, but worked to build support for its measures with some of ACHCEW's erstwhile supporters, then reintroduced the measures in the NHS Reform and Health Care Professions Bill in November 2001, which became law in June 2002.

co-opted by powerful interests like large charities, care providers, and the medical profession, preferring self-help and direct action. Most notable in this respect is the Disabled People's Direct Action Network (DAN) which undertook a variety of 'actions' (a word borrowed from the environmental movement), aimed at inaccessible public transport, and protesting against what it sees as the Blair government's failure to honour a pre-election pledge to strengthen the Disability Discrimination Act's accessibility requirements. That, and proposals to decrease disability payments to beneficiaries, resulted in DAN's best-known action in 1997 when the group staged a highly visible demonstration outside Downing Street, chaining themselves to the gates and splattering themselves with red paint to represent people 'killed by neglect'.

The key feature of DAN's actions is that they use publicity in much the same way that ACHCEW used it in its battle over the abolition of CHCs—to create a self-contained situation full of conflict which will attract media attention and thus apply pressure to other decision-making processes. DAN gives journalists advance warning of actions so there will be plenty of coverage. Indeed, its press releases are sent out in advance of actions bearing notes to editors such as:

N.B. Photo journalists: There will be dramatic photo opportunities DAN actions are non violent, typically high profile and confrontational Arrests are likely. ([*sic*], DAN 1998)

While espousing non-violence, DAN's actions are designed to provoke an equally confrontational reaction, which, it is hoped, will lead to policy change; indeed, Scalmer (2002: 176) argues out that shock and 'hysterical critique' are necessary preconditions for attracting that media and policy community attention. For DAN, there is nothing quite so likely to stir the emotions and make a media impact as images of disabled men and women being hauled into wheelchairs by police and ambulance officers and taken away. The point here is that, where a group lacks a voice in decision-making moments, or where it has good reason for rejecting the model of engagement used by decision-makers, then more 'reasonable' means of attracting publicity may not be effective. In a media environment which focuses on the theatrical, the deliberate use of theatre is a particularly effective means of having their voice heard.

Such effectiveness comes at a cost, however. What gets lost in such theatrical media accounts, as noted in Section 5.1.4, are the technical and moral complexities of issues, as well as the material and discursive forces at work; and the everyday experiences of people rather than the exceptional. In the ACHCEW case, what was lost was the point that its functions were being given to organizations which were *more* accountable to citizens rather than less, which would draw their membership from a wider demographic base, and which had more extensive watchdog powers. In disability movement actions, what gets lost is the fact that the social model of disability is itself controversial because it can serve to undermine attempts to solve physical problems (Humphrey 2000), leaving people with genuine medical needs sidelined by the movement and by the policy priorities it advocates. This returns us to the concerns about interest groups raised in Chapter 4: unless they themselves are inclusive and internally democratic, there is no reason to expect that the arguments they make are representative of the claims that might be made by those for whom they claim to speak. If we rely purely on dramaturgy to gain access to the media, and rely on the media as our means of building publicity, then it seems that we privilege those points of view which can easily be dramatized and exclude those which cannot.

The solution may well be one that Dryzek (2000: 108) puts forward. A movement may make a strategic choice to split itself into radical and engaged wings, one which works in civil society, sets the agenda, and challenges the exercise of state power, the other which works with the state to integrate the new voice into state decision-making, as the green movement has sometimes done in Germany. This is precisely what has happened with the disability movement: groups like DAN have forced issues onto the public agenda while the British Council of Disabled People and others get invited to join working parties to write anti-discrimination legitislation and onto the board of the Disability Commission. The fact that activists help open up the agenda but more 'reasonable' others get invited to join in the subsequent conversation may not be a problem. From the standpoint of the deliberative system, what matters is that the public conversation is changed rather than who precisely is speaking at any one moment. However, this can only be a partial solution: activists cannot determine which bits of a complex message survive publicity's filtering process, and thus cannot determine entirely how the problem is reconstructed by government for action.[10]

5.5   CONCLUSIONS

It is now time to sum up and draw out the implications for the quest to establish legitimating bonds between participants and non-participants in deliberative democracy.

---

[10] In the context of women's movement activity surrounding childcare and unpaid work, Grey (2003) shows that movements have very limited policy success if they hold firmly to their discursive frames; they have significantly more success when they reframe debate in terms that are consonant with dominant discourses, but at the cost of dropping key demands which were only supported by the rejected discourse.

The first step was to highlight the often unrecognized but always implicit importance of the news media in democratic theory, having as it does a role in determining what issues become seen as 'problems' in the public sphere and thus what issues get political attention or not. However, while few academics argue that the present-day media performs that role in the pure way imagined by Thomas Carlyle, I have been at pains to point out that the reasons for this go well beyond 'input' problems: they concern the very political economy of news, including what counts as news in the first place. These structural features mean that certain kinds of issues get covered easily in the news media while others do not. In particular, those who have arguments to advance through the media must do so by personalizing, polarizing, and dramatizing their issues such that they construct a narrative with all the conventions which accompany the narrative form. This was seen in action particularly in the case of the NHS poll where television's narrative conventions significantly constrained how much reason-giving, supposedly a key feature of small group deliberations, could be shown. Instead, the televised version featured extensive coverage of combat between celebrities. The end result was that non-participants did not get exposed to many of the arguments which were made in the poll event.

The Leicester citizens' jury case shows that a newspaper, with its greater space and lack of visual constraints, was able to transmit the key arguments to non-participants once they had been made in the jury itself. Prior to the jury, however, the newspaper's coverage reflected the protestors' claims much more than the health authority's. Thus it seemed that the jury itself provided an 'opportunity structure' (Tilly 1978: 56) in which the range of arguments could be shared, but that the media on its own, without a deliberative site on which to focus, did not. In this case, accountability was dispersed throughout the public sphere when a deliberative forum provided a focal point. The implication here is that macro-deliberative democracy might only share a reasonably comprehensive range of available arguments among citizens when it focuses on micro-deliberative moments, which means we cannot entirely abandon micro deliberation in favour of macro.

The reasons why the Leicester jury attracted coverage in the first place had a lot to do with the fact that it was addressing an issue which had already been elevated to 'problem' status—had become salient, that is—and because it was connected with another decision-making moment, unlike the NHS poll or the Belfast jury. In both Belfast and Leicester, the fact that the process itself was new helped made it 'news'. Given a lack of newness, of salience, or of connection with a decision-making moment, the NHS poll made next to no impact on the public sphere.

Where salience is absent, it can be created by dramaturgical means. Both ACHCEW and the more radical arm of the disability movement used political theatre which emphasized conflict to generate salience and gain media coverage. By so doing they hoped to force decision-makers to accommodate their wishes. They both gained some success: the disability movement was successful in having government agencies established and human rights legislation amended, while ACHCEW won a stay of execution, albeit temporarily. But dramaturgy can undermine deliberative democratic values, either by sidelining inconvenient complexities or inconvenient viewpoints. Normatively, therefore, I would suggest that drama has a role in opening up deliberative space so that excluded voices can be included; but is dangerous when allowed to go further into the pursuit of specific policy goals, simply because such communication may very well exclude important perspectives.

Can deliberative democrats therefore rely on the media to transmit arguments, to be the means by which bonds of accountability are created between participants and non-participants? At least in the cases I examined, it seems this is only so where the following conditions are met: that a particular deliberative system has a micro level deliberative focal point, a forum in which arguments can indeed be made freely; where the issue is already salient; where it is the subject of an actual decision; and where it can be easily narrated. Without them, mediated deliberation is at best an unreliable builder of links between participants and non-participants.

6

Reason and Persuasion

> Great public events cannot be carried by the influence of mere reason.
> —Robert Peel (1846)

The last of the major grounds on which legitimacy battles were fought in my cases is rationality. Rationality issues, broadly defined, were raised by my interviewees on 105 occasions, only slightly less than representation issues, and were one of the two major motivations for local National Health Service (NHS) managers to experiment with deliberative processes (see Section 3.3). Indeed, it is frequently argued in health policy settings that if something is irrational it is therefore illegitimate (Tenbensel 2002: 175n.). This reflects a technocratic frustration with politics as usual, with strategic game-playing and the undermining of important public initiatives for selfish ends, or simply with decision-making processes which do not seem to take important facts and values into account (Gutmann and Thompson 1996: 12; see also Fischer 1990). Micro-deliberative processes like citizens' juries and deliberative polls have rationalizing benefits simply because they systematically inform participants about the issues and encourage people to check their understandings, interpretations, and opinions with each other. While hardly perfect, it is better than driving policy by uninformed 'non-attitudes' or 'pseudo-opinions' (Converse 1964; Fishkin 1991: 82; Neuman 1986: 23).

Questions about rationality connect with my theoretical concerns in several ways. As will be seen, there are connections with all three of the motivations problems: speech culture, limited agendas, and pre-deliberative commitments. Rationality is also an essential part of the concept of legitimacy I have been working with. The reasons for a proposal, including substantive judgements about its rightness, are necessary for judging whether or not it should be implemented or obeyed (see Section 2.1). However, I have also argued that appeals to rationality, even from experts who have spent time considering the details of an issue, should not have decisive force: they should have weight only inasmuch as they are offered in a process of public deliberation.

Nonetheless, some deliberative theorists and practitioners worry because it is not at all obvious that people are persuaded solely by what even they agree is reasonable. As in the observation from Peel above, and as thousands of years of rhetoric have taught us, persuasion requires argumentation which engages the heart as well as the mind, but this risks reopening the doors of deliberative forums to manipulation of emotions for strategic ends, a door which rationalists try to keep firmly closed (Chambers 1996; Habermas 1984; Spragens 1990). If this tension between reason and persuasion is unresolveable then once again there seems to be no way of reaching legitimate agreements in deliberative democracy: any process will either fall foul of the rationality requirement, or will fail to persuade.

In this chapter I explore that tension in theory and practice. I begin by looking at how the majority of public actors have come to conceptualize rationality, and some of the problems with that construction both in descriptive and normative terms. I then return to the cases to see how these issues arose and were dealt with, and conclude by summing up the strengths and weaknesses of the different deliberative models on these dimensions.

6.1 BUREAUCRATIC RATIONALITY, BUREAUCRATIC ARGUMENT

For many public actors rationality has come to require two things: first, instrumental action, the selection and implementation of good means to consistent and clarified ends; and second, that choices about rational actions be made against objective standards which are universally applicable, such as the rules of evidence, or the methods of scientific enquiry, or the values of efficiency and effectiveness (Dryzek 1990: 3–4; Elster 1983: 16–7; Fischer 1990: 41–3, 61). On this account, a well-resourced, well-informed and well-trained policy analyst should, after gathering the facts and evidence, be able to identify, select, and implement rational courses of action from the comfort of her office chair.

This account of instrumental rationality has been advanced both as a description and as an ideal. The description met its death at the hands of March and Simon (1958), who noted that while the ideal of instrumental rationality relies on clear problem definition, full information, and adequate resources, such conditions are rarely met in the real world of decision-making. Instead, rationality is almost always 'bounded'—for March and Simon by cognitive limits, but also by inequalities and competitive pressures between actors, structural distortions, and the political economy (Forester

1984: 24)—such that the instrumental ideal can rarely be approximated, let alone achieved, although different institutional settings apply different sorts of pressures. Furthermore, scholars working in a more Foulcauldian mode have argued that rationality itself is context-dependant; that what counts as rational bends to suit the interests of the powerful in a given situation (Flyvbjerg 1998; Hindess 1988). Nevertheless, the instrumental ideal continues to exert considerable normative force among policymakers.

Instrumental norms penetrated expert thinking in each of my cases. The extent of that can be most clearly seen in the way that Leicestershire Health Authority managers talked about their case. In contrast to my media, Community Health Council (CHC) and local council interviewees, who described the debate in more 'political' terms—the seat-of-the-pants search for a resolution to a crisis—the health authority people reconstructed the Leicester debate in terms of an idealized, instrumentally rational process selection:

And so we had a problem really, which was how do we look at not just one set of factors in relation to how the services ought to be—in other words, the service model for the future—but also how do we make the decision about where those services ought to be based.... Is the model that we're looking to adopt for the next ten years seen in the public's eyes as one they could support? In other words, is there a compelling case for reorganizing services?...

I mean in many respects we were on the horns of a dilemma really. How do you gain consensus when in fact there are different views within the system? There was a clinical view that said yes, we think it's right to organize these services in such a way. On the other hand, loyalties towards a particular hospital were very, very pressing, and how do we get not necessarily just an informed view, but how do we test out of some of those assumptions with a group of people? So we decided to do it that way. (Leicestershire Health Authority manager)

This interviewee claimed three things here which were not supported by other evidence. He claimed ownership of the idea to run a citizens' jury, when in fact the suggestion was made by Patricia Hewitt; he claimed that theirs was the decision to go with that model, when in fact the decision had been made for them by central and local politicians and the CHC, under pressure from the media; and he claimed it was the calm, logical, instrumentally rational selection of a good means to a well-defined end, when the real situation was anything but calm and the problem anything but well-defined. I will get to issues of problem definition next, but the point I want to stress here is how striking the mismatch was between descriptions of events. This shows how powerful the instrumental rationality norm was, leading the health authority manager to reconstruct events to fit the norm of how things *should* have happened.

Policymakers try to overcome the 'boundedness' of instrumental rationality by a variety of strategies. Depending on the nature of the challenges faced, these include satisficing, making do with the first workable solution rather than the best possible; networking to improve problem definitions, information, and resources; bargaining and adjusting positions with competing actors (Lindblom 1965); or more communicative solutions (Forester 1984). Put another way, to deal with boundedness issues, managers are required to consult various stakeholders about issues, options, and plans; they need to discuss issues with others, use arguments for and against proposals, weigh evidence, and attempt to persuade others to their point of view. As Majone (1989: 1) stresses, 'public policy is made of language. Whether in written or oral form, argument is central in all stages of the policy process.'

But this means that there is a mismatch between what public managers actually do, and what instrumental rational norms tell them is the 'right' way of going about things. This mismatch can have unfortunate consequences. For one, it can lead public managers to miss the ways in which power, discourses, networks, and institutions shape the policy agenda, and determine what counts as a problem in the first place (Kingdon 1984), so blinding them to potential problems with, and challenges to, their programmes. Another problem is that it may blind different participants to the ways in which the evidence wielded in favour of a proposal, and the persuasive power of that evidence, depends to a large degree on discursive frames (Hajer 1993). There is no reason to suspect that even instrumentally rational actors sitting down together will count each others' evidence as relevant, let alone valid. Perhaps more seriously, given a 'deep-seated animosity towards politics— particularly democratic politics' (Fischer 1990: 21), public managers may resent the political, discursive processes which are necessary for them to get their well-thought-out plans accepted. All this may lead them to reject the diverse grounds of others' arguments while at the same time finding it impossible to live up to the ideal themselves. They may bewail the irrationality of others, to the detriment of democracy, while unable to be rational in this way either.

The solution, for some theorists, is to question not just the descriptive grounds of the instrumental ideal, but its normative grounds as well; that is, to advance a more democracy-friendly account of rationality in which the linguistic aspect plays a more central role (Dryzek 1990; Fischer and Forester 1993; Habermas 1996: 3). In communicative rationality, processes of discussion and persuasion, rather than being bemoaned, are celebrated for helping form bonds of understanding 'across the boundaries of scientific paradigms, political theories, cultures, or normative positions, even in the absence of transcendent criteria', so long as the discussion is under dispersed and competent democratic control (Dryzek 1990: 11), although this approach rarely touches public managers.

The communicative approach helps lessen the tension between rationality and persuasion as well. While acknowledging Aristotle's observation that emotional appeals (*pathos*) can be stronger than logical argument, Dryzek (2000: 52–4) blunts the more rationalist criticism by pointing out that such appeals can be 'subjected to rational justification, because emotions often rest on beliefs,' which themselves can be checked for accuracy. For example, expressing public anger at particular circumstances can be perfectly justified by the unfairness of those circumstances. The same goes for character-based appeals (*ethos*): O'Neill (1998) points out that under the time constraints of real deliberation, participants may have no choice but to take *ethos* into account, but can nonetheless make rational judgements about those appeals. I will highlight some examples later.

The next question is, on what terms does rationality get fought over in the cases? In Sections 6.2 and 6.3 I discuss the two most important grounds of contention: problem definitions and attachments to particular outcomes. I then look at how participants in these deliberative moments reasoned together and worked to persuade each other before, in Section 6.5, offering some thoughts on the strengths and weaknesses of the different processes in allowing for rationalization in this richer, communicative sense.

6.2   RATIONALITY AND PROBLEM DEFINITIONS

I argued in Chapter 3 that legitimacy requires that problem definitions be contestable, and agendas broad enough to at least engage with, if not solve, the larger social, political, and economic issues which provide the context for local issues. This is both to make deliberative events more motivationally attractive, and to ensure that deliberators do not overlook the impact of a given situation on groups which might otherwise be invisible. However, this requirement can conflict with the practice of instrumental rationality in a technocratic environment. While instrumental rationality requires a well-defined problem so that remedial action can address what is 'really' going on, if the problem is defined by experts in advance of any consultative process, this can shut out competing definitions (Schratz and Walker 1995: 11), which then undermines the legitimacy of any subsequent deliberation. In all of my micro-deliberative cases, this turned out to be a problem to some degree: all were commissioned by public managers to address a particular problem, and so it should not come as a surprise that one of the most important legitimacy battles concerned limited problem definitions and the scope of deliberation.

In its initial stages in particular, the Leicester debate can be seen as an instance of contested problem definitions. The health authority's problem was an artefact of what Kingdon (1984) calls 'comparative drivers': the decision to compare the resources devoted to chronic and acute ailments and the subsequent discovery that chronic services were at a relative disadvantage.[1] Given that definition, the hospital service reorganization looked like a sensible response. However, as noted in Chapter 5, the 'problem' for the protestors and petition-signatories was the closure of accident and emergency services, or entire hospitals, in smaller centres around the country. The proposed changes at Glenfield Hospital were interpreted as making any future closure easier, and so was to be resisted.

Judgements of rationality depended on which problem definition the protagonists were allied with. For the health authority and for the CHC, who had been involved in the authority's early consultations, someone was irrational if they thought that the reorganization was about closing Glenfield. Such people were simply mistaken about the facts (as determined by the authority's frame of reference), and going off half-cocked:

I did go to the local media and said, 'Glenfield Hospital is not closing, it's not about closing of hospitals. It's actually about building services.' And I did say a lot of people do feel that they were signing petitions to stop closure of hospitals. (CHC officer)

For the protestors, irrationality was pretending that closure was *not* a possibility. So, the health authority found its first job was not so much to persuade people that it had chosen the right means to a given end, but to change the terms of debate such that its problem definition became accepted, something they never completely achieved. Indeed, the problem definition battle became one of the questions the citizens' jury had to decide: 'are you convinced of the need for change?', as well as, 'which is your preferred option?' (OPM 2000: 3).

Similar problems occurred in the deliberative poll, where there was a clear gap between what the organizers and expert panellists thought the debate was about, and the aims and values of the lay participants. Recall that the NHS poll was set up largely as a social scientific experiment to see whether lay people, confronted with information about the unsustainability of the current system, would accept the need for some form of explicit priority-setting, as opposed to the implicit processes which have always been a feature of medical practice, as well as asking what principles they would recommend to guide

---

[1] This is an example of an issue that has been identified in public management studies: 'what gets measured gets managed'. The phrase is used by Schick (1996) to describe how some issues become 'problems' simply because they can be easily quantified, with the result that management focuses on lowering or raising the relevant *number*, ignoring issues which are less easily reducible to numerical indicators.

such decisions. In other words, the problem definition included the assumption that explicit priority-setting was the right way to go, and that rationality required that public opinion shift in that direction. This was indicated in comments by one of the poll organizers:

I expected people to become more accepting of rationing; and I think that what we underestimated was people's unbelievable attachment to the NHS and unwillingness to contemplate it changing dramatically in the way it was structured.

Two of the NHS poll panellists implied very similar prejudgements in responses to questions during the plenary sessions, demonstrating a lack of respect for lay values and knowledge by drawing contrasts between 'obsessions' on the one hand and being 'serious' on the other:

The waiting list issue is a very complex one. The first thing I'd say is that it's a very small proportion of the total NHS. There's a tendency for the tail to be wagging the dog, and I don't think that obsessions with clearing waiting lists are at all helpful. (Public health academic)

If you want to reduce inequalities in health, if you're really serious about it—and I'm not sure that everybody is—but if you are serious, you should be prepared to redirect resources away from those who have already had a good innings towards those who are unlikely ever to get it. (Health economist)

By contrast, lay participants placed a great deal more emphasis on the value of ensuring equal access to a full range of services regardless of age, lifestyle, or other factors, and were willing to pay higher taxes to keep things that way. Indeed, the perceived egalitarianism of the NHS is one of the reasons that support for the institution remains very high, despite public acknowledgement of its many faults and failures (Park, Jowell, and McPherson 1998). These attitudes were very robust—surprisingly so, to the poll organizers— such that while the poll raised general acceptance of the probable need to ration services from 10 per cent pre-deliberation to 33 per cent after, attitudes against specific bases for rationing (such as position on a waiting list, quality of life, cost of treatment, and so on) actually hardened after deliberation. That is, people became less accepting of specific policy changes even while some at least recognized the general need.

While no one would say this so bluntly, I got the feeling that some took this 'robustness' as evidence for lay irrationality, a failure to face facts, especially when 'emotional attachments' to particular situations or institutions mean that 'you reach a point where rational argument simply doesn't prevail' (Politician, London). However, the argument I want to put forward here is that the NHS poll does not so much provide evidence of lay irrationality, as evidence that two conflicting problem definitions were in play, based on conflicting values between policymakers and lay participants (Schon and Rein 1994). It is of concern, therefore, to note that the deliberative poll format really does not allow much room for such conflicts to be exposed and discussed: the problem definition is set in concrete in the questionnaire which cannot be changed during deliberation without undermining the logic of the social scientific experiment. One of the poll's organizers admitted as much to me when she said that she would want to 'unpick' the reasons for people's robust attitudes more than she was able to using a broad question-naire. *The NHS Plan* process is equally vulnerable to criticism on this point: the various participants were asked to design the implementation, not to question the fundamental principles. The citizens' jury model seems less susceptible as the jurors have the power to call witnesses and ask their own questions, and have on occasion rebelled against manipulative agendas or witnesses, while the openness and composition of the steering group is clearly important if a variety of perspectives are to be brought to bear on the initial problem definition and agenda-setting:

One of the big problems we've always found here is if people are going to attack the jury process, if they're going to attack on the grounds of legitimacy, one of the things they will say is 'Who decided the question, who decided how you are going to recruit these people, who decided what information they're going to get?' Something we tried to do to counter that to some extent is to ensure right from the design process, the early stages of design, that it's as open as possible, where possible including the local media. (Jury manager)

Despite this, the citizens' jury model still faces problems if the process is only used by local agencies, as this limits agendas to those things that can actually be decided and acted on at the local level. Small-scale deliberations are constrained by how near or far they are from the centre of power, by how much influence they have over the legal and economic frameworks which limit what they can achieve. In the Leicester jury, one of the factors which created the acute/planned 'problem' in the first place was a national shortage of clinical staff, a factor which was not within the remit of the Leicestershire Health Authority to address, and which caused the Leicester jurors some frustration. The Belfast jurors were even more constrained, not just by the terms of the brief they had been given, but by the fact that Northern Ireland health policy had to fit into policy frameworks determined in Westminster and by the terms of the Good Friday Agreement. *The NHS Plan* process was commissioned at the highest level in the Department of Health (DoH), but even then participants were constrained by decisions taken by cabinet to drive through the 'modernization' agenda.

The activist-driven, 'insurgent' model is the least susceptible to such agenda problems, as I have stressed before. Activists in such groups seek to influence the terms of macro deliberation before getting involved in micro processes, maintaining a delicate balance between engagement with the state and insurgent activity against it (Dryzek 2000). This is precisely the strategy pursued by the disability movement both in working to set up government institutions such as the Disability Rights Commission on the one hand, but explicitly challenging the dominant frame of reference, the 'medical model of disability', through direct action on the other hand. This can be an extremely difficult balance to maintain, something which disabled academics Barnes and Oliver (1995: 115) put nicely:

> To get too close to the Government is to risk incorporation and end up carrying out their proposals rather than ours. To move too far away is to risk marginalisation and eventual demise. To collaborate too eagerly with the organisations for disabled people risks having our agendas taken over by them, and having them presented both to us and to politicians as theirs. To remain aloof risks appearing unrealistic and/or unreasonable, and denies possible access to much needed resources.

This is not to say that the removal of all agenda constraints is possible: one is always constrained to some extent by prior agreements, even prior democratic agreements, while even governments face constraints on their ability to act, self-imposed or otherwise, particularly economic constraints like the need to attract and retain investment and trade, or the need to maintain international agreements on human rights, justice, labour, and so forth. Nonetheless, within the confines of my particular group of cases, the point to stress is that deliberative events are significantly more constrained, and face greater legitimacy challenges, when they are run at a distance from the real locus of decision-making power.

Not only is the removal of agenda constraints not always possible, in the case of micro-level practices it may not be desirable either. This is because micro deliberations do not work well with over-broad agendas. The Belfast jury was criticized by one of its managers on such grounds. Two of the three questions were to elicit people's values surrounding health and social services generally, as well as public involvement in health decision-making, an 'issue that was not really having a major policy decision made about it' instead of 'something quite concrete..., something that's quite live' (Jury manager). Because the questions were so broad, and not focused on a particular policy event, the responses were fairly broad too: indeed, on the second question the responses were pretty much what one would expect from any undeliberative opinion poll, demanding services available free to all regardless of other factors, shorter waiting lists, more clinical staff, and fewer managers. An identical criticism was made of the NHS poll:

...it was vague, doing the classic deliberative thing: no clear question, the body commissioning it had no powers to act upon that anyway, it was a media stunt, and it had four million different questions. If you look at the size of the questionnaire, I mean, you know. SCPR have a very different understanding of what they mean by 'deliberative'. (Department of Health manager)

Instead, a citizens' jury agenda needs to be quite focused if it is to deliver a thorough, well-deliberated, and thus more rational response to a given question. But herein lies the rub: greater focus leads to better quality deliberation on a given question, and thus more legitimacy from an instrumentally rationalist point of view, but less legitimacy in terms of agenda constraint. Micro deliberations have their uses when the problem is well-defined and affects a clearly identifiable and contained group of people, but the broader the problem and the more diffuse the impacts, the less likely it is that a citizens' jury or any other micro-deliberative practice is going to be able to deliver legitimacy *on its own*, simply because they cannot possibly deal with all the competing problem definitions. This is a further reason for democrats not to neglect the broader strategies of engagement and contestation, to re-emphasize macro models of deliberation rather than putting all one's eggs in the micro process basket. Micro processes might perform very useful and valuable roles within a macro-deliberative system, but they cannot solve all the legitimacy challenges at once.

6.3   PRE-DELIBERATIVE COMMITMENTS AND RATIONALITY

The second major ground on which rationality was contested was the presence of attachments to a cause, to an issue, to particular decisions or particular institutional forms: the pre-deliberative commitments problem, in other words. The problem was seen to be greatest for those who had the greatest stake in an issue, for whom it was most salient. This came out during the Leicester citizens' jury:

...we had one consultant who decided not to turn up as a way of protesting. That consultant felt as though we'd reached the right solution, we had the right recommendation and we'd taken four years to get there, and now we were going to overturn it by asking the people what they thought about it. It was then in some ways like an affront to the value of doing it as managers and clinicians. (Health authority manager)

The managers' response to this was to give such people a subsidiary deliberative role as witnesses or steering group members, and to involve 'ordinary' citizens in the actual deliberation: this is one of the key reasons why the citizens' jury model appealed. However, as argued in Chapters 2 and 5, salience is necessary both to motivate participation and to achieve publicity. This may mean that the very engagement which disqualifies some people from having an active decision-making role is required in order to get participants into the forum in the first place, or to get non-participants to attend to its proceedings.

This conflict was apparent in the way interviewees talked about emotions and pre-deliberative attachments. On the one hand, some interviewees recognized that emotional attachments to an institution like the NHS provide it with a general salience which helps motivate participation. As the report on the NHS poll noted, 'the NHS has come to occupy a special symbolic place in British national life', becoming 'a source of great national pride', particularly because it is comprehensive, free at the point of delivery, and available to all regardless of means. It was this salience which was one of the reasons why Social & Community Planning Research (SCPR) chose the NHS as a poll topic in the first place. In addition, some talked about what might be called 'righteous anger', the idea that people can have rational justifications for feeling angry about a situation in which important interests, values, or principles have been affected. In Leicester, both the health authority and the CHC acknowledged this point:

There was a lot of emotion around the subject. People had worked hard to create these services and so cared about them deeply. (Health authority manager)

... I could see why [the 'save Glenfield' campaign chairman, Mike Turner] was angry. He'd raised a lot of money, he had done a good job, he had got this centre open for women—breast care is incredibly emotive as well, incredibly—and a few weeks later he saw that all of that work, all that energy, apparently looked as if it was worthless. They weren't going to close the service down, but for him they were closing it down because it wasn't in Glenfield, and he was bloody angry that he hadn't been informed, that he hadn't been told. (CHC officer)

On the other hand, interviewees frequently set up contrasts between rationality and emotional engagement in terms such as these:

... the charities are generally set up by people that are... quite emotive. But the jury were a little bit more detached I think, and I think they did a fantastic job. (Journalist, Leicester)

... at the end of the day you've got to put your personal feelings aside, and it is what is best for the community, what is best for the resources. (City councillor, Leicester)

The point is that while these attachments were necessary for motivating participation, they were also seen as undermining the rationality of decision-making, because attachments are not equally distributed, which leads to some options not getting a fair hearing in some cases. Putting it another way, some issues matter more than others for reasons which have little to do with their severity and more to do with the social processes by which salience is constructed, a situation which would be anathema to a rationalist public servant attempting to apportion resources on 'objective criteria' rather than on the basis of who 'shouts the most'.

The uneven distribution of such attachments can clearly be seen in the gap between the disorders that were most salient for patients and those that were salient for the wider public. Four interviewees noted how difficult it was in general to motivate patient involvement on issues surrounding acute illnesses and comparatively easy to get involvement surrounding chronic illnesses. An NHS manager in Leeds put it this way:

I'm thinking social care, mental health, learning disabilities, where patients, users, clients and their families have a vested interest in continued involvement, and of course a lot of expertise in managing their own conditions, their own care.... These patients are experts, they're part of the system, they've been in the system and will continue to be in the system and therefore have ownership and investment in it. It will be far more difficult where you have your large acute hospital or your primary care trust where either it's in a very deprived area, if you're thinking primary care, where people don't actually go to the doctor's very much, or you've got people passing through the system at a rate of knots, having time-limited procedures, and getting people involved in those settings is always going to be far more difficult.

That is, chronic illnesses or disability are major factors over the whole lives of their sufferers—indeed, in severe cases they could be said to define their lives—whereas acute illnesses are just one episode which claims the attention, and the political interest, of sufferers.

Salience is reversed for the rest of the public, with acute illness attracting a great deal more attention. The Leicester case is a demonstration of this: acute services not only received more public resources in the first place (unfairly so, in the eyes of the health authority), but it was the threat to acute services which motivated petitioners much more than any subsequent inconvenience to long-term patients:

... the people in the General [wanted] to keep the General as it is ... [but] Glenfield has got incredibly powerful support networks, more so than any hospital that I've ever come across ... it's almost on a level with something like Great Ormond Street.[2] It does children's heart surgery which is probably why, and it also has intensive care and ... it's all very strong with heart [disease]. And the General just hasn't, and it's awful really. It's older, it's got a lot of very old parts, very crumbly bits of building, but it's still the centre for diabetes and renal which are not very sexy areas of medicine. (Journalist)

---

[2] A well-known children's hospital in London.

It is therefore interesting to note that the Leicester citizens' jury provided a forum in which these competing patient/public claims could be sorted through, as the journalist quoted above continued:

One of the things they did do, which I thought was brilliant, they recognized the fact that kidney patients were very much the underdogs in all this. Heart and kidney had to go together [but] at the moment they're at separate hospitals, so one of them would have to move. The heart group were the loud shouters, but the Kidney Patients Association, they also had very good reasons for wanting to see services stay at the General. And what ended up happening is that the jury took that on board, and although they found that the Glenfield should stay, and the General should become this planned care centre, they asked that a satellite centre should be set up at the General for patients to go to for treatment. They recognized that a lot of patients had moved closer to the General so they could go and have their three hours treatment. I think it was great that the jury members picked up on the fact that they needed to provide something. They didn't take the choices as read, they didn't sit and say, 'Right we need to decide this or this because that's what the health authority's told us'.

One reason why the jurors were able to sort through these competing claims was to do with the scheduling of different presentations. The 'loud shouters' went first, but the Kidney Patients Association were given equal time in a later time slot, which meant that they could be asked questions in light of the evidence given by the 'save Glenfield' campaigners, something which the campaigners did not have the opportunity to do. In other words, the volume of 'shouting' was equalized between witnesses. Another reason, however, was because of the separation of roles between the 'passionate' and the 'detached'. The former—that is, the interest groups—helped set the agenda by sitting on the steering group and, as witnesses, provided the necessary competing viewpoints to the jury, but they were not allowed to have any decision-making role. Implicit in this, I suggest, is a judgement that their attachments would have overwhelmed their reasoning powers, ensuring that the process would degenerate into politics as usual.

What evidence is there for that judgement? In my cases, the evidence is limited. Neither the citizens' jury nor the deliberative poll model can give guidance either way because, by separating roles, they assume an answer to that question. *The NHS Plan* process made no such assumptions, being a forum in which the 'passionate' were themselves the deliberators, and as such offers more hope. From the limited reports of participants I have available, it showed that the various interests could indeed work through their differences and reach 'working agreements' (Dryzek 2001), at least on procedures for taking the next steps if not always on substantive detail.

Nonetheless, this may be much easier where the deliberations are in camera. The risk of degeneration into strategic game-playing remains considerable where deliberation takes place in the glare of publicity, and where participants' prior commitments have already constrained their freedom to engage in authentic deliberation (Kuran 1998; Mackie 2002). This point was alluded to by a DoH official when talking about the reaction of various groups to the decision to abolish the CHCs:

... all the patients' groups that I know were consulted as part of this have said, 'Oh, absolutely, you're doing the right thing now.' Most people don't like CHCs in private but they weren't [saying that] in public.

In other words, the risk is that deliberators with prior commitments to others will play to the gallery rather than engage in the spirit of authentic deliberation. That is, the *audience* of speech acts in deliberation may not be one's substantive opponent at all, but third parties watching from the sidelines, either already committed to one side or the other, or still making up their minds about the issue. In turn, this would mean that the strategic goal of a deliberating party may no longer be to persuade his or her interlocutors, but to score points off them for the benefit, even entertainment, of the audience. Should the deliberator decide that the encounter is swinging the other way, he or she may then try to exploit other channels of influence rather than continuing to play the deliberative game (Hendriks 2002*a*). Indeed, a citizens' jury conducted by Niemeyer (2004) was almost killed off before it began when developers with an interest in one side of the argument tried to disrupt funding and had questions raised in the Queensland state parliament.

This brings me to an unpalatable possibility. Combine the observation above with the representation and publicity requirements outlined in the previous chapters, and we are faced with yet another irony of deliberative democracy. It may well be that representation and publicity are required to create legitimating bonds between participants and non-participants, but with the unfortunate consequence that rationality and deliberative authenticity are undermined. Try to contain such outside influences, and the deliberations themselves may be more authentic, but have much less impact on, and legitimacy for, the wider community.

There may be some hope of resolving this conflict if simply participating in deliberation encourages people to internalize deliberative norms, which can either mean that people would not be tempted to 'cheat' in the first place or, if they did, suffer the public opprobrium of those who *had* internalized the norms (Goodin 1992: 135). My cases proved to be an inadequate test of either possibility. The NHS poll and the Belfast jury were too far removed from real decision-making to make it worth anyone's while kicking up trouble even if they had disagreed with the outcomes. In the Leicester case, the jurors' recommendations were broadly in line with the protesters' preferences and so there was no reason for them to continue the campaign; we can only speculate on what might have happened if the decision had gone the other way (see Section 4.3). In the case of *The NHS Plan* process, it might be thought that the Association of Community Health Councils of England and Wales (ACHCEW) campaign to stop the abolition of the CHCs is an example of an actor choosing to play to the gallery, but they were never offered the opportunity to deliberate in good faith, and so we cannot tell what effect deliberative norms might have had on their actions had they been involved. However ACHCEW's actions can be seen in another light: because the DoH had not met the principle of inclusion adequately when putting together *The NHS Plan* deliberations, ACHCEW was quite justified in calling public attention to this exclusion, thus casting public opprobrium on the department when deliberative norms were transgressed. While it is reasonable to doubt the deliberative purity of ACHCEW's motives here—they worked to foreclose debate rather than open it—their actions nonetheless reinforce the point I made in Chapter 4 about one of the positive possible roles of interest groups in the macro-deliberative system being to challenge exclusion both of people and of issues from deliberative processes.

Still, we are left without much resolution on this point: it may well be that deliberative norms have a disciplining effect on those with pre-deliberative commitments; or it may well be that we cannot have both good deliberation and deliberation that *matters*, given current institutional arrangements at least.

6.4   REASONING TOGETHER

While there is a clearly negative role that emotional attachments to particular issues can play in deliberative democracy, on the positive side are some benefits to do with motivating engagement in deliberation in the first place, both in terms of the decision to participate and the way in which one engages with one's fellow deliberators, taking them and their arguments seriously. I have already mentioned the benefits of emotional attachments in generating salience; in this section, I show that expressing the emotions surrounding a particular issue helps to form communicative bridges between participants.

This point speaks to some questions raised by Dryzek (2000: 65–6) about the incidence in actual deliberations of the speech culture problem raised by difference democrats, particularly by Sanders (1997) and Young (1996): namely, that deliberation represses difference because it privileges norms of argumentation that are specific to powerful groups (see Section 2.4).[3]

---

[3] Doganay (2004) offers a case study which seems to confirm Sanders' and Young's fears, but her example has many fewer micro-deliberative features than even my cases, and so cannot be taken as a rigorous test of deliberative theorists' claims.

The criticism supposes that deliberative norms would force people to engage together in much the same way that a university seminar sometimes would, with reasons being challenged, examined, defended, and opposed on all sorts of grounds. However, people in real deliberations do not deliberate this way all the time: they also deliberate by swapping stories. Consider this example from the broadcast version of the NHS poll,[4] in which participants spent about half their time telling stories and drawing lessons from them, and about half their time in more abstract discussion. To get some flavour of how the former works, here is one exchange from a small group discussion:

One: Who are all these people who complain about the health service? I haven't met anybody who says, 'Oh, it's terrible.' Are any of you saying it's terrible?

Two: I think it's absolutely appalling, the health service. My mother was stricken with cancer, and it developed rapidly. Now my mother needed a syringe driver, and we couldn't get a syringe driver to inject the morphine in every so often. And my mother was in agony waiting for this. My brother said 'I'll go and buy one.' They said, 'They're a thousand pounds.' He said, 'I'll buy one!' 'But you can't, there's only so many in the area and they're all being used.' And I think that is absolutely appalling. If you could break a window in a shop and steal one, we would have done it.

Three: If you do have a serious problem, then there's no waiting list, and you do get excellent service. That is certainly the case in Scotland. A friend has had to move near to Glasgow Royal Infirmary for him to get instant treatment, but it was available.

Four: I have a friend whose wife is being treated at the moment and has to travel from where she lives, 30–40 miles, and there's no facility to get her to where she has to have the treatment, and she can't drive after the treatment, and her husband is self-employed, and she has to have this treatment every three days a week for a month. Now he has to give up three working days to take his wife to treatment.

Five: There are centres of excellence and you just can't have those all over the country because of the expense of putting small regional hospitals with expertise in nearly every area, which means people will have to travel.

Four: Yeah, but it's that thing of not providing a facility for her to get there. Yes, there is that centre of excellence for that person, but if they can't get there, it might as well be on Mars.

This does not sound too much like the dry, committee-style approach bemoaned by Young. It sounds more like what Rorty (1998) calls 'sentimental education'. Rorty contends that moral education that appeals to people's sentiment is most likely to change people's thoughts and habits. This senti-

---

[4] The transcript should be read keeping in mind the differences between the poll event itself and the broadcast version, discussed in Chapter 5.

mental education consists of telling 'long, sad stories' that begin, 'you should care about this person because this is what it is like to be in her situation.'[5] This is the *pathos* of Aristotle, the most powerful persuasive tool in an orator's armoury (Remer 2000: 76). This work of building empathy not only opens others' eyes to one's problems, it also creates a sense of being listened to, which further binds participants into the deliberative process, and to each other. Indeed, the swapping of stories helps develop bonds of friendship between participants that in some cases can last lifetimes, as it did for five members of the Belfast jury who continued to be involved in regular consultations for the Eastern Health and Social Services Council (EHSSC) for several years, while another two fell in love and married soon afterwards.

It is unclear from my cases whether 'being heard' is enough, or whether there needs to be some substantive change in a deliberative outcome for the losers in a process to accept it as legitimate. In *The NHS Plan* case, the losers were the CHCs, and they protested vigorously, but that may well be because they had not been part of the consultations in the first place. In the Leicester case, the relative losers were the Kidney Patients Association who argued against shifting acute services from the General Hospital because many kidney patients had moved closer to the General in order to minimize travel time for their three or four weekly dialysis treatments, but their concerns were at least addressed when the jury recommended that a satellite centre for kidney patients be set up at the General, so that does not really test the question either.

Still, friendship and bond-forming between deliberators may well be a necessary if not sufficient condition for persuasion. This is because those who can show mutuality in a deliberative setting are not only enhancing the legitimacy of their claims by making the effort to demonstrate 'co-performance' (Schaar 1984); they are also at a distinct rhetorical advantage over those who cannot (Remer 2000: 76). Speakers in deliberation need to be 'appealing', likeable characters in some way (NHS poll organizer). I have both positive and negative evidence to support this contention from the cases. The negative evidence comes from the failure of Conservative health spokesperson Ann Widdecombe to form bonds with the NHS poll's lay participants in the terse exchange noted in Chapter 5. It was clear from the reaction of the audience and from subsequent 'vox pops' that the testiness, the implied criticism of the audience, and the implied criticism of the well-liked journalist running the show led people to discount Widdecombe's message. Other speakers elicited quite different reactions. One of the panellists, the late health economist Professor Alan Williams from the University of York, delivered an unpopular message about his preference for prioritizing the young rather

---

[5] See Forester (1999) on the importance of stories in policy and planning processes.

than the elderly, but was able to do so without drawing fire from the audience by the humorous, self-deprecating way with which he prefaced his remarks:

(*with a wry smile*), Well, I don't think you suddenly become old, it creeps up on you (*laughs, as does the audience; cameras cut to a big smile from the questioner*), it's certainly crept up on me. At the age of 71, I've ceased denying that I'm old.

Another, Professor Paul Dieppe of the Department of Social Medicine, University of Bristol, made a plea for the present system, and earned rare spontaneous applause from the audience not just for his stand, but for the passion with which he delivered it. He was asked by the compere whether he agreed with a comment about using more of the private sector's capacity, and responded,

No, absolutely not, I disagree very strongly with that. I think we should take the private sector into the NHS rather than the other way round, because I think one of the most divisive things (*applause breaks out*), I think one of the most divisive things is we have people working in a dual economy. It leads to the biggest inequalities in the health service and it's divisive in the staff.

Note that, in part, what was going on in the NHS poll was an implicit appeal to *ethos*, the authority a speaker has by virtue of the kind of person he or she is (Remer 2000: 76). Professors, especially medical ones, have enormous status, which gives them a head start over politicians who lack such status in the rhetorical race. But this does not guarantee winning that race: the deliberative poll participants were not persuaded that the private sector should have more of a role in delivery of health services either, despite the fact that it was medical authority figures who were trying to convince them. This is an instance of the kind of rational judgement of *ethos* that O'Neill (1998) suggests is possible.

That it is possible, however, is not to say that it happens all the time. Two interviewees noted an incident in the Belfast jury concerning GP fundholding, a measure by a former Conservative government to devolve budgets to GPs which was blamed for helping create a two-tier health system, one for the rich, another for the poor (Klein 2000: 196). The Belfast jurors were not persuaded that fundholding was a good idea, at least in part because of who delivered the message:

We had a GP fund-holder from Belfast, and they didn't like him, it was clear they didn't like him, he didn't convince them about fund-holding, and so they wanted— (*pause*)—one of the witnesses they wanted was a non-fund-holding GP from a rural area, which we got, and they really liked him, they could associate with him, even though a lot of them were from Belfast. (Jury organizer)

On the other hand, just being 'a nice guy' is not sufficient either. While the NHS poll audience reacted well to Simon Hughes, then the Liberal Democrat health spokesperson, for speaking in terms that meshed well with the audience's stated opinions about the NHS, the vox pops after his session stressed that since Hughes was not in power he could promise all sorts of things but could not make any of them happen. Once again, proximity to power matters when it comes to persuasion, as much as in assessments of legitimacy, and again the audience showed themselves capable of making rational judgements about *ethos*. Nonetheless, the substantive content of people's positions is not sufficient to persuade. As Aristotle argued, logical explanation is only one, and by no means the strongest, of the rhetorical proofs: *ethos* is often stronger, *pathos* stronger still.

There are two main implications of this discussion of practical reasoning for legitimacy in deliberative democracy. First, it seems clear that even in the far-from-perfectly-deliberative worlds of my cases, 'reasoning together' is quite consistent with a range of communicative styles, and although a great deal would depend on the skills and prejudices of the moderator of any deliberative event (Dryzek 1987)—they have a great deal of power to encourage or discourage different communicative styles—this did not cause problems in any of my cases. In my own experience as a moderator, participants of all sorts of backgrounds will challenge the authority of someone who tries to shut them up unreasonably, either within the forum or by withholding consent later. This means that the motivational concerns of Sanders (1997) and Young (1999) may well be theoretical possibilities but empirical rarities in genuinely deliberative processes.

Second, while lay participants clearly had the ability to make rational judgements about the rhetorical claims made through *ethos* and *pathos*, they did not always do so. Who delivers a message is at least as important as the content of the message itself: they need to be likeable characters and possessed of some rhetorical skill if they are going to move their audiences. We can connect this with the discussion of narrative in Chapter 5: when it comes to persuasion, the narrator matters, and the narrative requirements of personalization and polarization matter, more than the actual content of the story, the proposals themselves. This means that those who would discuss the important material and discursive forces which shape political problems are at a distinct rhetorical disadvantage even in deliberative democracy; and that the door remains open to manipulation, to the perpetuation of politics as a 'spectacle' (Edelman 1988) which many advocates of deliberative ideals sought to undermine. It could be that attempts to manipulate public communication can themselves be subject to scrutiny and challenged: if someone tries, for example, to reduce a debate to *ad hominem* attacks, this can be exposed and ridiculed in turn by their interlocutors. However, as I argued in Chapter 5, it is important to get in first in debate: mud sticks, such that those at whom it is flung may end up spending more time trying to clear their own characters than having their substantive arguments assessed. Thus I have offered a solution to one of deliberation's motivational problems, only to have that solution potentially undermine the substantive requirements of legitimacy.

6.5 CONCLUSIONS, TENSIONS, AND IMPLICATIONS

Three sets of conclusions arise from this discussion of rationality and persuasion. The first is that my earlier, more tentative conclusion about the importance of deliberating at the right level of the hierarchy has been borne out by closer examination of the cases, but it may be a double-edged sword. On the one hand, deliberation should be done as close to the real decision-makers as possible so that people get to deliberate about things which really matter, rather than getting involved in very sophisticated and empowering processes which end up not changing things all that much. This is because of the requirement that agendas not be too restricted, which improves the motivational attractiveness of deliberation and its substantive legitimacy by addressing more fundamental issues and their consequences for as broad a range of people as possible. On the other hand, the closer deliberation is to the locus of power, the greater the incentive for those with pre-deliberative commitments to get involved in strategic game-playing, but this remains just a logical possibility. My cases were not an adequate test of Goodin's idea that participation in deliberation disciplines this kind of behaviour, the positive view of ACHCEW's campaign notwithstanding.

The opportunity for strategic manipulation of a deliberative process is opened by the necessary role of rhetoric in persuading, although rhetoric too has positive and negative aspects. On the one hand, appeals of *pathos* and *ethos* are necessary for building communicative bridges between participants and for motivating the involvement of those who are not normally empowered to speak in committee-style processes. Indeed, it appears to be one of the normal ways in which people communicate with each other, either sharing stories and then drawing out general lessons from them, or making general claims and illustrating or countering those claims with particular tales. This applies just as much in macro as in micro deliberation; perhaps more so, given the tendency for mediated public discourse to favour narrative styles over more abstract discussion. Also, rhetoric can be a powerful tool to challenge limited agendas or exclusion of particular groups: the Leicester interest groups' 'save Glenfield' campaign and ACHCEW's campaign to maintain the CHCs can be seen in this light. On the other hand, such appeals can sometimes override substantive considerations, considerations which are also a necessary component of the legitimacy of any deliberative outcome. Deliberators in the NHS poll seemed to make rational judgements about the safety of relying on *ethos* claims when it came to someone they liked: 'Trust me, I'm a doctor,' is not always an effective rhetorical strategy; nor is, 'Believe me, I'm a nice guy'. When it came to someone they disliked, however, the *ethos* judgement overwhelmed the substantive content of what the person was saying. The points Ann Widdecombe made in the NHS poll did not get a fair hearing because she got most people's backs up; the same went for the GP presenting the pro-fundholding viewpoint in the Belfast citizens' jury. The lesson here is that while O'Neill (1998) may well be right that people can make rational judgements of *ethos* and *pathos* claims, they seem to exercise their judgement better when it is someone they can relate to who is talking. This leaves plenty of room for worries about the discursive advancement of unjust ideas by a powerful, likeable character—history is littered with persuasive dictators—or the ability of one side to blacken the name of its opponents, neutralizing their substantive arguments.

The third set of conclusions concerns the ability of the different processes under study to handle these tensions. Micro-deliberative processes generally do not handle the agenda-setting issues well, not just because they have been used at low levels in the hierarchy, but also because they work best with relatively constrained agendas. Despite that basic flaw, some micro-deliberative processes handle the rationality tensions better than others. The deliberative poll is particularly weak, despite its interest as a social scientific experiment. Within the confines of the poll, deliberators have no influence whatsoever over the agenda and content of the questionnaire: to give them some influence would undermine the logic of the experiment which is the dominant purpose of any deliberative poll. Nor, even in the relatively small amount of time the poll gives people to debate the issues together, do many of the issues that people decide are important in their small group sessions come up in the plenary sessions, let alone make it into television coverage, and are not captured in the questionnaire. In the case of the NHS poll, none of the issues raised in the small group discussion recorded in Section 6.4 were reflected in the questionnaire or subsequent report. It may be possible to open up the initial agenda-setting process beyond the very limited circles of people who have typically decided poll topics to date. One of the Australian deliberative polls provides a model, in which a series of focus groups were run in indigenous communities around the country to identify the key issues which should be discussed in the main event (Issues Deliberation Australia

2001).[6] Still, the particular way in which the deliberative poll format uses the media opens it up to strategic manipulation more than others: because it is broadcast, and because it puts 'significant' people centre stage, it can easily become a soapbox for panellists to address the television audience, scoring points off their opponents, rather than an opportunity for them to deliberate with the poll participants, let alone each other (Gibson and Miskin 2002).

The citizens' jury is much less susceptible to these problems. Those with pre-deliberative commitments are assigned a subsidiary role as witnesses, which means they have less opportunity to manipulate the deliberations rhetorically. The deliberative quality is much higher given that jurors spend several days deliberating together in camera, rather than just a few hours in the deliberative poll, some of which is in front of the cameras, which introduce new distortions. Another benefit of this is that it allows participants time to get to know each other, to get comfortable with each other, so that when difficult issues do come up, they can be dealt with properly: people have time both to get angry and to have that anger acknowledged and discussed (on the importance of which, see Stone, Patton, and Heen 2000). Many people can have an influence on the agenda because of the way in which steering committees are normally made up of members of relevant interest groups or 'stakeholders', to use the presently fashionable term. To a more limited extent, lay participants get the chance to call witnesses, write recommendations, and even, on occasion, challenge the terms of reference where they feel it is too limiting. Even the decision to run a jury has been the result of activism rather than academic entrepreneurship, as happened in Leicester. Nonetheless, as for any micro-deliberative process, there are still limits to the breadth of issues that a citizens' jury can deal with, and thus question marks remain over its democratic impact.

Of the more macro-deliberative processes, *The NHS Plan* process also suffered some agenda constraint issues because that agenda was set by a very small group in the DoH, with limited public involvement used more to legitimate that agenda than to make much in the way of substantive recommendations (see Mort, Harrison, and Wistow 1996), the department's protestations notwithstanding. At least it was run near the peak of the health policy hierarchy, and so mattered far more than the other processes. What it did show was that, within those constraints, even a semi-deliberative process helped those interest groups, NHS staff, and DoH managers with strong pre-deliberative commitments to work together and come to agreements without

---

⁶ Fishkin has been silent on agenda-setting questions in published work on deliberative polls. See Fishkin (1996, 2003), Fishkin, Luskin, and Jowell (2000, 2002).

fur flying. Just being part of the process seemed to help a great deal: the only significant opposition came from the CHCs and that may have had more to do with the fact that they and their champions on the CHC were not included in the process at any stage. One can only speculate on what would have happened had they been included—their interest in their own perpetuation may well have overwhelmed the deliberative spirit even if they had been involved from the start, but evidence is inconclusive on this point.

The model which is least vulnerable to the limited agendas problem is that of the disability movement. They maintain a stance independent of government and private care agencies precisely in order to challenge effectively the overarching, and limiting, agendas of those agencies, dismissing micro deliberation for some of the reasons I have advanced here. However, the model seems in principle to be much more susceptible to criticism on rhetorical grounds, because there seems to be no reason why only those views which political theorists consider to be just or rational will be successful, given what I have suggested is an asymmetry in persuasive power between likeable characters and those who do not successfully create communicative bridges. If that is the case—and certainly my assertion would require more empirical investigation before it can be made with any great confidence—then we are left with a worry which undermines macro deliberation as the solution I have been advancing to micro deliberation's legitimacy problems. This means there is no single solution, that different institutions have features which help with legitimacy but others which undermine it. In Chapter 7, I try to pull all this together, summarizing the legitimacy criteria, and putting together some picture of how different institutions might be arranged in a deliberative system to maximize their strengths and minimize their weaknesses.

7

The institutions of a legitimate deliberative democracy

It is now time to pull together the various insights and conclusions from the theoretical and empirical work to answer the institutional question I posed in Chapter 1: what do we need to do to current deliberative institutions to make them more legitimate, given the problems of scale (not everyone can deliberate together) and motivations (not everyone may want to, because of pre-deliberative commitments and limited agendas)? When casting around the deliberative democratic literature for answers to that question, one comes up relatively empty-handed: it is dominated either by ideal end points without much in the way of how we should move from our current position towards those ideals—a complaint Gunnell (1986) makes of a great deal of political theory—or what sometimes feels like tinkering with micro processes, which, as seen in some of my cases, can leave mass politics relatively untouched (see also Gutmann and Thompson 2004: 143). Indeed, some of the institutional recommendations do not appear to have much that is either deliberative or democratic about them although all sorts of micro-level practices may well have important, legitimate, deliberative, and democratic functions in the broader deliberative system, regardless of how many deliberative principles they instantiate themselves (Ryfe 2002: 369).

In this chapter, I want to offer my own vision of what the next steps from current institutions towards a legitimate deliberative democracy might look like—an exercise more in institutional intervention than 'from scratch' design (Pettit 1996: 55). To get there, I begin by drawing together the key insights into the nature of a legitimate deliberative democracy that have arisen from the case studies and theoretical discussion so far. I then compare the various processes featured in my cases, as well as the micro and macro models of deliberation, in terms of their strengths and weaknesses when it comes to legitimacy. After a brief discussion of some existing approaches to institutionalizing deliberative democracy, I put forward my own modest proposal.

Often with good reason, critical theorists distrust institutionalization, especially the 'foisting of institutions and practices on already oppressed groups by outsiders who cannot know the true interests of these groups' (Dryzek 1990: 30). As Dryzek goes on to say, this does not mean that institutions are intrinsically bad things: it could mean that they should be chosen by those subject to them, just as the institutions themselves embody the principles of democratic inclusion and publicity in their internal workings. This puts a question mark over efforts by small groups of state actors— for example in the Department of Health (DoH)'s Strategy Unit—to impose deliberative models without those institutions themselves being the result of more widespread public discussion than was the case with *The NHS Plan* process. Equally, however, it is not always the case that the use of state power is a bad thing, especially at a time when enormous economic, technical, and informational power is concentrated in relatively few hands. Individuals and small collectivities sometimes need large collectivities to take effective action on their behalf to restrain others, whether big businesses or bad neighbours, at least to drag the recalcitrant into discussion and enforce procedural fairness if not to impose particular solutions. Thus, the state can be a force for democratization against expressions of private power. While the state needs restraint so that it does not come to overwhelm private lives, it sometimes needs to be unleashed too. Given that, I shrink less from proposing models and recommending their implementation than many critical theorists once did; it is how those models are justified to whom, and who has the decisive voice, that is more important to me than who actually does the proposing.

7.1   PRINCIPLES OF A LEGITIMATE DELIBERATIVE DEMOCRACY

Throughout this book I have identified important elements of legitimacy in a complex deliberative democracy. In this summary, I connect the legitimacy principles with the institutional design principles that follow from them, drawing particularly on Goodin (1995) for the latter.

7.1.1   The rightful source is those affected

I have taken the legitimate source of political authority to be 'those affected', which may be a relatively small group in a particular locality, or may include people well beyond particular political or cultural boundaries. 'Those affected' can be judged both objectively and subjectively: it is important that the managers of deliberative processes think about who a given proposal might affect and actively seek to involve them (which is one of the benefits of stratified random selection as currently practised), but it is also important that groups of people can nominate themselves, highlighting exclusion, inadvertent or otherwise. We can judge how closely a given practice matches the source ideal by assessing the degree to which it involves more rather than fewer people (Dryzek 1996*a*: 5); plus, as difference democrats might suggest, more *kinds* of people; plus, I would want to insist, the *relevant* kinds: it is no good involving a fixed set of traditionally defined groups on every decision, as some corporatist systems do, if the various proposals impact significantly on groups that are not represented by those traditional categories.

One-off micro-deliberative processes can obviously be criticized on the basis of sheer numbers: the sixteen jurors in Leicester were only 0.003 per cent of the county's population; the deliberative poll's much larger group was an even smaller proportion—five times smaller—of the UK population; while only one in fifty-nine got the opportunity to participate at all in *The NHS Plan* process.[1] This is, of course, inevitable, but it highlights how far particular deliberative experiments are from the ideal expressed by Benhabib (1996), Cohen (1989), and others.

This problem is not so great if micro-deliberative processes are ongoing institutions rather than one-off moments. On this view, micro-deliberative processes would be much more common than they are, and we should simply aim to ensure that every citizen gets the chance to participate directly in deliberative decision-making regularly—even several chances a year as the Swiss get in regular referendums. Legitimacy would be created along more Athenian lines, because it is fair that everyone regularly governs and is governed in turn (Manin 1997). While this solution creates legitimacy for the system as a whole, it nonetheless leaves question marks over particular decisions, and it is in particular decision-making moments that arguments over legitimacy become acute.

A further counter-argument is to highlight one of the benefits of random selection: that it ensures participants of many different kinds, which is just as important as large numbers. This is one of the primary justifications of some deliberative designs, but I have argued that this view is mistaken when it confuses representation with representativeness. For particular decision-making moments, decision-makers need to be authorized by, and accountable to,

---

[1] Based on a Leicestershire population of 610,300 and a UK population of 58,789,194 according to the 2001 national census, available from http://www.statistics.gov.uk.

non-participants, not just descriptively representative of them, topics I take up again shortly.

7.1.2   Decision-making processes should meet the criteria for good deliberation

There are parallels between deliberative requirements and the appropriate procedural standard for legitimate decision-making: inclusiveness to ensure that all relevant interests, values, and information are brought to the table, including differing problem definitions; adequate time to hear all the arguments and debate a range of options without unreasonably tight agenda restrictions; communicative and cognitive competence, such that participants are able to engage with each other and sort through good arguments from bad, based on a range of evidence which may or may not have the status of accepted and final 'truth'; and equality between participants and freedom from rhetorical manipulation (but not rhetoric per se) to ensure that the good argument dominates. All these elements go together to make up communicative rationality. Expert knowledge is an essential ingredient in such reasoning, but it should not trump good democratic procedure; but nor does good procedure trump good substance. In a world where we cannot have perfect procedure, and cannot know all there is to know, procedure and substance should stand in tension with each other, each providing a critical benchmark.

Given that, legitimate processes need to encourage participants to take each other seriously, to recognize a variety of entities as agents with legitimate claims, what Gutmann and Thompson call reciprocity. In practice this means that different communicative styles and different kinds of knowledge and experience are respected, requiring participants to treat someone relating a personal story about their experiences as seriously as another person relating research results. This is not to say that different types of knowledge are treated the same way. 'Tacit knowledge' (Squires 2003) based on long, personal experience is best communicated through direct sharing of the experience or through storytelling, even encouraging people to get angry when necessary; while 'codified knowledge' can and should be tested more rigorously against standards of evidence. Nonetheless, both experience and expertise are valuable.

Clearly there were problems with achieving this ideal in the cases I surveyed. In the deliberative poll, for example, experts and lay people talked past each other for much of the event thanks to incompatible problem definitions, inadequate respect for others' agency, and a process that did not allow enough time and direct contact for those issues to be debated. I have argued that that was because of the way in which the experiments were embedded deep in a technocracy which privileges expertise ahead of communicative norms and lived experience (Fischer 1990). To redress the balance, several changes might be necessary. First, because the skills and orientation of a process's moderator are critical, they should be trained to be aware of the way technocratic power is deployed in such cases and seek to combat it at all the stages of decision-making, from agenda-setting to implementation and everything in between. Second, it would help technocrats take lay deliberation more seriously if micro deliberations were actually making binding decisions, or were significant inputs into higher-level decision-making moments, rather than being purely advisory as in the Belfast case, or just of academic interest alone as in the deliberative poll. Third, and perhaps most importantly, it would help if the decision to deliberate were not taken purely by public managers, as at present, but were somehow triggered either from within the informal public sphere, or from the formal public sphere, or by constitutional rules. All these changes would require some institutional change (described in Section 7.1.3) but all would be helped by the fact that there exist supportive elements within bureaucratic discourse, particularly under the influence of the Third Way and 'the new localism' (Pratchett 2004), which preaches recognition of lay knowledge—indeed, I argued in Chapter 3 that while the history of public and patient involvement initiatives in the NHS since the 1970s is partly one of increasingly sophisticated means of central control, it is also one of increasing acceptance of the idea that 'ordinary people' matter to public policy in ways they once did not. The presence of such discursive resources can make the difference between successful institutional change or failure for change to take root.

7.1.3   If not everyone can be 'in', then we need to know if and how insiders speak for outsiders

The ideal remains the full involvement of every citizen in every collective decision that affects them, including the involvement of those who speak for the natural world. In large-scale, complex societies, however, rarely will all (or even very many) of those affected be (*a*) easily identifiable; (*b*) able or willing to give their attention to every issue that affects them; and (*c*) able to 'fit' into one deliberative moment, actual or virtual. This is the scale problem of deliberative democracy. Therefore, we need some way of deciding who has a good claim to speak for, and decide for, others.

Note the distinction between speaking and deciding in that formulation. In classic deliberative theory, there should be no such distinction: no one can decide without having also been a speaker for or against certain positions and having listened to counterarguments, changing their minds in the face of the better arguments. However, as the case studies and other literature have shown, in real deliberation in the large scale there is frequently a distinction between audience, speakers, and deciders. Even within micro deliberations, once the group size gets over about seven members the better orators start to take more time and those with less confidence are in the spotlight less often. But in the macro version, deliberation in a number of different sites or via numerous discursive threads may not—indeed, I suspect rarely will—result in a clear-cut 'decision', which is simply transmitted to the state for action. Rather, a final decision-making process must take place to sort through competing proposals that have not perfectly engaged with each other, whose partisans have not had their preferences transformed by exposure to each others' arguments, and thus have not been able to reach even working agreements let alone consensus.

The distinction is important because legitimate claims to 'decide for' are distinct from legitimate claims to 'speak for', and individual deliberators may not be able to make both types of claim at once. Drawing on Mansbridge (1999), I have argued that it is at the decision-making end of a deliberative system that the problem of legitimacy is most acute: it is there that binding collective decisions are made, and so at that point we want to be clear that there are strong bonds between the actual deciders and those on whose behalf they have decided, taking into account the wishes of those others. This requires formal bonds of accountability and authorization, but only some kinds of insiders can demonstrate such bonds to outsiders. At the same time, such bonds should *not* be tight at the informal end of the deliberative system, because those bonds would interrupt the free exchange of experience and the free participation in discourse, illegitimately clamping down on the creative aspects of the public sphere. This means that different kinds of 'speakers' will be more important at the informal end. Sections 7.1.4, 7.1.5, and 7.1.6 summarize those distinct roles and claims.

7.1.4   For binding collective decisions, the strongest way of ensuring insider–outsider bonds is through elected, principal–agent representation

The most obvious solution to the scale problem is representation, and the strongest form of that is when representatives are electorally bound to their principals. This is because of the effective power this gives the principals—it gives them the power to remove agents who do not perform, assuming that they have sufficient autonomy in terms of adequate information about past and likely performance, a reasonable range of choices and freedom from manipulation.[2] The strength of this norm was seen in effect in the two citizens' jury cases and in *The NHS Plan* where decision-making power was restricted to those representatives who were accountable to the electorate, not given to unaccountable jurors or even bureaucrats working in the modernization teams.

Principal–agent relationships need not be established by election: they can also be established by appointment. This is what I have called the 'champion' role, someone who possesses enough power to challenge powerful others by virtue of their specialist position in, and knowledge of, a field. Interest groups in particular have a role in monitoring the public sphere, highlighting both successes and failures, and using their power to open up deliberative space where debate has been foreclosed, although champions can and do come from all walks of life, from the formal public sphere, from the economic sphere, from the bureaucracy, as well as from grass-roots organizations. Being a self-appointed champion is not enough, however: that status must be confirmed through a public act of consent by the people on whose behalf the champion acts, perhaps by asking them to sign a petition. Even with that confirmation, they should have advisory power only, not decision-making power.

The ideal of tight bonds between principals and agents meets practical difficulties when applied to deliberative democracy. This is because representatives in deliberative democracy are expected to argue with each other to develop a common position (the trustee role); but if representatives have been instructed to take particular positions on issues (the delegate role), as opposed to simply re-presenting their principals' experience, they face difficulties explaining to people why it was that they changed their minds. To manage these inherent tensions, representatives at the formal end of the deliberative system should perform what Young (2000: 125) calls 'representation as relationship'. They should bring non-participants' values, wishes, and experiences to the forum and transmit back to their principals the reasons for and against those points of view, in an ongoing process of two-way communication. Performance, ideally, should be judged in terms of how well that relationship is functioning—is there goodwill between the parties, do they

---

[2] Plus an electoral system which adequately translates voter wishes into action. This, of course, is a vexed issue. The public choice orthodoxy holds that there is no electoral system that delivers results which are not simply artefacts of the process (Riker 1982), although Mackie (2003) provides a detailed refutation of Riker and the Rochester school, arguing that arbitrariness results only when certain simplifying assumptions are made which do not track real-world conditions. For discussion of the strengths and weaknesses of different models, see Lijphart and Grofman (1984).

feel that they have clear, adequate, and undistorted information (Mansbridge 1998), and that problems can be resolved—rather than just in terms of whether substantive goals were realized or not. The better these relationship aspects function, the less acute Dryzek's (2001) objection to this solution becomes—while there is nothing terribly deliberative about mass elections right now, there may well be practical things that can be done to improve their deliberative qualities, and I will make some suggestions along those lines shortly.

The problem is different at the informal end of the deliberative system. To impose strict rules of principal–agent accountability on the informal public sphere would be to impose crippling costs on anyone, or any small group, trying to have their voice heard, no matter how just their claims, while at the same time undermining the 'playful', intuitive spirit of more informal communication which generates both creative solutions to political problems and helps challenge and reshape problem definitions in the first place. Middle democracy presents a halfway case: it might be possible to insist, for example, that interest groups demonstrate accountability linkages back to those they claim to represent if they want their proposals and arguments to have weight in a given forum, but accountability between specific forums and the wider public might better be promoted through publicity mechanisms than by formal elections. If micro-deliberative processes became common, it would be hard to imagine 'those affected' electing representatives to sit on citizens' juries, for example, not least because of the time and expense involved in setting up the different electorates relevant to every different topic.

For those reasons I would recommend that strict principal–agent bonds only apply at the formal end of the deliberative system; and that communication between elected representatives and other citizens is of high enough quality to ensure that citizens can send clear instructions and make informed judgements about performance. The latter requirement, however, faces difficulties of its own, which I will come to in Section 7.1.6.

7.1.5   Legitimacy is boosted when insiders share descriptive features with outsiders

While descriptive representation cannot create accountability between deliberators and non-deliberators, and so cannot on its own solve the legitimacy problem, it is nonetheless better if agents have both direct principal–agent bonds and are descriptively representative of outsiders. This is not for essentialist reasons; rather, it is because those who share experiences with certain groups of outsiders are more likely to represent those outsiders' experience more accurately and, it is hoped although by no means certain, take their interests more into account in decision-making; and for the practical reason that deliberating groups should be *seen* to be inclusive of a range of viewpoints.

At the formal end of the deliberative system, if representatives are attending to their relationships, faithfully reporting the wishes of their principals as well as communicating the ongoing debates back to them, then the quality of the relationship is more important than descriptive characteristics. However, it is because such representative relationships cannot be performed perfectly that description is desirable: it adds another level of assurance that different voices get to make binding collective decisions. Where descriptive representation takes on more importance is in middle democracy, where principal–agent bonds cannot be so tight. The descriptive breadth of the deliberating body is one way of showing that the first 'source' criterion is being met, that a variety of perspectives have been heard, and that the body is as neutral as can be, independent of any one group, or narrow coalition, in society—as was remarked on in the Leicester citizens' jury case.

Descriptive ideals face significant practical challenges too. There is disagreement about which cleavages matter on any given topic, and so which differences need to be represented in any given forum, although most difference democrats might agree that differences of gender, ethnicity, and socioeconomic status matter, no matter what the issue (Phillips 1995: 46–7). Also, the mathematics involved in creating a descriptively representative body on just a few dimensions means that size quickly gets out of hand, even if we make some fairly modest assumptions about the extent of diversity and speaking time (Goodin 2003). These facts speak in favour of some ad hoc political institutions, with smaller-scale deliberative systems forming around a particular issue and then dissolving once the decision is made and implemented. This could clash with the stability requirement (Section 7.1.8), however, and I will make some suggestions for managing that conflict shortly.

7.1.6   Insider–outsiders links can also be established by means of publicity

The other way of establishing links with non-participants is through publicity. It has both prospective and retrospective features: the prospective is the idea that one must give an account of one's reasons before a proposal can be put into action; the retrospective is the idea that one's actions are publicized so they can be scrutinized to ensure they match previous undertakings, and that they meet both procedural and substantive standards. Publicity helps establish 'relationship' representation by sharing information, proposals, and reasons throughout the deliberative system, not just within a given forum. In this study I have concentrated on the way that is done through the news media, rather than other things like networks in the informal public sphere, because of the media's reach and central role in monitoring the public sphere and triggering debate, much like other 'champions'.

The big advantage of thinking of accountability as publicity is that we do not have to worry quite so much that few of those affected are in the room when a given issue is discussed, so long as people have taken part in the discursive threads which are brought to the table by the participants, to the extent that they are all 'inside' the wider, macro deliberation. Some, of course, can afford to be more attentive than others, and this is where champions can play a part, monitoring the discussion and alerting others if something is amiss.

Just like the other solutions to the scale problem, the publicity solution is not perfect either. First, like the descriptive solution, publicity lacks an effective, final sanction without some principal–agent bonds. Second, salience matters for generating public and media attention and motivating participation, yet, in my cases, salience depended on whether or not the topic could be communicated using a few simple messages (even better, one simple message); whether it could be polarized, dramatized, and individualized; whether it connected with the identity, symbolism, and concerns of the dominant consensus rather than minority interests (see Hall et al. 1978); and whether or not it was connected with major decision-making moments, and thus the concerns of powerful decision-makers. This leaves out some of the most important features of many political issues. Third, media coverage of a given deliberative moment is usually one-way: the arguments made in a micro-deliberative forum can reach outsiders but they have no means of arguing back within the confines of that micro-deliberative event. In such cases, it may be valuable if those affected have the opportunity to grant or withhold consent once a decision has been reached, and I will suggest some mechanisms by which that can happen later on. Fourth, moving beyond the ideal of a self-contained forum in which all those affected are present introduces an important role distinction between orators and audiences, between those who are speaking and those the speakers are trying to persuade. When that happens, speech tends to become oriented not to mutual understanding between orators, but to swaying an audience at the expense of one's interlocutors (Bessette 1994: 221), using as many of the tools of rhetoric as one has mastered. Indeed, as I suggested in Chapter 5, it may well be good strategy to sling some mud first, splattering one's political opponents so that they have to spend more energy fending off character attacks, trying to rebuild their *ethos*, before they can begin to be taken seriously in the public forum. Relying on public rhetoric to carry one's cause is a very dangerous strategy unless one is well resourced, and prepared to launch a few pre-emptive attacks.

7.1.7   Decision-making and implementation power have positive and negative impacts

I have argued that one aspect of the motivations problem is solved when more people have substantive control rather than merely symbolic involvement, and exercise that control over broad rather than narrow domains; this helps improve the quality of the recommendations as well. Participants in both citizens' juries started demanding binding decision-making power because the limited agendas caused frustration; the lack of connection to a real decision-making moment meant the recommendations of the Belfast jury and the deliberative poll were less detailed and less useful than those which emerged from the Leicester jury and *The NHS Plan* process.

However, the more an issue matters in these ways, the more severe another aspect of the motivations problems becomes. In deliberation where there is a speaker–audience distinction, the pre-deliberative commitments problem becomes more acute because the pay-off is greater for successfully persuading one's audience rather than engaging constructively with one's fellow delib- erators. Worse, there is evidence from other deliberative experiments that in present institutional arrangements where power is unevenly distributed, power will simply speak to power: that is, powerful interests may well choose not to play the deliberative game at all, but apply pressure to decision-makers using other channels (Hendriks 2002*a*). This depends, however, on the audience not having the critical capacity to spot such things as attempted manipulation, or not having effective means of intervening, and from my cases there is some cause for optimism on both points. On the issue of lay participants' critical capacities, recall, for example, the deliberative poll par- ticipants who liked what the Liberal Democrats' Simon Hughes had to say but dismissed it because he was not in any danger of having to put his money where his mouth was; or the fact that the Leicester jurors did not allow the 'sexy' nature of heart and breast services to overwhelm the less salient needs of kidney patients. However, deliberators' feelings *against* other individuals did lead them to discount those people's substantive contributions. On the second issue of having effective power to do something about attempted manipulation, this would depend on ultimate decision-makers closing off other channels of influence, making the deliberative process the only game in town, as central and local government officers effectively did in the Leicester case, or by regulations restricting certain kinds of lobbying, or including deliberative specifications in 'duty to consult' legislation, or through the use of insurgent action to challenge such illegitimate outcomes.

I have noted how it may be easier both to motivate participation and to raise deliberative quality by holding the deliberations in camera—this reduces the pressures created by previous commitments to peers and principals, lessening the likelihood that participants will play to the gallery instead of engaging honestly with each other. Such a move results in more substantive quality and more legitimacy between participants; but it lowers legitimacy for outsiders who have no access to the reasons for and against proposals. This weakness could be counteracted if deliberation is held in private but the reasons for and against proposals are publicized afterwards, but this does not solve the problem of pre-deliberative commitments completely: deliberators in camera need to come out again and face their peers who may not understand if their agents have given way on what they consider to be key grounds. I think that publicity is essential, most obviously because of the practical difficulties inherent in the principal–agent ideal. It therefore must be used, but with awareness of its limitations.

7.1.8   Deliberative institutions need some stability if they are to empower those who do not already hold powerful positions

Democratic citizens need institutions and procedures to have a certain amount of stability: if the rules change all the time, only those who can bear the cost of relearning the rules will be enfranchised (Flathman 1972). There are two caveats to this principle. First, institutions themselves should result from the deliberation of those subject to them; and second, because the first kind of decision must itself be taken by fallible people using imperfect institutions, and because institutions can tend to lose touch with shifting social realities and power relations, all such institutional design decisions should be subject to periodic review (Goodin 1996*b*: 40–1).

The concern with knowing how to access political institutions implies not just some amount of stability, but also requires that citizens be well informed and educated about the institutions that are available to them so that they can, if they choose, take up an issue or engage in a discussion without facing too many barriers to participation. That is not to say that participation should be costless—in particular, the deliberative ideal implies that people do have to face some costs in terms of learning about issues and the effects on others before coming to a decision.

7.2   PROCESSES COMPARED

In Table 7.1, I compare the strengths and weaknesses of the different processes covered in the thesis, both in their case-specific and more general forms, against the legitimacy criteria set out in Section 7.1 (the numbers in brackets refer to the subsections above).

The micro-deliberative processes share some advantages and disadvantages. On the plus side, they help address the motivations problem in various ways. The first is by shoulder-tapping citizens who might otherwise not have the efficacy needed to get involved in collective decision-making; indeed, because participants are often actively recruited by market research firms to fit a given stratification profile, they work hard to persuade the reluctant to come on the grounds that 'the whole thing would fail without them' (Deliberative poll manager, London). By confining those who have pre-deliberative commitments to a subservient role, such processes lower the chances that the deliberation will be manipulated for strategic ends, although that is by no means assured. By giving various stakeholders a role in agenda-setting on the steering group, the citizens' jury process handles this better by binding them more closely into the whole decision-making process; a deliberative poll wheels experts in and out, giving them little stake and even less incentive to take the process seriously. So long as they are seen to be an important preliminary to some other major decision-making event—as was the case in Leicester—such events provide a focal point in which the major arguments for and against a proposal can not only be tested against each other but also transmitted more comprehensively and accurately through the media; without such a focal point, mediated public discourse is the stuff of symbol over substance, which I think is something we should regret for the most part.

However, micro processes share significant downsides. The first of these concerns the restrictions on the agenda imposed by micro-deliberative techniques. Now, there certainly is evidence that the citizens' jury model is suitable for grappling with highly complex and ill-defined problems (Niemeyer 2004), but even then organizers and facilitators need to be selective about what issues and perspectives are presented to the jurors. Four days is not long enough to engage with every problem definition, every viewpoint, and every level of analysis, and while in some cases that might not matter all that much, in other cases it certainly *does* matter, as the Leicester jurors found out when they discovered that what they really wanted to be addressing was issues of staff recruitment and retention. As for deliberative polls, the time available for intense deliberation in that format is clearly much more

Table 7.1. Legitimacy pros and cons of deliberative processes and models

	Pro	Con
Citizens' juries	• Shoulder-tapping citizens who would otherwise not get involved (7.1.1) • Rationalizes micro-level debate through interest group 'quarantine', tight agenda, information, and deliberation (7.1.2) • Deliberators descriptively representative in a limited way, with some openness of stratification process (7.1.5) • Gives focal point for all sides of an argument, leading to better quality media coverage of issue (7.1.2, 7.1.6) • Can be applied on an ad hoc basis, which increases flexibility in descriptive and agenda terms (7.1.8)	• Very small numbers with no external accountability, so advisory only—not much democracy (7.1.4, 7.1.7) • Only major cleavages represented (7.1.5) • Grandview problem: deliberative transformation of representative sample into an unrepresentative one (7.1.5) • Tight agenda requirement means it is too 'local' to have an impact on broad issues—tool by which centre controls local agencies, not for citizens to control the centre (7.1.8) • Does not necessarily rationalize macro-level debate if interest group preferences left untransformed (7.1.2) • Because completely ad hoc, impossible for citizens to access unless called upon by commissioners (7.1.8)
Belfast citizens' jury	*as for juries generally, plus:* • Lack of external accountability did not cause a problem in practice—deliberative norms meant participants acted *as if* they were held to account (7.1.4) • Made institutional recommendations (7.1.8)	*as for juries generally, plus:* • Salience undermined thanks to research orientation and lack of clear connection to a decision-making moment, which led to media coverage for the process only, not for its substantive recommendations (7.1.6) • Question too broad, therefore answers too broad to be useful (7.1.2)

| Leicester debate | *as for Belfast jury, plus:*
• Issues already salient—end point of a longer, public process driven by interest groups and government allies, not by Health Authority—leading to improved publicity, accountability, and pressure on HA to follow through (7.1.4, 7.1.6, 7.1.8)
• Consent given to activists' champion role via petition (7.1.1)
• Media presence on steering committee and during deliberation improves links with outsiders (7.1.6) | *as for juries generally, plus:*
• Tiny number of jurors may have been overwhelmed by large number of petitioners and/or power of interest groups if decision had gone another way, regardless of substantive considerations (7.1.1, 7.1.2, 7.1.7) |
| Deliberative polls | • Shoulder-tapping citizens (7.1.1)
• Rationalizes same as citizens' juries, but to lesser degree (7.1.2)
• Deliberators descriptively representative, much more than citizens' jury (7.1.5)
• Media publicity an integral part of the process, which guarantees some wider attention (7.1.6)
• Can be applied on an ad hoc basis which increases flexibility (7.1.8) | • Small groups unlikely to include all but major cleavages thanks to proportionality requirement (7.1.1, 7.1.5)
• TV creates grand-standing, a focus on celebrity, personalization, and polarization (7.1.2, 7.1.6)
• Social scientific experiment drivers restrict agenda too much (7.1.2)
• Results no more nuanced than an ordinary opinion poll (7.1.2)
• Does not necesssarily rationalize macro-level debate if interest group preferences left untransformed (7.1.2)
• No external accountability, so advisory only (7.1.4, 7.1.7) |

(Continued)

Table 7.1. (*Continued*)

	Pro	Con
		• Grandview problem: deliberative transformation of representative sample into an unrepresentative one (7.1.5) • Unsuitable for television in the long term—not easily transformed into narrative terms (7.1.6, 7.1.8) • Because completely ad hoc, impossible for citizens to access unless called upon by commissioners (7.1.8)
NHS poll	• as for deliberative polls generally	*as for deliberative polls generally, plus:* • No agenda control beyond a very small group (7.1.2) • Salience minimal thanks to lack of connection to a decision-making moment, which leads to lack of publicity through other media (7.1.6) • Deliberatively poor—little bridging of problem definition and values gap between experts and lay participants (7.1.2)
NHS Plan process	• Broad involvement thanks to a range of techniques, with some limited shoulder-tapping in the focus groups (7.1.1) • Popular input into agenda through the postcards, public meetings, and focus groups (7.1.2) • Allowed range of interests to come to working agreements (7.1.2)	• Public involvement may have been a legitimating mask for changes that would have happened anyway (7.1.2, 7.1.7) • Agenda too dominated by DoH (7.1.2) • Forgot to include all stakeholders, especially the CHCs and the Commons Health Committee (7.1.1) • Realities of electoral politics mean that representatives unlikely to be called to account specifically for the successes and failures of *The NHS Plan*, although the NHS might well be a salient issue (7.1.4)

	• Final decisions made by representatives with clear principal–agent bonds (7.1.4) • Enormous government resources put into publicizing the decisions and new institutions, with the reasoning defended in parliament and in open committee, proceedings of which available online (7.1.6)	• Because completely ad hoc, impossible for citizens to access unless called upon by commissioners (7.1.8)
Disability activism	• Participatory norms help create broader base of involvement (7.1.1) • Non-state actors set the agenda and define problems themselves, challenging attempts to limit them (7.1.2) • Descriptively representative, in some respects, of all those who suffer disability (7.1.5) • Generate salience for issues that might otherwise pass unnoticed (7.1.6) • Alter decisions by changing problem definitions on which decisions depend (7.1.7) • Stability of groups helps citizens to find out how to join and how to have an impact on policy—provides a relatively stable, non-state channel for action (7.1.8)	• Usually no representative link between activists and others so should not be decisive (7.1.3) • Not descriptively representative of non-members on features correlated with the active/inactive variable (7.1.5) • Too dependent on rhetoric and dramaturgy to convey messages, at the cost of complexities—may narrow agenda in unintended ways, and opens the door to strategic manipulation (7.1.2, 7.1.7)

restricted, while the quantitative research imperatives mean that the topics under discussion cannot be renegotiated by participants. These issues are made worse by the way in which the techniques have typically been used by the bureaucracy in Britain—by local agencies rather than central ones. This is a concern for the legitimacy of deliberative democracy if citizens only get to deliberate on the small stuff, never on the big issues that frame the local ones—why put yourself out or go through such an intense process if it is not going to change things?

The second major disadvantage is that the scale problem is most acute at this level: in practical politics there are few reasons why the deliberation of a dozen, or even a few hundred, people without representative bonds would weigh more heavily than the express preferences of hundreds of thousands, even millions. Where this may not be the case, I have argued, is where the micro-deliberative event is held to break a deadlock which has arisen in mass politics; it should not be used to foreclose mass debate.

The macro processes solve these problems in various ways, but introduce others. Among the positives, they bring many more people into any given deliberation, which greatly reduces the scale problem, and they allow for a greater range of views and experience to shape the deliberative agenda, particularly if no one commissioning body can control that agenda. They create salience for an issue simply by choosing to focus on it and spreading communication about it throughout the deliberative system: government-led processes can wield significant resources to publicize events, while the mechanisms of parliament ensure that eventual decisions must be defended in public; activists in civil society can use dramaturgical means to create salience, attracting attention to exclusion and manipulation. Government-led processes have enhanced legitimacy if those making the decisions are subject to electoral sanction, although voting decisions are a great deal more complex than a simple indication of policy preferences (Catt 1996). Perhaps a more certain way would be to subject particular decisions to a referendum once a macro-deliberative process has run its course. Activist-led deliberation has the great advantage of challenging the agendas of the powerful.

Among the negatives, not everyone is equally powerful in macro deliberation: some speak more than others, some can only be listeners and are not able to challenge the arguments of those privileged enough to get time on the podium or space in the media, which means that the uses and abuses of rhetoric become much more important in macro than in micro deliberation. Furthermore, the reliance on the news media to transmit arguments around the deliberative system means that only certain arguments get through: what gets lost is the complexity, and the impersonal features of social and political issues. Finally, all the various inputs from the public sphere still have to be gathered and decisions made. This is the role of an elected assembly and its committees, perhaps a parliament reformed along deliberative lines (Uhr 1998), but still a body of decision-makers effectively accountable to the people they represent.

Thus, if there is one key lesson to be drawn from this study, it is that no one institution can be perfectly legitimate because not all the principles can be instantiated at once: we cannot have both ideal deliberative quality and full publicity as the conditions of the latter undermine the former; we cannot have tight principal–agent bonds and ideal deliberation because participants need to be free to change their minds; we cannot endow any one micro-deliberative process with much power on its own without undermining the rights of outsiders to have a say on a particular political question.

However, different types of institution can make different legitimate contributions to a wider deliberative system. We can think about this in two ways. The first is to adapt the social research idea of triangulation, using multiple methods to look at the same data. It is done because particular research tools are only good at answering particular kinds of questions and deliver particular kinds of results (Berg 2001); in the same way, democratic deliberation should be the result of several different processes, because different processes motivate different kinds of representative to take part, sharing different kinds of knowledge, creating inclusiveness and legitimacy for the deliberative system despite the individual peculiarities of its parts (Goodin 1996*b*: 41–2). The second approach is to use timing and sequencing, and the Leicester example helps us think about this. It seems clear that the citizens' jury 'worked' in part because of when it was held, not just because of internal qualities of the process itself. Recall how important it was for local people to wrest control of the decision-making process back from the health authority. One can plausibly imagine that had the authority tried to run a jury right at the start of its decision-making process in 1996, it might still have faced a revolt further down the track, for several reasons. At best it would only have generated publicity for the process (as in Belfast) and not the issue; therefore, there would still have been a lack of public visibility about the issue, the arguments, and the recommendation, which means that non-participants would still not have possessed grounds for agreeing with the decision when it came to be announced, regardless of how well designed the micro process was. The corollary of those observations is that perhaps any reasonably deliberative process would have created a legitimate decision at the right point in time, that is, after a broad public debate outside the health authority's control.

If we are going to think in sequence terms, it is useful to think about the steps in a decision-making process, and how different institutions might make useful contributions to each of them. I use Catt's four stages

(1999)—define, discuss, decide, implement. Of course, no stages model is perfect: the stages lend an unearthly, rational glow to policy processes in which problems are constantly redefined and decisions taken at various steps (Sabatier 1999). Despite those imperfections, they nonetheless have analytic usefulness when it comes to thinking about linkages between particular devices and the roles they are expected to play (see also John 1998). This is very similar to the 'reflexive proceduralist' approach recommended by Saward (2003a), although he contrasts his approach with deliberative democracy, while I have come to similar conclusions by working through the tensions and implications within deliberative democracy itself. So, what I do in Section 7.3 is to take those four decision-making stages and see what kind of process is more likely to make a positive contribution at each stage, and where its negatives will be minimized.

7.3   MODELLING A LEGITIMATE DELIBERATIVE DEMOCRACY

To step from these principles to recommending specific practices within the boundaries of a book would strike some deliberative democrats as odd, to say the least. Gutmann and Thompson (1996: 358) argue that '[t]he best forum for considering the design of deliberative institutions is likely to be one in which deliberation, however nascent, has a prominent place', not inside an academic's head, democratic deliberation within notwithstanding (Goodin 2000). I agree, but only in part. When it comes to deliberating about deliberative institutions, it would help greatly if the people had some ideas to work with, and if academic books have any impact at all on wider public conversations, this is one way that I, as a citizen who has thought about these things, can contribute.

Among those deliberative democrats who have taken that next step, there are those who concentrate on the formal public sphere, those who stress the informal public sphere, those who recommend institutions of middle democracy, and a very small number who try to address the whole in some way. The first of these have focused on protecting the quality of deliberation within the formal public sphere, but they have tended to do so at the expense of the democratic character of that deliberation, ascribing either no role, or a very limited one, to other citizens (Bessette 1994; Rawls 1997). As Gutmann and Thompson (1996: 358–9) remark, 'deliberative labor should not be divided so that representatives give reasons while citizens merely receive them'. We can and should go further if we are to meet the legitimacy requirements, and we can do so, I think, without seriously undermining the deliberative benefits focused on by Bessette and Rawls.

Concentrating on the informal end of the public sphere can lead to the opposite mistake, focusing too heavily on the democratic value of popular control as expressed by such things as grass-roots networks, without taking seriously enough either the fragmented, multiple nature of the informal public sphere which results in disjuncture rather than communication across different experiences on the one hand (Fraser 1992); or the distortions, manipulations, and sometimes sheer irrationality of mass communication and mass action on the other. While some proponents of this kind of approach do use principles of communicative rationality to distinguish between what might be crudely called 'good' networks and 'bad' networks, I do not think they pay enough attention to the complexities of public communication processes which oversimplify, personalize, and polarize debates; that is, to the fact that while a network may be communicatively rational internally, it cannot be as communicatively rational as it would like externally if it is to have an effect on public action—although Dryzek (2000: 167–8) and Young (2001: 676) are at least sensitive to this point. This is where the distinction between debate and decision may be useful. It may be essential that an active informal public sphere exists to challenge the status quo and bring new claims and new experiences to public attention, but decision-making mechanisms should not be beholden to such processes without some kind of intervening institutions which bring all the various threads together. Otherwise we run the risk of what we might call thorubocracy,[3] rule by those who can command public attention purely by shouting loudly enough.

It is to intervening institutions in middle democracy that by far the most attention has been paid. For some this is because it is relatively easy to apply deliberative principles to a small, self-contained practice; for others it is because that is where attention should be focused. Among the latter, Fung (2003: 339) argues that, 'given the fragmentation of cultural and political life, effective large-scale public sphere reforms may consist largely in the proliferation of better minipublics rather than improving the one big public'. However, I, along with Gutmann and Thompson (2004), think this view is mistaken because, as we have seen with the experience of micro deliberation in the NHS, it gives away too much control of problem and scope definition to large governmental and non-governmental organizations, especially big businesses and central 'coordination' agencies who define the terms on which

---

[3] A term coined for me by Elizabeth Minchin of the Classics Program, Australian National University. It is based on *thorubos*, used by Plato (1997) to mean the din and racket made in the assembly in response to a speaker.

such deliberative events are held, if not directly commissioning them themselves.

Instead, we need to take all three realms seriously: the informal for its creativity, proximity to the people, and (sometimes latent) power to challenge the status quo; the formal for its ability to collect together the results of various kinds of democratic deliberation, make legitimately binding collective decisions, and resist other sources of power; and the intermediate for its ability to connect the other two in rationalized ways. My suggestions encompass all three, making sure they are intricately connected with each other. However, I emphasize again that my proposals are about next steps on from current institutions, not ideal end points.

First of all, it is important to recognize that the four decision-making stages are only conceptually distinct; real political processes are much messier with some stages happening simultaneously or being widely separated in time; with some actors concentrating on an activity belonging to one stage while others concentrate on something quite different. Furthermore, discussion and decision define problems as much as they define implementation, while implementation itself creates new problems (Pressman and Wildavsky 1979). Nonetheless, I have argued that legitimacy problems arise in large measure because of the wrong techniques, even the wrong kinds of representatives, being activated at the wrong times in a decision-making process and so such a scheme—highly stylized, I readily admit—helps us think about what the right process at the right moment might be.

The scheme, in Table 7.2, starts with the source norm: many different kinds of people can raise issues and put them up for public discussion through the media, through dramaturgical action, and through activist networks. I do not want to be too prescriptive at this point, because part of the value of such activity is that it is created by its members rather than parachuted in from above. However, grass-roots democracy can be hard work. Given that, it helps if people can learn from the successes and failures of their peers, and in this regard Schlosberg (1999) commends the work of central information clearing houses who distribute ideas and issues to their members, as well as the 'monitorial' role of mass media (Zaller 2003). Central and local government agencies can also help by sharing information and resources to help such networks set up—some government websites are making initial efforts to act as community information clearing houses in just this way,[4] while the simple provision of server space and information technology expertise would be a significant boost to local networks' capacity to organize and communicate.

---

[4] Albeit in nascent form only: for example, see Wellington City Council in New Zealand, http://www.wellington.govt.nz/services/commdirectory/index.html.

Table 7.2. A deliberative system: roles at different decision stages

	Decision stages			
	Define	Discuss	Decide	Implement
Activist networks	• Raise issues and work to make them salient	• Research impacts and offer solutions • Voice perspectives	• Monitor process	• Monitor results and challenge if necessary
Experts	• Research and raise issues	• Conduct research on impacts • Offer solutions		• Monitor results and challenge if necessary
Bureaucracy	• Research and raise issues	• Manage macro-deliberative processes • Gather the arguments and supply to decision-makers		• Implement decisions
Micro techniques		• Provide deliberative focal point for arguments made by others	• Recommend course of action, including dissenting opinions	• Evaluate implementation
Media	• Research and raise issues, make them salient	• Present the arguments for and against different solutions from various sources	• Report the decision and the reasons for and against	• Monitor results and challenge if necessary
Elected assembly	• Instigate macro-deliberative processes	• Debate the arguments from the broader public sphere	• Make binding collective decisions • Communicate reasons for and against the decision	• Monitor implementation
Direct techniques	• Instigate macro-deliberative processes (petitions)		• Make binding collective decisions (referendums)	

This should be in addition to providing access to research resources, either through public libraries with improved access to research databases, or perhaps through allowing networks access to university library databases at substantially discounted rates, perhaps even subsidized salaries for research officers.

However, only some of the things that need discussion can be handled at once, so there needs to be some way in which the 'official' public agenda—that around which macro-deliberative processes will be deliberately set up—can be established which is not simply the result of a small group's more or less arbitrary exercise of power. This could be done by allowing citizen-initiated referendums, but because it requires significant resources to qualify a proposition for the ballot they tend to be the tools of the already powerful and well organized, regardless of how low the qualifying signature threshold is set (Parkinson 2001*a*). It could be done by opening up the agenda-setting processes of elected assemblies, putting a parliamentary committee in charge that gathers submissions from activists and experts and schedules issues for deliberation according to some publicly debated criteria—the expert advisory element of this would help act as a balance to concerns that public agendas are themselves socially, even rhetorically, constructed, while the agenda would have to be flexible enough to cope with new issues that arise between elections. This could also be a useful function for something like the 'deliberation day' proposed by Ackerman and Fishkin (2002), in which citizens get together before elections not so much to decide on who should lead them, but what the government should focus on for the coming term. However, rather than following Ackerman and Fishkin's recommendation of using the deliberative poll process, a process I think is too contaminated by survey research imperatives to be of much practical use, I would recommend that deliberation day use a larger scale and more deliberative process like the Electronic Town Hall pioneered by the AmericaSpeaks organization (www.americaspeaks.org, reviewed in Fung 2003), in which thousands of people are split into groups of ten, each with a moderator and a minute taker, and each linked electronically to all the others in order to share issues, take quick polls and reactions, and vote on proposals once they had been discussed. While the Electronic Town Hall has only been tried in single locations, there is no reason why such networks could not span multiple locations, involving hundreds of thousands of participants. Nor is there any reason why it would have to take place at one time: topics could be taken one at a time over a series of events with a final meeting to decide priorities. However, the specific process used is less important than the general requirement that many different kinds of people have an opportunity to contribute to the agenda-setting: it should not be elite-dominated, as issues that affected non-elite groups may not get taken seriously enough; it should not be 'consumer'-dominated either, as this would run the risk of focusing only on individual or local goods and services rather than collective issues—in health, focusing on getting more pills for more problems rather than strategies to change behaviour and counteract pill demand, for example (Davis 1992).

Once the agenda was set, something like parliamentary committees could be responsible for overseeing the next phase of the process: seeking and debating solutions. Here we can draw on *The NHS Plan* process for inspiration. Experts and interest groups could be asked to participate in a series of workshops to go through the issues and thrash out possible solutions, based on consultative events as well as research, but not come to final decisions. Their ideas could then be presented to citizens, in micro-deliberative events who would argue through the various options and make recommendations on the way forward, perhaps using the three-step process of Renn et al. (1993) which uses the citizens' jury as its core. This would be essential for managing the concerns about rhetorical manipulation of macro deliberation which came out in Chapter 6. Both the consultative and deliberative processes would be monitored and reported on by the media to ensure that the various arguments made it out into the public sphere. The key issues here are that micro deliberation occurs only after a broad and relatively unprescriptive process of issue generation and debate, and that it is plugged into a real decision-making moment—both of which generate the salience required to meet the publicity criteria and to motivate participation from a variety of actors.

With all this debate and discussion, decisions still need to be made. In cases where consensus emerged, it would simply be a matter of elected representatives passing any necessary enabling legislation and monitoring performance. In the more likely event that a number of competing options found significant favour for one reason or another, it would either be up to elected representatives to make that decision or, if they found it impossible to come to some working agreement, to refer it to the public in a referendum.

The referendum process as it exists in various countries is far from perfect, and it is something I have been highly critical of in the past (Parkinson 2001*a*, 2001*b*). The key flaws are that complex issues tend to be broken down into 'this option or nothing', yes/no questions, and that public debate through the media without any micro-deliberative focal point fails to meet any of the criteria of communicative rationalization. To counter these failings, there is no reason why a referendum has to be a yes/no question. It might well be a choice between three or more options, perhaps with a run-off in cases where two options receive similar levels of support—New Zealand's 1993 decision to change electoral system is an example of another type where four electoral options were presented, followed by a run-off vote between the existing system and the top-polling alternative in the previous round. Of course, any voting procedure is theoretically open to strategic manipulation, with binary option and multi-stage processes dependent on how the options are carved up in the first place (McLean 1987); to deal with this, the advice emerging from the micro deliberations could include a recommendation on dividing up any subsequent referendum. So long as the referendum is not a substitute for deliberation, but the final decision-making event at the conclusion of a longer deliberative process which has been engaged in a variety of forums by different kinds of representatives and well-covered by the media, the rationality issues will be less pressing. At the same time, legitimacy would be further enhanced by the opportunity for everyone to grant consent.

The final stage is implementation and evaluation, and this is where the bureaucracy, interest groups, the media, and experts come back into the equation, monitoring results and making challenges if necessary.

While the scheme I have sketched out does not *solve* the scale and motivations problems, it produces positive movement on all my legitimacy criteria, while reducing the impact of the dangers. It addresses the scale problem by taking a macro view of deliberative democracy, giving citizens a prominent, and sometimes decisive, role in the deliberative system, even though they do not all deliberate together at every stage on every issue. Yet it does so at the same time as limiting the risks of rhetorical manipulation by emphasizing rhetoric's positive role in agenda-setting but limiting its reach at the other stages. The limits are reinforced by giving micro processes a pivotal role, providing a focal point for media coverage and so improving the likelihood that the media will transmit the various arguments accurately. At the same time it gives representatives of all kinds a role, thus improving the inclusiveness of the system, but leaves practical decision-making in the hands of those representatives over whom citizens retain electoral power, ensuring effective public accountability. It addresses the motivational problems by featuring a broadly inclusive agenda-setting process and because it is oriented to collective decision-making, which engages the whole public hierarchy, not mere advice at the local level. Decisions reached through such a process therefore matter in ways that local micro deliberations do not, which means that those with specific goals to achieve have an incentive to pursue those goals through this public channel rather than standing aloof or doing end runs around the process. While the incentives for strategic manipulation are consequently greater, they are managed not only by the central role of micro-deliberative processes in making recommendations but also to the degree that interest groups, experts, bureaucrats, and the media monitor the whole process on behalf of other citizens, publicizing underhanded action and publicly shaming transgressors. Finally, while it has many ad hoc features that improve its ability to include relevant voices on different issues, it nonetheless retains some stability so that citizens can learn how to access it.

It might be objected that the system appears quite inefficient: would it not be better simply for leaders and experts to decide things and then work to sell the new concepts to people, bringing them along rather than having a sceptical public hold progress back? It would certainly slow things down at the agenda-setting, deliberation, and decision stages, but that, to my mind, is no bad thing if it creates legitimacy for the resulting agreements and thus minimizes the inefficiencies involved in having perpetually to fight fires after decisions have been announced, slowing down the implementation phase. This is an open empirical question, but the hope of an optimistic answer receives some anecdotal support from one of my Belfast interviewees, who observed that while the highly consultative environment in place in Northern Ireland was resisted strongly by the local bureaucracy, on the grounds that 'both the local civil society and the bureaucracy would grind to a halt under the pressure to participate', and that it would require too many resources, these fears have not been borne out in practice. Decision-making was slower, but had by no means stopped and was, in the interviewee's opinion, of better quality than before.

Finally, as Dryzek (1996*b*) argues, institutional arrangements are just the 'hardware' for collective decision-making—there also needs to be 'software' in the form of supportive discourses, which make the difference between new arrangements taking root or withering. To my knowledge there have been no comprehensive surveys of discourses of democracy in the UK,[5] but the brief survey in Chapter 3 suggests that there may indeed be elements in UK political discourse that would support my scheme. Present discourse recognizes, gives agency to, and ascribes positive motivations to 'ordinary people', which would seem to encourage schemes for closer connection with them, although it would certainly be a challenge to have the championing role of interest groups more widely accepted. As for the role of the mediating and formal institutions, there is already evidence that some key decision-makers would at least consider such a scheme, evidence in the shape of the raft of measures brought in following *The NHS Plan*, including the National Institute for Clinical Excellence (NICE) citizens' council, patients' forums, and so forth. The challenge would be applying the model at the parliamentary level itself, not just imposing it on local government agencies.

---

[5] A model for such a survey exists in the shape of a recent collection by Dryzek and Holmes (2002).

8

Questions and conclusions

I opened this book with a question about why a large number of protestors should grant legitimacy to the decisions reached by a small number of people plucked out of obscurity by a market research firm. The search for an answer to that question has led me to reconsider the nature of deliberative democracy: not only its account of legitimacy, but its institutional forms as well. This final chapter draws out the general conclusions reached on that journey, highlighting some limits and still-unanswered questions, before giving the Leicester protestors some answers to the question I posed on their behalf.

I have shown that the classical deliberative account of legitimacy is incomplete, because it cannot account for why non-participants should grant legitimacy to the outcome of any deliberative moment. I have argued that attending to three critical aspects of legitimacy—representation, publicity, and rationality—leads us to reconsider the very nature of deliberative democracy, moving away from the micro conception towards a more macro or public sphere-oriented account. The rethink allows us to loosen the tight institutional restrictions some early theorists had inadvertently imposed on deliberative designs, allowing us to think about legitimacy as being created across multiple deliberative moments in a wider deliberative system. This rethink helps with the scale problem by involving many more people in deliberative democracy than any one micro-deliberative process could ever manage, even though not all of them can deliberate in the technical sense specified by Cohen, Walzer, and others. Such a move opens the door to the risk of strategic manipulation of the deliberative democratic process, but it is a risk we can manage by thinking in sequential terms, separating out decision-making from agenda-setting, discussion, and implementation, and giving different processes and participants different legitimate roles at different points of the decision-making cycle. By being oriented nonetheless to making decisions, the scheme further addresses the motivational difficulties presented by having citizens participate only in relatively local, unimportant, advisory deliberative events.

Nonetheless, while we can imagine a deliberative system that is more legitimate than current arrangements, no one event can ever be fully legitimate and at the same time strictly deliberative, because not all the elements of legitimacy, democracy, and deliberation can be present in one process. This is imposed on us by the fact of scale and the consequent requirement of salience: that which makes an issue salient and thus transmissible throughout the deliberative system is that which opens it to manipulation, undermining the substantive requirements of legitimacy. I have suggested some ways in which this tendency can be fought, but it will be, of necessity, a constant battle.

There are numerous questions outstanding, and some objections to overcome. First, the whole edifice is built on a narrow empirical foundation. I have examined only four processes in any depth, with the occasional contribution from a fifth, and done so in only one country on one kind of issue. There were good reasons for that, and the cases were reasonably well representative of several variables on Mansbridge's deliberative continuum. Still, in other countries, on other issues, or using different techniques, the outcomes may well have been different. The narrow empirical basis would be more of a problem if my aim had been to do a comprehensive evaluation of the processes I looked at, but it was not: the aim was to mine others' experience with implementing deliberative principles to see what legitimacy issues actually arose and what their solutions might be. Nonetheless, it would be interesting to use these results to form the basis of research to assess how widespread the issues and attitudes uncovered here are, in the UK and elsewhere. Such a study could confirm the validity of my intuitions, or undermine them, and force a rethink.

Moreover, because the cases were embedded in a liberal, technocratic system, not a fully deliberative one, it is impossible to say how similar processes would have functioned under quite different institutional pressures, and so the cases may not have tested those processes under terribly fair circumstances. Still, even given those limitations, it was remarkable that the Leicester debate and *the NHS Plan* did produce something close to fully legitimate outcomes. I can only speculate on what might have happened had those circumstances been closer to the ideal.

There are three main gaps in the research that I would like to see filled. First of all, I have limited my consideration of representation to principal–agent and descriptive ideas, without taking the symbolic aspects more seriously, asking whether they can play a role in building links between insiders and outsiders (Edelman 1976). When it comes to decision-making I can think of obvious problems with that, similar to those faced by the publicity solution—a lack of accountability and openness to manipulation—but perhaps the symbolic can make a contribution at the discussion stage which I have not considered here. The second gap concerns the issue I raised but was unable to answer about how participants feel themselves to be accountable to outsiders even though there are no formal mechanisms holding them to that. This is related to the third gap, to do with publicity in the public sphere. I confined my discussion of this to the news media, but the media is broader than news, and the public sphere broader than the media. Perhaps a broader examination of those alternatives may throw up more solutions to the problems which come with the media, particularly their structural inability to transmit some kinds of arguments because of the need to narrate a story.

In terms of my own model of a legitimate deliberative democracy, there is an enormous amount of technical detail of how the system would work which I have glided over, detail like the roles of existing institutions like parties, interest groups, cabinet, powerful central policy agencies, and so on. Just as important as doing the detailed design, however, is knowing whether any supportive discourses exist for all of this, or whether other preliminary work would need to be done before anything like my scheme, or even some of its elements, could be contemplated. Therefore a detailed study of discourses of democracy in Britain and elsewhere would be very useful, particularly if it paid attention to the discursive allegiances of politicians, public servants, and other powerful public actors.

Finally, what about the questions I asked right at the beginning, on behalf of the protestors standing outside the Leicester City Football Club back in March 2000? What reasons did they have for conferring legitimacy on the process? On what grounds could they be persuaded to accept the outcome without being inside the room themselves, hearing the arguments, and participating in the debate directly?

From what I have argued, there were several. First, their own representatives were inside the jury room, making presentations to the jurors and arguing their case, and if they did a bad job, then those leaders could be replaced. Second, while the witnesses were not privy to the in camera deliberations and so could not transmit those arguments back to their members, the jury report was widely distributed so they could at least read through the jurors' reasoning and, presumably, consent to or challenge it later; local newspaper and television journalists covered the proceedings over the four days as well, ensuring that the wider population was able to follow the key arguments. Third, the jurors were at least broadly descriptively representative of the county population—more representative than those who had taken part in the initial planning process at any rate—while the random selection process also ensured that no one making the recommendations had more than an ordinary citizen's interest in the outcome. Fourth, the health authority agreed to be bound by the decision, a decisiveness which enhanced some measure of democratic control and undermined bureaucratic diktat. Fifth, it was agreed to be a more rational process than the polarized shouting which had prevailed up to that point, a rationality which increased the likelihood that the result would be legitimate on substantive grounds. Sixth, and perhaps most importantly, the citizens' jury was not the entire deliberative process, but just its focal point—up until then, the protestors and the wider population had taken part in a mass challenge to the health authority's decision, and mobilized support from elected representatives and other champions, which meant that participation in the public conversation surrounding the issue had been very much broader than just the sixteen jurors. These six points mean that the protestors had good reason indeed to grant legitimacy to the process, reasons which were both internal to the jury process itself, and external, related to its role as the focus of a larger deliberative system.

The most serious shortcoming was that this particular deliberative system was focused only on Leicestershire, while the issues which constrained both the scope of the deliberation and the available solutions were determined in Whitehall and by the myriad factors making up the political economy of the UK's health service. To be more fully legitimate, deliberative democracy needs to be much bigger than local consultations on local issues. It needs to be integrated into central government as well, even into the international system, and to engage with the power of large private interests. Otherwise political life will involve, perhaps as it already does, democratic deliberation on issues which do not matter very much, technocracy or thorubocracy on some of those which do, and plutocracy for everything else.

References

Abramson, Jeffrey B. (1994). *We, the Jury: The Jury System and the Ideal of Democracy.* New York: Basic Books.

Ackerman, Bruce (1991). *We the People 1: Foundations.* Cambridge, MA: Harvard University Press.

Ackerman, Bruce, and James S. Fishkin (2002). 'Deliberation Day', *Journal of Political Philosophy,* 10 (2): 129–52.

Almond, Gabriel, and Sidney Verba (1963). *The Civic Culture.* Princeton, NJ: Princeton University Press.

Anderson, Richard (1998). 'The Place of the Media in Popular Democracy', *Critical Review,* 12 (4): 481–500.

Aristotle (1997). *The Politics of Aristotle.* Trans. P. L. P. Simpson. Chapel Hill, NC: University of North Carolina Press.

Audit Commission (2003). *Achieving the NHS Plan: Assessment of Current Performance, Likely Future Progress and Capacity to Improve.* London: Audit Commission for Local Authorities and the NHS in England and Wales.

Bandura, Albert (1982). 'Self-efficacy Mechanisms in Human Agency', *American Psychologist,* 37(2): 122–47.

Barber, Benjamin (1984). *Strong Democracy: Participatory Politics for a New Age.* Berkeley & Los Angeles, CA: University of California Press.

Barker, Anthony (1982). 'Governmental Bodies and the Networks of Mutual Accountability', in *Quangos in Britain,* A. Barker (ed.). London: Macmillan.

Barker, Rodney S. (2001). *Legitimating Identities: The Self-presentations of Rulers and Subjects.* Cambridge: Cambridge University Press.

Barnes, Colin and Michael Oliver (1995). 'Disability Rights: Rhetoric and Reality in the UK', *Disability and Society,* 10(1): 111–16.

Barnes, Marian (1999). *Building a Deliberative Democracy: An Evaluation of Two Citizens' Juries.* London: Institute of Public Policy Research.

Bartlett, Will, Carol Propper, Deborah Wilson, and Julian Le Grand (eds.) (1994). *Quasi-markets in the Welfare State.* Bristol: SAUS Publications.

Baumgartner, Frank R., and Beth L. Leech (1998). *Basic Interests: The Importance of Groups in Politics and in Political Science.* Princeton, NJ: Princeton University Press.

BCODP (2002). *Website.* British Council of Disabled People available at http://www.bcodp.org.uk

Beetham, David (1991). *The Legitimation of Power.* Basingstoke: Macmillan.

—— (ed.) (1994). *Defining and Measuring Democracy.* London: Sage.

—— and Christopher Lord (1998). *Legitimacy and the European Union.* Harlow: Addison-Wesley/Longman.

Bell, Daniel (1993). *Communitarianism and its Critics.* Oxford: Clarendon Press.

Benford, Robert D. and Scott A. Hunt (1992). 'Dramaturgy and Social Movements: The Social Construction and Communication of Power', *Sociological Enquiry*, 62(1): 36–55.

Benhabib, Seyla (1996). 'Toward a Deliberative Model of Democratic Legitimacy', in *Democracy and Difference*, S. Benhabib (ed.). Princeton, NJ: Princeton University Press.

Beresford, Peter and Jane Campbell (1994). 'Disabled People, Service Users, User Involvement and Representation', *Disability and Society*, 9(3): 315–25.

Berg, Bruce L. (2001). *Qualitative Research Methods for the Social Sciences*. Boston: Allyn & Bacon.

Bessette, Joseph M. (1980). 'Deliberative Democracy: The Majority Principle in Republican Government', in *How Democratic is the Constitution?* R. A. Goldwin and W. A. Schambra (eds.). Washington, DC: American Enterprise Institute for Public Policy Research.

—— (1994). *The Mild Voice of Reason: Deliberative Democracy and American National Government*. Chicago: University of Chicago Press.

Besterfield, Dale, Carol Besterfield-Michna, Glen Besterfield, and Mary Besterfield-Sacre (1995). *Total Quality Management*. Englewood Cliffs, NJ: Prentice-Hall.

Bevir, Mark, and Roderick A. W. Rhodes (2003). *Interpreting British Governance*. London: Routledge.

Birch, A. H. (1971). *Representation*. London: Pall Mall.

Blair, Tony (1998). *The Third Way: New Politics for the New Century, Fabian Pamphlet 588*. London: Fabian Society.

Bohman, James and William Rehg (eds.) (1997). *Deliberative Democracy: Essays on Reason and Politics*. Cambridge, MA: MIT Press.

Boston, Jonathan, John Martin, June Pallot, and Pat Walsh (1996). *Public Management: the New Zealand Model*. Auckland: Oxford University Press.

Bowie, Cameron, Ann Richardson, and Wendy Sykes (1995). 'Consulting the Public about Health Service Priorities', *British Medical Journal*, 311: 1155–8.

Broome, John (1984). 'Selecting People Randomly', *Ethics*, 95(1): 38–55.

Brown, Stephen (1980). *Political Subjectivity: Applications of Q Methodology in Political Science*. New Haven, CT: Yale University Press.

Burnheim, John (1985). *Is Democracy Possible?* Cambridge: Polity Press.

Burns, Carol (2000a). 'Hospitals Shake-up: People to Speak Out', *Leicester Mercury*, 24 March 2000.

—— (2000b). 'Jury Will Decide on City Hospitals', *Leicester Mercury*, 23 March.

Button, Mark and Kevin Mattson (1999). 'Deliberative Democracy in Practice: Challenges and Prospects for Civic Deliberation', *Polity*, 31(4): 609–37.

Cairney, Paul (2002). 'New Public Management and the Thatcher Healthcare Legacy: Enough of the Theory, What about the Implementation?', *British Journal of Politics and International Relations*, 4(3): 375–98.

Capella, Joseph and Kathleen Jamieson (1996). 'News Frames, Political Cynicism, and Media Cynicism', *Annals of the American Academy of Political and Social Science*, 546: 71–84.

Carlyle, Thomas. (1993) [1840]. *On Heroes, Hero-worship, and the Heroic in History.* Berkeley, CA: University of California Press.

Carson, Lyn and Brian Martin (1999). *Random Selection in Politics.* Westport: Praeger.

Catt, Helena (1996). *Voting Behaviour: A Radical Critique.* London: Leicester University Press.

—— (1999). *Democracy in Practice.* London: Routledge.

Chambers, Simone (1996). *Reasonable Democracy: Jürgen Habermas and the Politics of Discourse.* Ithaca, NY: Cornell University Press.

—— and Anne Costain (eds.) (2000). *Deliberation, Democracy, and the Media.* Lanham: Rowman and Littlefield.

Channel 4 (1998). *The Prescription.* Television, Episode 1, 4 July 1998, 8:00 p.m.; Episode 2, 5 July 1998, 2:30 p.m.; Episode 3, 5 July 1998, 7:00 p.m.

Chowcat, Ian (2000). 'Moral Pluralism, Political Justification and Deliberative Democracy', *Political Studies*, 48: 745–58.

Christiano, Thomas (1996). 'Deliberative Equality and the Democratic Order', in *Political Order: Nomos 38*, I. Shapiro and R. Hardin (eds.). New York: New York University Press.

Coffey, Amanda and Paul Atkinson (1996). *Making Sense of Qualitative Data: Complementary Research Strategies.* Thousand Oaks, CA: Sage.

Cohen, Joshua (1989). 'Deliberation and Democratic Legitimacy', in *Contemporary Political Philosophy: An Anthology*, R. E. Goodin and P. Pettit (eds.). Oxford: Blackwell.

—— and Joel Rogers (1992). 'Secondary Associations and Democratic Governance', *Politics and Society*, 20(4): 393–472.

Cohen, Stanley (1973). *Folk Devils and Moral Panics: The Creation of the Mods and Rockers.* St. Albans: Paladin.

Commons Select Committee on Health (2000). *Minutes of Evidence.* London: Her Majesty's Stationery Office. Available at http://www.parliament.the-stationery-office.co.uk/pa/cm199900/cmselect/cmhealth/957/0110205.htm; accessed 19 August 2005.

Converse, Philip (1964). 'The Nature of Belief Systems in Mass Publics', in *Ideology and discontent*, D. Apter (ed.). New York: Free Press.

Coulter, Angela and Christopher Ham (eds.) (2000). *The Global Challenge of Health Care Rationing.* Buckingham: Open University Press.

Cox, Eva and Robert D. Putnam (2002). *Democracies in Flux: The Evolution of Social Capital in Contemporary Society.* Oxford: Oxford University Press.

Crook, Richard C. (1987). 'Legitimacy, Authority and the Transfer of Power in Ghana', *Political Studies*, 35: 552–72.

Crosby, Ned (1998). 'Using Citizens' Juries: A Process for Environmental Decision-making', in *Making Better Environmental Decisions*, K. Sexton, A. A. Marcus, K. W. Easter, and T. D. Burkhardt (eds.). Washington, DC: Island Press.

Czikszentmihalyi, Mihaly and J. LeFevre (1989). 'Optimal Experience in Work and Leisure', *Journal of Personality and Social Psychology*, 65: 815–22.

Dahl, Robert (1961). *Who Governs? Democracy and Power in an American City.* New Haven, CT: Yale University Press.

—— (1967). *Pluralist Democracy in the United States: Conflict and Consent.* Chicago: Rand McNally.

—— (1971). *Polyarchy: Participation and Opposition.* New Haven, CT: Yale University Press.

—— (1989). *Democracy and its Critics.* New Haven, CT: Yale University Press.

DAN (1998). *DAN Goes to Jail for the Right to Ride* [Press release]. Disabled People's Direct Action Network, 6 April 1998. Available at http://www.dimenet.com/cgi-bin/getlink?actions,9R; accessed 24 October 2000.

Davies, Stella, Susan Elizabeth, Bec Hanley, Bill New, and Bob Sang (1998). *Ordinary Wisdom: Reflections on an Experiment in Citizenship and Health.* London: King's Fund.

Davis, Peter (ed.) (1992). *For Health or Profit? Medicine, the Pharmaceutical Industry, and the State in New Zealand.* Auckland: Oxford University Press.

Dawson, Diane (2001). 'The Private Finance Initiative: A Public Finance Illusion?' *Health Economics,* 10(6): 479–86.

Day, Patricia, and Rudolf Klein (1987). *Accountabilities: Five Public Services.* London: Tavistock.

Denver, David, Gordon Hands, and Bill Jones (1995). 'Fishkin and the Deliberative Opinion Poll: Lessons from a Study of the *Granada 500* Television Program', *Political Communication,* 12(2): 147–56.

DETR (1998). *Guidance on Enhancing Public Participation in Local Government.* London: Department of the Environment, Transport and the Regions.

DHSS (1983). *NHS Management Inquiry (The Griffiths Report).* London: Department of Health and Social Security.

Dienel, Peter and Ortwin Renn (1995). 'Planning Cells: A Gate to "Fractal" Mediation', in *Fairness and Competence in Citizen Participation,* O. Renn, T. Webler, and P. M. Wiedemann (eds.). Dordrecht, The Netherlands: Kluwer.

Doğanay, Ülkü (2004). 'Rethinking Democratic Procedures: Democracy and Deliberative Experiences in Turkey's LA21 Process', *Political Studies,* 52(4): 728–44.

DoH (2000). *The National Plan: Analysis of the Response to the Consultation Exercise Carried out in May/June 2000.* London: Department of Health.

Dolan, Paul, Richard Cookson, and Brian Ferguson (1999). 'Effect of Discussion and Deliberation on the Public's Views of Priority Setting in Health Care: Focus Group Study', *British Medical Journal,* 318(7188): 916.

Driedger, Diane (1989). *The Last Civil Rights Movement: Disabled People's International.* London: Hurst and Company.

Driver, Stephen and Luke Martell (2000). 'Left, Right and the Third Way', *Policy and Politics,* 28(2): 147–61.

Dryzek, John (1987). 'Complexity and Rationality in Public Life', *Political Studies,* 35(3): 424–42.

—— (1990). *Discursive Democracy.* New York: Cambridge University Press.

—— (1996*a*). *Democracy in Capitalist Times: Ideals, Limits, Struggles*. New York/ Oxford: Oxford University Press.

—— (1996*b*). 'The Informal Logic of Institutional Design', in *The Theory of Institutional Design*, R. Goodin (ed.). Cambridge: Cambridge University Press.

—— (2000). *Deliberative Democracy and Beyond: Liberals, Critics, Contestations*. Oxford: Oxford University Press.

—— (2001). 'Legitimacy and Economy in Deliberative Democracy', *Political Theory*, 29(5): 651–69.

—— (2005). 'Deliberative Democracy in Divided Societies: Alternatives to Agonism and Analgesia', *Political Theory*, 33(2): 218–42.

—— and Leslie Holmes (eds.) (2002). *Post-communist Democratization: Political Discourses across Thirteen Countries*. Cambridge: Cambridge University Press.

Dunsire, Andrew (1973). 'Administrative Doctrine and Administrative Change', *Public Administration Bulletin*, 15 (December): 39–56.

Eckersley, Robyn (2000). 'Deliberative Democracy, Ecological Risk, and "Communities-of-Fate"', in *Democratic Innovation: Deliberation, Association, and Representation*, M. Saward (ed.). London: Routledge.

Edelman, Murray (1976). *The Symbolic Uses of Politics*. Urbana, IL: University of Illinois Press.

—— (1988). *Constructing the Political Spectacle*. Chicago: University of Chicago Press.

Elliott, Valerie (1996). 'Blair to Give Public More Say with Citizens' Juries', *The Times*, 28 October 1996, 2.

Elster, Jon (1983). *Sour Grapes: Studies in the Subversion of Rationality*. Cambridge: Cambridge University Press.

—— (1997). 'The Market and the Forum: Three Varieties of Political Theory', in *Contemporary Political Philosophy: An Anthology*, R. E. Goodin and P. Pettit (eds.). Oxford: Blackwell.

—— (1998). 'Introduction', in *Deliberative Democracy*, J. Elster (ed.). Cambridge: Cambridge University Press.

Emden, Cecil Stuart (1956). *The People and the Constitution*, 2nd edn. Oxford: Clarendon Press.

Estlund, David (1997). 'Beyond Fairness of Deliberation: The Epistemic Dimension of Democratic Authority', in *Deliberative Democracy: Essays on Reason and Politics*, J. Bohman and W. Rehg (eds.). Cambridge, MA: MIT Press.

Fairclough, Norman (1992). *Discourse and Social Change*. Cambridge: Polity Press.

Farrell, Catherine M. and Jane Jones (2000). 'Evaluating Stakeholder Participation in Public services—Parents and Schools', *Policy and Politics*, 28(2): 251–62.

Fennema, Meindert and Marcel Maussen (2000). 'Dealing with Extremists in Public Discussion: Front National and "Republican Front" in France', *Journal of Political Philosophy*, 8(3): 379–400.

Ferlie, Ewan, Lynn Ashburner, Louise Fitzgerald, and Andrew Pettigrew (1996). *The New Public Management in Action*. Oxford: Oxford University Press.

Fischer, Frank (1990). *Technocracy and the Politics of Expertise*. London: Sage.

Fischer, Frank and John Forester (1993). *The Argumentative Turn in Policy Analysis and Planning.* Durham: Duke University Press.

Fisher, B. Aubrey and Donald G. Ellis (1990). *Small Group Decision Making: Communication and the Group Process,* 3rd edn. New York: McGraw-Hill.

Fishkin, James S. (1991). *Democracy and Deliberation.* New Haven, CT: Yale University Press.

—— (1996). 'The Televised Deliberative Poll: An Experiment in Democracy', *Annals of the American Academy of Political and Social Science,* 546: 132–40.

—— (1997). *The Voice of the People: Public Opinion and Democracy,* 2nd edn. New Haven, CT: Yale University Press.

—— (2003). 'Consulting the Public through Deliberative Polling', *Journal of Policy Analysis and Management,* 22(1): 128–33.

—— and Robert Luskin 2000: 184–8. 'Broadcasts of Deliberative Polls: Aspirations and Effects', *British and Robert Luskin Journal of Political Science,* 36(1).

—— —— and Roger Jowell (2000). 'Deliberative Polling and Public Consultation', *Parliamentary Affairs,* 53(4): 657–66.

Flathman, Richard E. (1972). *Political Obligation.* New York: Atheneum.

Flinders, Matthew (1999). 'Setting the Scene: Quangos in Context', in *Quangos, Accountability and Reform: The Politics of Quasi-government,* M. Flinders and M. Smith (eds.). Basingstoke: Macmillan/Political Economy Research Centre, University of Sheffield.

Flyvbjerg, Bent (1998). *Rationality and Power: Democracy in Practice,* trans. S. Sampson. Chicago: University of Chicago Press.

Foley, Paul and Steve Martin (2000). 'A New Deal for the Community? Public Participation in Regeneration and Local Service Delivery', *Policy and Politics,* 28(4): 479–91.

Forester, John (1984). 'Bounded Rationality and the Politics of Muddling Through', *Public Administration Review,* 44: 23–30.

—— (1999). *The Deliberative Practitioner: Encouraging Participatory Planning Processes.* Cambridge, MA: MIT Press.

Frankena, William K. (1968). 'Two Notes on Representation', in *Representation: Nomos 10,* J. R. Pennock and J. W. Chapman (eds.). New York: Atherton Press.

Fraser, Nancy (1992). 'Rethinking the Public Sphere: A Contribution to the Critique of Actually Exisiting Democracy', in *Habermas and the Public Sphere,* C. Calhoun (ed.). Cambridge, MA: MIT Press.

Fukuyama, Francis (1989). 'The End of History?' *The National Interest,* 16: 3–18.

Fung, Archon (2003). 'Survey Article: Recipes for Public Spheres: Eight Institutional Design Choices and Their Consequences', *Journal of Political Philosophy,* 11(3): 338–67.

—— (2005). 'Deliberation before the Revolution: Toward an Ethics of Deliberative Democracy in an Unjust World', *Political Theory,* 33(2): 397–419.

Gamble, Andrew (1994). *The Free Economy and the Strong State: The Politics of Thatcherism,* 2nd edn. Basingstoke: Macmillan.

Gavin, Neil and David Sanders (2003). 'The Press and its Influence on British Political Attitudes under New Labour', *Political Studies*, 51(3): 573–91.

Gergen, Kenneth J. and Mary M. Gergen (1991). 'Toward Reflexive Methodologies', in *Research and Reflexivity*, F. Steier (ed.). London: Sage.

Gibson, Rachel and Sarah Miskin (2002). 'Australia Deliberates? A Critical Analysis of the Role of the Media in Deliberative Polling', in *Constitutional Politics: the Republic Referendum and the Future*, J. Warhurst and M. Mackerras (eds.). St Lucia, Australia: University of Queensland Press.

Giddens, Anthony (1998). *The Third Way: The Renewal of Social Democracy*. Cambridge: Polity Press.

Goodall, H. Lloyd (1990). *Small Group Communication in Organizations*, 2nd edn. Dubuque, IA: W.C. Brown.

Goodin, Robert (1982). *Political Theory and Public Policy*. Chicago: University of Chicago Press.

—— (1992). *Motivating Political Morality*. Cambridge, MA: Blackwell.

—— (1996*a*). 'Enfranchising the Earth, and Its Alternatives', *Political Studies*, 44: 841–4.

—— (1996*b*). 'Institutions and Their Design', in *The Theory of Institutional Design*, R. Goodin (ed.). Cambridge: Cambridge University Press.

—— (2000). 'Democratic Deliberation Within', *Philosophy and Public Affairs*, 29(1): 81–109.

—— (2003). 'Representing Diversity', *British Journal of Political Science*, 34(3): 453–68.

—— (ed.) (1995). *The Theory of Institutional Design*. Cambridge: Cambridge University Press.

—— and John Dryzek (1980). 'Rational Participation: The Politics of Relative Power', *British Journal of Political Science*, 10(3): 273–92.

Goodwin, Barbara (1992). *Justice by Lottery*. Hemel Hempstead: Harvester Wheatsheaf.

Grafstein, Robert (1981). 'The Failure of Weber's Conception of Legitimacy: Its Causes and Implications', *Journal of Politics*, 43(2): 456–72.

Gray, John (1996). *After Social Democracy: Politics, Capitalism and the Common Life*. London: Demos.

Grey, Sandra (2002). 'Does Size Matter? Critical Mass and New Zealand's Women MPs', *Parliamentary Affairs*, 55(1): 19–29.

—— (2003). 'Talking Work: Discourse Coalitions and Unpaid Work Debates in New Zealand'. Paper read at Public Policy Network conference, 30–31 January 2003, Victoria University of Wellington.

Gunnell, John G. (1986). *Between Philosophy and Politics: The Alienation of Political Theory*. Amherst, MA: University of Massachusetts Press.

Gutmann, Amy and Dennis Thompson (1996). *Democracy and Disagreement*. Cambridge, MA: Belknap Press of Harvard University Press.

—— (2004). *Why Deliberative Democracy?* Princeton, NJ: Princeton University Press.

Habermas, Jürgen (1975). *Legitimation Crisis*. Trans. T. McCarthy. Cambridge, MA: Beacon Press.

—— (1984). *The Theory of Communicative Action*, trans. T. McCarthy. Boston, MA: Beacon Press.

—— (1989). *The Structural Transformation of the Public Sphere: An Inquiry into a Category of Bourgeois Society*. Cambridge: Polity Press.

—— (1995). 'Reconciliation through the Public Use of Reason: Remarks on John Rawls's *Political Liberalism*', *Journal of Philosophy*, 92(3): 109–31.

—— (1996). *Between Facts and Norms: Contributions to a Discourse Theory of Law and Democracy*, trans. W. Rehg. Cambridge: Polity Press.

Hajer, Maarten (1993). 'Discourse Coalitions and the Institutionalization of Practice: The Case of Acid Rain in Britain', in *The Argumentative Turn in Policy Analysis and Planning*, F. Fischer and J. Forester (eds.). Durham, NC: Duke University Press.

—— (2005). 'Setting the Stage: A Dramaturgy of Policy Deliberation', *Administration and Society*, 36(6): 624–47.

Hall, Declan and John Stewart (1996). *Citizens' Juries in Local Government: Report for the LGMB on the Pilot Projects*. London: Local Government Management Board.

Hall, Stuart, Chas Critcher, Tony Jefferson, John Clarke, and Brian Roberts (1978). *Policing the Crisis: Mugging, the State, and Law and Order*. London: Macmillan.

Hallas, Jack (1976). *CHCs in Action: A Review*. London: Nuffield Provincial Hospitals Trust.

Ham, Christopher (2004). *Health Policy in Britain: The Politics and Organisation of the National Health Service*, 5th edn. Basingstoke: Palgrave.

Hamel, Jacques, Stéphane Dufour, and Dominic Fortin (1993). *Case Study Methods*. Newbury Park, CA: Sage.

Harrison, Stephen and Maggie Mort (1998). 'Which Champions, Which People? Public and User Involvement in Health Care as a Technology of Legitimation', *Social Policy and Administration*, 32(1): 60–70.

Harrison, Stephen, and Christopher Pollitt (1994). *Controlling Health Professionals: The Future of Work and Organization in the NHS*. Buckingham: Open University Press.

Hendriks, Carolyn (2002a). 'Institutions of Deliberative Democratic Processes and Interest Groups: Roles, Tensions and Incentives', *Australian Journal of Public Administration*, 61(1): 64–75.

—— (2002b). 'Navigating the Murky Waters of Civil Society in Deliberative Democracy'. Paper presented at Australasian Political Studies Association, Australian National University, Canberra.

Hindess, Barry (1988). *Choice, Rationality, and Social Theory*. London: Unwin Hyman.

Hogg, Christine, and Charlotte Williamson (2001). 'Whose Interests Do Lay People Represent? Towards an Understanding of the Role of Lay People as Members of Committees', *Health Expectations*, 4(1): 2–9.

Hood, Christopher (1991). 'A Public Management for all Seasons?' *Public Administration*, 69 (Spring): 3–19.

—— (1998). *The Art of the State: Culture, Rhetoric and Public Management*. Oxford: Oxford University Press.

House of Commons (2000). *Official Report*. London: Her Majesty's Stationery Office.
—— (2002). *Official Report*. London: Her Majesty's Stationery Office.
Humphrey, Jill (2000). 'Researching Disability Politics, or, Some Problems with the Social Model in Practice', *Disability and Society*, 15(1): 63–85.
Hunter, David, and Stephen Harrison (1997). 'Democracy, Accountability and Consumerism', in *Healthy Choices: Future Options for the NHS*, S. Iliffe and J. F. Munro (eds.). London: Lawrence & Wishart.
Issues Deliberation Australia (2001). *Group Discussion Outline: 'Australia Deliberates: Reconciliation—Where to From Here?'* Adelaide.
Iyengar, Shanto (1996). 'Framing Responsibility for Political Issues', *Annals of the American Academy of Political and Social Science*, 546: 59–70.
Jacobs, Lawrence, Theodore R. Marmor, and Jonathan Oberlander (1999). 'The Oregon Health Plan and the Political Paradox of Rationing: What Advocates and Critics Have Claimed and What Oregon Did', *Journal of Health Politics, Policy and Law*, 24(1): 161–80.
Jefferson Center (1998). *The Citizens Jury: Effective Public Participation*. Minneapolis: Jefferson Center for New Democratic Processes.
John, Peter (1998). *Analysing Public Policy*. London: Continuum.
Jorgenson, Jane (1991). 'Co-constructing the Interviewer/Co-constructing "Family"', in *Research and Reflexivity*, F. Steier (ed.). London: Sage.
Joss, Simon and John Durant (eds.) (1995). *Public Participation in Science: The Role of Consensus Conferences in Europe*. London: Science Museum.
Judge, David (1999). *Representation: Theory and Practice in Britain*. London: Routledge.
Kateb, George (1992). *The Inner Ocean: Individualism and Democratic Culture*. Ithaca, NY: Cornell University Press.
Kavanagh, Dennis (1987). *Thatcherism and British Politics: The End of Consensus?* Oxford: Oxford University Press.
Kellner, Douglas (1995). *Media Culture: Cultural Studies, Identity, and Politics between the Modern and the Postmodern*. London: Routledge.
Kerbel, Matthew, Sumaiya Apee, and Marc Ross (2000). 'PBS Ain't so Different: Public Broadcasting, Election Frames, and Democratic Empowerment', *Harvard International Journal of Press/Politics*, 5(4): 8–32.
Kerr, Peter and David Marsh (1999). 'Explaining Thatcherism: Towards a Multidimensional Approach', in *Postwar British Politics in Perspective*, D. Marsh (ed.). Cambridge: Blackwell.
Kingdon, John W. (1984). *Agendas, Alternatives and Public Policies*. Boston: Little, Brown.
Klein, Rudolf (1990). 'The State and the Profession: The Politics of the Double Bed', *British Medical Journal*, 301(6754): 700–2.
—— (2000). *The New Politics of the NHS*, 4th edn. Harlow: Prentice-Hall.
—— Patricia Day, and Sharon Redmayne (1996). *Managing Scarcity: Priority Setting and Rationing in the National Health Service*. Buckingham: Open University Press.

Klein, Rudolf and Janet Lewis (1976). *The Politics of Consumer Representation: A Study of Community Health Councils.* London: Centre for Studies in Social Policy.

Klingemann, Hans-Dieter, Richard Hofferbert, and Ian Budge (1994). *Parties, Politics and Democracy.* Boulder, CO: Westview Press.

Kobach, Kris (1997). 'Spurn Thy Neighbour: Direct Democracy and Swiss Isolationism', *West European Politics*, 20(3): 185–211.

Koch, Jeffrey W. (1995). *Social Reference Groups and Political Life.* Lanham: University Press of America.

Kogan, Maurice and Katherine Bowden (1975). *Educational Policy-making: A Study of Interest Groups and Parliament.* London: Allen & Unwin.

Kukathas, Chandran (1996). 'Liberalism, Communitarianism, and Political Community', in *The Communitarian Challenge to Liberalism*, E. F. Paul, F. D. Miller and J. Paul (eds.). Cambridge: Cambridge University Press.

Kuran, Timur (1998). 'Insincere Deliberation and Democratic Failure', *Critical Review*, 12(4): 530–44.

Kymlicka, Will (1995). *Multicultural Citizenship: A Liberal Theory of Minority Rights.* Oxford: Clarendon Press.

Lane, Jan-Erik (1987). *Bureaucracy and Public Choice.* London: Sage.

Langer, John (1998). *Tabloid Television: Popular Journalism and the 'Other News'.* London: Routledge.

Larmore, Charles (1987). *Patterns of Moral Complexity.* Cambridge: Cambridge University Press.

Le Grand, Julian and Will Bartlett (1993). *Quasi-markets and Social Policy.* Basingstoke: Macmillan.

Lenaghan, Jo (1999). 'Involving the Public in Rationing Decisions: The Experience of Citizens' Juries', *Health Policy*, 49(1–2): 45–61.

—— Bill New, and Elizabeth Mitchell (1996). 'Setting Priorities: Is There a Role for Citizens' Juries?' *British Medical Journal*, 312(7046): 1591–4.

Letters to the Editor (1999). 'Hospital's Only Fault Is in Being too Popular', *Leicester Mercury*, 26 November 1999.

Lewis, Richard S. (1974). *The Voyages of Apollo: The Exploration of the Moon.* New York: Quadrangle.

Lijphart, Arend and Bernard Grofman (1984). *Choosing an Electoral System: Issues and Alternatives.* New York: Praeger.

Lindblom, Charles E. (1965). *The Intelligence of Democracy: Decision Making Through Mutual Adjustment.* New York: Free Press.

Lindenmann, Walter (1997). 'Setting Minimum Standards for Public Relations Effectiveness', *Public Relations Review*, 23(4): 391–408.

Lipset, Seymour M. (1984). 'Social Conflict, Legitimacy and Democracy', in *Legitimacy and the State*, W. Connolly (ed.). Oxford: Blackwell.

Luban, David (2002). 'The Publicity of Law and the Regulatory State', *Journal of Political Philosophy*, 10(3): 296–316.

Luskin, Robert, James S. Fishkin, and Roger Jowell (2002). 'Considered Opinions: Deliberative Polling in Britain', *British Journal of Political Science*, 32(3): 455–87.

Macedo, Stephen (1999). *Deliberative Politics: Essays on Democracy and Disagreement.* New York: Oxford University Press.

MacGregor, Brent (1997). *Live, Direct, and Biased? Making Television News in the Satellite Age.* London: Arnold.

Mackie, Gerry (2002). 'Does Democratic Deliberation Change Minds?' Paper presented at Democratic Theory: The Canberra Papers, Australian National University, Canberra.

—— (2003). *Democracy Defended.* Cambridge: Cambridge University Press.

Majone, Giandomenico (1989). *Evidence, Argument, and Persuasion in the Policy Process.* New Haven, CT: Yale University Press.

Manin, Bernard (1987). 'On Legitimacy and Political Deliberation', *Political Theory*, 15(3): 338–68.

—— (1997). *The Principles of Representative Government.* Cambridge: Cambridge University Press.

Mansbridge, Jane (1992). 'A Deliberative Theory of Interest Representation', in *The Politics of Interests: Interest Groups Transformed*, M. Petracca (ed.). Boulder, CO: Westview Press.

—— (1998). 'The Many Faces of Representation', in *Working Papers on Political Theory and Ethics, 98-17.* Cambridge, MA: Politics Research Group, Kennedy School of Government, Harvard University.

—— (1999). 'Everyday Talk in the Deliberative System', in *Deliberative Politics: Essays on 'Democracy and Disagreement'*, S. Macedo, (ed.). New York: Oxford University Press.

March, James G. and Herbert Simon (1958). *Organizations.* New York: John Wiley & Sons.

—— and Johan P Olsen (1995). *Democratic Governance.* New York: Free Press.

Marmor, Theodore R. (1994). *Understanding Health Care Reform.* New Haven, CT: Yale University Press.

May, J. D. (1978). 'Defining Democracy', *Political Studies*, 26: 1–14.

McAdam, Doug (2000). 'Movement Strategy and Dramaturgic Framing in Democratic States: The Case of the American Civil Rights Movement', in *Deliberation, Democracy and the Media*, S. Chambers and A. Costain (eds.). Lanham: Rowman and Littlefield.

McIver, Shirley (1997). *An Evaluation of the King's Fund Citizens' Juries Programme.* Birmingham: Health Services Management Centre, University of Birmingham.

McLean, Iain (1987). *Public Choice.* Oxford: Blackwell.

McLuhan, Marshall (1987). *Understanding Media: The Extensions of Man.* London: ARK Paperbacks.

Milburn, Alan (2001). *Shifting the Balance of Power in the NHS: Speech at the Launch of the NHS Modernisation Agency.* Available at http://www.dh.gov.uk/NewsHome/Speeches/SpeechesList/SpeechesArticle/fs/en?CONTENT_ID=4000938&chk=vNg%2B0G; accessed 14 June 2003.

Milewa, Timothy, Justin Valentine, and Michael Calnan (1998). 'Managerialism and Active Citizenship in Britain's Reformed Health Service: Power and Community in an Era of Decentralisation', *Social Science and Medicine*, 47(4): 507–17.

—— —— —— (1999). 'Community Participation and Citizenship in British Health Care Planning: Narratives of Power and Involvement in the Changing Welfare State', *Sociology of Health and Illness*, 21(4): 445–65.

Mill, John Stuart (1974). *On Liberty*. Harmondsworth: Penguin.

Miller, David (1992). 'Deliberative Democracy and Social Choice', *Political Studies*, 40 (Special Issue): 54–67.

Moran, Michael (1999). *Governing the Health Care State: A Comparative Study of the United Kingdom, the United States and Germany*. Manchester: Manchester University Press.

Mort, Maggie, Stephen Harrison, and Gerald Wistow (1996). 'The User Card: Picking through the Organisational Undergrowth in Health and Social Care', *Contemporary Political Studies*, 2: 1133–40.

Moscovici, Serge (1985). 'Social Influence and Conformity', in *Handbook of Social Psychology*, G. Lindzey and E. Aronson (eds.). New York: Random House.

Mouffe, Chantal (1999). 'Deliberative Democracy or Agonistic Pluralism?' *Social Research*, 66(3): 745–58.

Mullen, Penelope (2000). 'Public Involvement in Health Care Priority Setting: Are the Methods Appropriate and Valid?' in *The Global Challenge of Health Care Rationing*, A. Coulter and C. Ham (eds.). Buckingham: Open University Press.

Nagel, Thomas (1991). *Equality and Partiality*. New York: Oxford University Press.

Negrine, Ralph (1989). *Politics and the Mass Media in Britain*. London: Routledge.

Neuman, Johanna (1996). *Lights, Camera, War: Is Media Technology Driving International Politics?* New York: St Martin's Press.

Neuman, W. Russell (1986). *The Paradox of Mass Politics*. Cambridge, MA: Harvard University Press.

New, Bill (ed.) (1997). *Rationing: Talk and Action in Health Care*. London: BMJ Publishing.

NHS Management Executive (1992). *Local Voices: The Views of Local People in Purchasing for Health*. London: Department of Health.

NICE (2002). *UK's First Citizens Council Being Established by NICE* (press release). London: NHS National Institute for Clinical Excellence.

Niemeyer, Simon (2004). 'Deliberation in the Wilderness: Displacing Symbolic Politics', *Environmental Politics*, 13(2): 347–72.

Norris, Pippa (2000). *A Virtuous Circle: Political Communications in Post Industrial Societies*. Cambridge: Cambridge University Press.

—— (ed.) (1997). *Passages to Power: Legislative Recruitment in Advanced Democracies*. Cambridge: Cambridge University Press.

North Down Borough Council (1998). Letter to Eastern Health and Social Services Council, 24 September 1998.

Northern Ireland Act. United Kingdom Parliament, 1998.

O'Neill, John (1998). 'Rhetoric, Science and Philosophy', *Philosophy of the Social Sciences*, 28(2): 205–25.

—— (2001). 'Representing People, Representing Nature, Representing the World', *Environment and Planning C: Government and Policy*, 19(4): 483–500.

O'Neill, Shane (2000). 'The Politics of Inclusive Agreements: Towards a Critical Discourse Theory of Democracy', *Political Studies*, 48: 503–21.

ODPM (1999). *Making the Difference: A New Start for England's Coalfield Communities*. London: Office of the Deputy Prime Minister. Available at http://www.urban. odpm.gov.uk/programmes/coalfields/report/index.htm; accessed 1 August 2001.

Oliver, Michael (1990). *The Politics of Disablement*. Basingstoke: Macmillan.

Olson, Mancur (1965). *The Logic of Collective Action: Public Goods and the Theory of Groups*. Cambridge, MA: Harvard University Press.

OPM (2000). *Leicestershire Health Citizens' Panel*. London: Office for Public Management.

Outhwaite, William (1994). *Habermas: A Critical Introduction*. Cambridge: Polity Press.

Page, Benjamin I. (1996). *Who Deliberates? Mass Media in Modern Democracy*. Chicago: University of Chicago Press.

Park, Alison, Roger Jowell, and Suzi McPherson (1998). *The Future of the National Health Service: Results from a Deliberative Poll*. London: Social and Community Planning Research.

Parkinson, John (2001*a*). 'Deliberative Democracy and Referendums', in *Challenges to Democracy: Ideas, Involvement and Institutions*, K. M. Dowding, J. Hughes, and H. Margetts (eds.). London: Palgrave.

—— (2001*b*). 'Who Knows Best? The Creation of the Citizen-initiated Referendum in New Zealand', *Government and Opposition*, 36(3): 403–21.

—— (forthcoming). 'Of Scale and Strawmen: A Reply to Fishkin and Luskin', *British Journal of Political Science*, 36(1) 2006: 189–91.

Parsons, Wayne (1995). *Public Policy: An Introduction to the Theory and Practice of Policy Analysis*. Cheltenham: Edward Elgar.

Pateman, Carole (1970). *Participation and Democratic Theory*. Cambridge: Cambridge University Press.

—— (1971). 'Political Culture, Political Structure and Political Change', *British Journal of Political Science*, 1: 291–305.

Pennock, J. Roland (1968). 'Political Representation: An Overview', in *Representation: Nomos 10*, J. R. Pennock and J. W. Chapman (eds.). New York: Atherton Press.

Peterson, R A. (1992). 'Understanding Audience Segmentation: From Elite and Mass to Omnivore and Univore', *Poetics*, 21(4): 243–58.

Pettit, Philip (1996). 'Institutional Design and Rational Choice', in *The Theory of Institutional Design*, R. Goodin (ed.). Cambridge: Cambridge University Press.

Phillips, Anne (1993). *Democracy and Difference*. University Park, PA: Pennsylvania State University.

—— (1994). 'Dealing with Difference: A Politics of Ideas of a Politics of Presence?' *Constellations*, 1(1): 74–91.

—— (1995). *The Politics of Presence*. Oxford: Clarendon Press.

Phillips, David (1980). 'The Creation of Consultative Councils in the NHS', *Public Administration*, 58(1): 47–66.

Pickard, Susan (1998). 'Citizenship and Consumerism in Health Care: A Critique of Citizens' Juries', *Social Policy and Administration*, 32(3): 226–44.

Pitkin, Hanna (1967). *The Concept of Representation*. Berkeley and Los Angeles, CA: University of California Press.

Plato, and Michael C. Stokes (1997). *Apology of Socrates*. Warminster: Aris and Phillips.

Poggi, G (1978). *The Development of the Modern State*. London: Hutchinson.

Pollitt, Christopher (1993). *Managerialism and the Public Services*, 2nd edn. Oxford: Blackwell.

—— Stephen Harrison, David Hunter, and Gordon Marnoch (1991). 'General Management in the NHS: The Initial Impact 1983–88', *Public Administration*, 69 (Spring): 61–83.

Pratchett, Lawrence (2004). 'Local Autonomy, Local Democracy and the 'New Localism'', *Political Studies*, 52(2): 358–75.

Pressman, Jeffrey and Aaron Wildavsky (1979). *Implementation: How Great Expectations in Washington Are Dashed in Oakland*, 2nd edn. Berkeley, CA: University of California Press.

Pretty, Jules, Rachel Hine, and Katharine Deighton (1999). *Participatory Appraisal for Community Assessment: Principles and Methods*. Colchester: Centre for Environment and Society, University of Essex. Available at http://www2.essex.ac.uk/ces/CommParticipation/ComPartPrinciplesnmethods.htm; accessed 19 August 2005.

Rawls, John (1996). *Political Liberalism*, 2nd edn. New York: Columbia University Press.

—— (1997). 'The idea of Public Reason Revisited', *University of Chicago Law Review*, 94: 765–807.

Raz, Joseph (1986). *The Morality of Freedom*. Oxford: Oxford University Press.

Rehg, William and James Bohman (1996). 'Discourse and Democracy: The Formal and Informal Bases of Legitimacy in Habermas' *Faktizität und Geltung*', *Journal of Political Philosophy*, 4(1): 79–99.

Remer, Gary (2000). 'Two Models of Deliberation: Oratory and Conversation in Ratifying the Constitution', *Journal of Political Philosophy*, 8(1): 68–90.

Renn, Ortwin, Thomas Webler, Horst Rakel, Peter Dienel, and Branden Johnson (1993). 'Public Participation in Decision Making: A Three-step Procedure', *Policy Sciences*, 26: 189–214.

—— —— and Peter M. Wiedemann (1995). *Fairness and Competence in Citizen Participation: Evaluating Models for Environmental Discourse*. Dordrecht, The Netherlands: Kluwer.

Richardson, J. J. and A. G. Jordan (1979). *Governing under Pressure: The Policy Process in a Post-parliamentary Democray*. Oxford: Robertson.

Ridgeway, Cecilia L (1983). *The Dynamics of Small Groups*. New York: St Martin's Press.

Riker, William H. (1982). *Liberalism Against Populism: A Confrontation between the Theory of Democracy and the Theory of Social Choice.* San Francisco, CA: Freeman.

Rorty, Richard (1998). 'Human Rights, Rationality and Sentimentality', in *Truth and Progress: Philosophical Papers,* Vol. 3. Cambridge: Cambridge University Press.

Rowe, Rosemary, and M. Shepherd (2002). 'Public Participation in the New NHS: No Closer to Citizen Control?' *Social Policy and Administration,* 36(3): 275–90.

Rudestam, Kjell Erik (1982). *Experiential Groups in Theory and Practice.* Monterey, CA: Brooks/Cole.

Ryfe, David M. (2002). 'The Practice of Deliberative Democracy: A Study of 16 Deliberative Organizations', *Political Communication,* 19:359–77.

Sabatier, Paul A. (ed.) (1999). *Theories of the Policy Process.* Boulder, CO: Westview Press.

Sanders, Lynn (1997). 'Against Deliberation', *Political Theory,* 25(3): 347–76.

Sartori, Giovanni (1987). *The Theory of Democracy Revisited.* Chatham, NJ: Chatham House Publishers.

Saward, Michael (1998). *The Terms of Democracy.* Cambridge: Polity Press.

—— (2003a). 'Enacting Democracy', *Political Studies,* 51(1): 161–79.

—— (2003b). 'The Representative Claim'. Paper presented at European Consortium of Political Research Joint Sessions: 27 March–2 April 2003, University of Edinburgh.

Scalmer, Sean (2002). *Dissent Events: Protest, the Media and the Political Gimmick in Australia.* Sydney: University of New South Wales Press.

Schaar, John H. (1984). 'Legitimacy in the Modern State', in *Legitimacy and the State,* W. Connolly (ed.). Oxford: Blackwell.

Schick, Allen (1996). *The Spirit of Reform: Managing the New Zealand State Sector in a Time of Change.* Wellington: State Services Commission.

Schlosberg, David (1995). 'Communicative Action in Practice: Intersubjectivity and New Social Movements', *Political Studies,* 43: 291–311.

—— (1999). *Environmental Justice and the New Pluralism: The Challenge of Difference for Environmentalism.* New York: Oxford University Press.

Schön, Donald and Martin Rein (1994). *Frame Reflection: Toward the Resolution of Intractable Policy Controversies.* New York: Basic Books.

Schratz, Michael and Rob Walker (1995). *Research as Social Change: New Opportunities for Qualitative Research.* London: Routledge.

Schudson, Michael (1996). 'The Sociology of News Production Revisited', in *Mass Media and Society,* J. Curran and M. Gurevitch (eds.). London: Arnold.

—— (1999). *The Good Citizen: A History of American Civic Life.* Cambridge, MA: Harvard University Press.

Schultze, Charles (1977). *The Public Use of Private Interest.* Washington: Brookings Institution.

SCPR (1998). *Deliberative Poll: The Future of the National Health Service—Project Instructions.* London: Social and Community Planning Research.

Secretary of State for Health (1997). *The New NHS: Modern, Dependable*. London: Her Majesty's Stationery Office.

—— (2000*a*). *Have Your Say on a Better NHS: Creating a 21st Century NHS* (postcard). London: Department of Health.

—— (2000*b*). *The NHS Plan: A Plan for Investment, a Plan for Reform*. London: Her Majesty's Stationery Office.

Shackley, Phil and Mandy Ryan (1994). 'What Is the Role of the Consumer in Health Care?' *Journal of Social Policy*, 23(4): 517–41.

Shakespeare, Tom (1993). 'Disabled People's Self-organisation: A New Social Movement?' *Disability, Handicap and Society*, 8(3): 249–64.

Shapiro, Ian (1999). 'Enough of Deliberation: Politics is about Interests and Power', in *Deliberative Politics: Essays on 'Democracy and Disagreement'*, S. Macedo (ed.). New York: Oxford University Press.

—— (2003). *The State of Democratic Theory*. Princeton, NJ: Princeton University Press.

Smith, Graham and Corinne Wales (1999). 'Citizenship and Locality: The Theory and Practice of Citizens' Juries', *Policy and Politics*, 27(3): 295–308.

—— (2000). 'Citizens' Juries and Deliberative Democracy', *Political Studies* 48(1): 51–65.

Spragens, Thomas A. (1990). *Reason and Democracy*. Durham: Duke University Press.

Squires, Judith (1999). 'Group Representation, Deliberation and the Displacement of Dichtomies'. Paper presented at Innovation in Democratic Theory: European Consortium of Political Research Annual Joint Sessions, 26–31 March 1999, Mannheim.

—— (2003). 'Representation and the Knowledge Economy'. Paper Presented at European Consortium for Political Research Joint Sessions, 27 March–2 April 2003, University of Edinburgh.

Staff reporter (2000). 'Community Health Council Replacement "is Undemocratic"', *Daily Telegraph*, 28 December 2000.

Stewart, John, Elizabeth Kendall, and Anna Coote (1994). *Citizens' Juries*. London: Institute for Public Policy Research.

Stokes, Geoffrey (ed.) (1997). *The Politics of Identity in Australia*. Cambridge: Cambridge University Press.

Stokes, Susan C. (1998). 'Pathologies of Deliberation', in *Deliberative Democracy*, J. Elster (ed.). Cambridge: Cambridge University Press.

Stone, Douglas, Bruce Patton, and Sheila Heen (2000). *Difficult Conversations*. Harmondsworth: Penguin/Harvard Negotiation Project.

Street, John (2001). *Mass Media, Politics and Democracy*. Basingstoke: Palgrave.

Sunstein, Cass (2001). *Republic.com*. Princeton, NJ: Princeton University Press.

Tenbensel, Tim (2002). 'Interpreting Public Input into Priority-setting: The Role of Mediating Institutions', *Health Policy*, 62(2): 173–94.

Thompson, Dennis F. (2002). *Just Elections: Creating a Fair Electoral Process in the United States*. Chicago: University of Chicago Press.

Threkeld, Simon (1998). 'A Blueprint for Democratic Law-making: Give Citizen Juries the Final Say', *Social Policy*, 28(4): 5–9.

Tiffen, Rodney (1989). *News and Power*. Sydney: Allen & Unwin.

Tilly, Charles (1978). *From Mobilization to Revolution*. New York: Random House.

Truman, David (1955). *The Governmental Process: Political Interests and Public Opinion*. New York: Knopf.

Uhr, John (1998). *Deliberative Democracy in Australia: The Changing Place of Parliament*. Cambridge: Cambridge University Press.

Urbinati, Nadia (2000). 'Representation as Advocacy: A Study of Democratic Deliberation', *Political Theory*, 28(6): 758–86.

van Eijck, Koen, and Kees van Rees (2000). 'Media Orientation and Media Use: Television Viewing Behavior of Specific Reader Types from 1975 to 1995', *Communication Research*, 27(5): 574–616.

Verba, Sidney, and Norman Nie (1972). *Participation in America*. New York: Harper & Row.

Walzer, Michael (1981). 'Philosophy and Democracy', *Political Theory*, 9(3): 379–99.

—— (1999). 'Deliberation, and What Else?' in *Deliberative Politics: Essays on 'Democracy and Disagreement'*, S. Macedo (ed.). New York: Oxford University Press.

Weale, Albert (1999). *Democracy*. New York: St Martin's Press.

Weber, Max, Guenther Roth, and Claus Wittich (1978). *Economy and Society: An Outline of Interpretive Sociology*. Berkeley, CA: University of California Press.

Webler, Thomas (1995). '"Right" Discourse in Citizen Participation: An Evaluative Yardstick', in *Fairness and Competence in Citizen Participation: Evaluating Models for Environmental Discourse*, O. Renn, T. Webler and P. M. Wiedemann (eds.). Dordrecht, The Netherlands: Kluwer.

Webster, Charles (1988). *Problems of Health Care: The National Health Service before 1957, Peacetime History*. London: Her Majesty's Stationery Office.

—— (2002). *The National Health Service: A Political History*, 2nd edn. Oxford: Oxford University Press.

Wilcox, Louise (2000). *Community Consultation: Reconfiguration of Acute Services in Leicester*. Leicester: Centre for Social Action, De Montfort University, commissioned by the Leicestershire Community Health Council.

Williams, Melissa S. (1998). *Voice, Trust and Memory: Marginalized Groups and the Failings of Liberal Representation*. Princeton, NJ: Princeton University Press.

Wood, Bruce (2000). *Patient Power? The Politics of Patients' Associations in Britain and America*. Buckingham: Open University Press.

Wright, Katharine (1998). *The NHS White Papers*. London: Social Policy Section, House of Commons Library.

Yin, Robert K. (1984). *Case Study Research: Design and Methods*. Beverly Hills, CA: Sage.

Young, Iris Marion (1996). 'Communication and the Other: Beyond Deliberative Democracy', in *Democracy and Difference*, S. Benhabib (ed.). Princeton, NJ: Princeton University Press.

Young, Iris Marion (1999). 'Justice, Inclusion, and Deliberative Democracy', in *Deliberative Politics: Essays on 'Democracy and Disagreement'*, S. Macedo (ed.). New York: Oxford University Press.

—— (2000). *Inclusion and Democracy.* Oxford: Oxford University Press.

—— (2001). 'Activist Challenges to Deliberative Democracy', *Political Theory*, 29(5): 670–90.

Zaller, John (2003). 'A New Standard for Judging News Quality: Burglar Alarms for the Monitorial Citizen', *Political Communication*, 20(2): 109–30.

Index

accountability 6, 18, 23–4, 29–31, 33, 120
  audit as a means of 29
  cause of motivations problem 38
  conflicting accountabilities 90, 93–4
  decisiveness creating accountability 80
  elections as a means of 29, 33, 90–1, 152–3, 164, 172
  media role in 29
  micro techniques and accountability 50, 79–80, 90, 97–8
  needed to legitimate representation 41–2, 49, 74, 154
  public versus intramural 29
  publicity as means of, *see* publicity
  quangos as unaccountable 46, 63, 90
  see also representation
Ackerman, Bruce 27, 170
activism, *see* interest groups
ad hoc assemblies, *see* legitimacy
advisory role, *see* decisiveness
agenda setting 12, 16, 34, 45, 50, 73, 116, 128–31, 164, 170–1, 172
  agenda constraints 55, 73, 96, 132–3, 144–5, 159
  and activism 131–2, 136, 145, 169–70
  and argumentation 127
  and dramatization 117–21
  and hierarchy 48, 71, 96, 131–2, 164, 167–8
  and legitimacy 48, 128, 133
  and motivations 36–7, 63–4
  and power 127, 135, 164
  and problem definition 129
  media influence on 101
  question framing 50, 131
agreements 3, 27, 36, 38, 65, 125, 132, 136, 152

AmericaSpeaks 170
argument 3, 40, 127, 138–9
  better arguments 3, 32, 37, 40, 152
  different in public and private 137
  policy making 127
  transmission of arguments, *see* media
Aristotle 128, 140, 142
assembly, *see* parliament
audience 4–5, 26, 100, 112, 137, 145, 152, 156; *see also* deliberative democracy, media
Australia 34, 67; *see also* deliberative poll
authenticity 31, 137
authority 18, 21, 23; *see also* health profession, legitimacy
authorization 23–4, 29, 31, 33
  needed to legitimate representation 41–2, 49, 74
autonomy 33, 152–3

Barker, Rodney 22
Barnes, Colin and Michael Oliver 132
BBC (British Broadcasting Corporation) 106, 114
Beetham, David 22–4, 102
Belfast, *see* citizen's jury
Benhabib, Seyla 3 n.1, 4 n.2, 149
Bessette, Joseph 1, 8, 166–7
Blair, Tony 51–2, 72
Bosom Buddies 85
bridge building, *see* communication
British Council of Disabled People 16, 121
Burnheim, John 75, 80

Carson, Lynn and Brian Martin 75
Catt, Helena 29 n.3, 165–6
centre-periphery relations, *see* deliberative techniques

inclusion 3, 7, 62, 72, 94, 119, 146, 155, 172
  and 'ordinary people' 69, 88
  impossibility of full inclusion 4–5, 35; *see also* scale
  inclusiveness and motivations 40, 172
  promoted by *NHS Plan* 88, 146
  promoted by random selection 75, 148
  rhetoric, unreasonable acts to force inclusion 119, 123, 143–4
information gathering, *see* research
information technology 4, 101, 168–70
injustice 26
Institute of Local Government Research 11
Institute for Public Policy Research (IPPR) 11, 14, 15, 48
institutions 21, 44, 173, 175–6
  activating different participants 165
  deliberative institutions 5–8, 17, 18, 20, 65–6, 147–8, 165, 166–73
  institutional change 151, 166
  stability and review 158
insurgent democracy, *see* interest groups
interests 5, 16, 28
  controlled by lottery 75
interest groups 24, 57, 62, 70, 84–9
  and agenda opening 131–2, 136, 145, 158, 164
  as champion for citizens 50, 69, 84, 86–7, 118–19, 153, 156, 172, 173
  contrast with ordinary person 58
  insurgent/collaborative distinction 132
  internal accountability and democracy 121, 154
  medical colleges 16, 118
  necessary for disabled voice 71
  patient advocacy groups 16, 118
  representation claims 88–9, 94, 121, 153
  role in deliberative democracy (feeding/bleeding) 66, 85, 88–9, 146, 153, 156

usual suspects, *see* participation
see also Community Health Councils, cooption, disability activism, public and patient involvement, rationality
internet, *see* information technology
issues, importance of, *see* salience
Iyengar, Shanto 103

journalists 19

Kateb, George 29 n.3
Kidney Patients' Association 136, 140
Kingdon, John 127
King's Fund 11, 48
knowledge, *see* expertise
Kuran, Timur 38
Kymlicka, Will 31, 34

Labour Party 51, 73, 120
  influence of deliberative democracy 51
  Third Way ideas 51–2, 72
language, *see* argument, persuasion, rhetoric
lay person 49, 53, 58, 63, 68–72, 82, 86, 97, 151, 173
  critical capacities 157
  informed vs. uninformed 12, 129–30
  see also expertise, interest groups
legality, *see* legitimacy
legislature, *see* parliament
legitimacy 17, 19, 21–5, 35, 42, 149
  accountability and authorization requirements for 41–2, 49, 100
  advantages of ad hoc assemblies 42, 155, 173
  agendas, *see* agenda setting
  appeals to authority 55
  appeals to science of processes 62
  behaviour of losers 96, 140
  being heard as legitimating 140
  citizens as rightful source 5, 23, 55, 68, 92, 94, 148–9, 155, 168